CONTENTS

multi-agency working:
a detailed study

UNIVERSITY OF
WOLVERHAMPTON
KNOWLEDGE · INNOVATION · ENTERPRISE

tkinson
e Wilkin
son Stott
Doherty
and
y Kinder

Local Government Association

INVESTOR IN PEOPLE

nfer

Published in January 2002
by the National Foundation for Educational Research,
The Mere, Upton Park, Slough, Berkshire SL1 2DQ

ACKNOWLEDGEMENTS

The authors would like to thank the staff from the different agencies within each of the initiatives visited who gave up their time to take part in the interviews. Their perspectives provided valuable data for this phase of the study. We are particularly grateful for the contributions of initiative staff and representatives of other agencies within the six authorities that agreed to act as case studies for the research.

We are very grateful to Michelle Robinson and Phil Craig for reading and commenting on drafts of this report. Thanks are also due to our colleagues at NFER: Sally Kendall, for acting as our internal reader; David Upton, for his editorial input; Simon Rutt for statistical input; Mary Hargeaves for her contribution to the final document and lastly, for secretarial support throughout the project, Hilary McElderry and Sue Medd.

EXECUTIVE SUMMARY

Background

This report relays the findings from the final phases of a study of multi-agency working involving professionals from the Education, Social Services and Health sectors of local authorities.

The research study comprised three phases (Phase One was described in the interim report, *Multi-agency Working: an Audit of Activity*). During Phase Two of the study, 30 multi-agency initiatives were selected and visited for the purpose of interviewing key individuals from each of the participating agencies – resulting in a total of 139 interviews. Six of these initiatives were then visited again for a more detailed case-study analysis and observation during Phase Three.

The report includes analysis and discussion of the different types, or models, of multi-agency activity; the rationale for their development; agencies' and individuals' involvement in multi-agency activities, their roles and professional backgrounds; the impact of multi-agency activities; and the challenges and key factors in their success.

Different types of multi-agency activity

♦ Five different models of multi-agency activity were evident within the sample: decision-making groups; consultation and training; centre-based delivery; coordinated delivery; and operational-team delivery. Thus, some models focused on direct delivery to a range of target groups, whilst in others the primary aim or purpose was decision-making or providing consultation and training to other agencies.

♦ Agencies came together for different reasons and, for each of the different models, different levels of engagement with professionals from other agencies were evident. A continuum may be described from decision-making groups, where professionals from different agencies maintained their distinct role, to operational teams, where professionals worked closely in close proximity and therefore the merging of roles was more likely.

Rationale and development

♦ Although a variety of rationales and aims for multi-agency working were presented, the aims centred on three main areas: improving services, outcomes for children and families and multi-agency working.

Whilst some aims were common to all multi-agency activity, some were specific to particular types.

♦ Differences emerged in the way in which professionals judged what was considered to be established and what was not, such as where individual agencies still felt there were issues for them that needed to be addressed. These may provide some useful pointers to the progression of multi-agency work in the future.

♦ Whilst the appointment of key staff, gaining the commitment of agencies and consultation were felt to be key processes in development, difficulties in these areas in the early stages were also reported.

Agency and professional involvement

♦ The background to the multi-agency initiatives set up clearly varied enormously – both in terms of the personal backgrounds of those involved, and the context of agency relationships within the authority. Interviewees also described a range of ways in which both individual professionals and agencies became involved in multi-agency work.

♦ Interviewees described their own backgrounds in terms of having a wide range of training and qualifications, and a wide range of roles within a variety of different agencies. Over a third of those involved in the initiatives under study had worked in multiple agencies during their career, indicating this as a beneficial experience for multi-agency working.

♦ The background contexts of the different authorities clearly varied considerably from area to area in terms of interviewees' perceptions of the general multi-agency working and relationships which existed prior to the initiative, and their perceptions of the relationships between specific agencies. Different traditions of interagency relations were evident in each of the services.

Roles and responsibilities

♦ Conflicting views, however, arose about whether roles were determined primarily by the skills and expertise of the professionals involved or whether this was secondary to the personal qualities of individuals.

♦ Roles and responsibilities generally undertaken in multi-agency work were, according to interviewees, the multi-agency steering or management group, which was a key phenomenon in all types of multi-agency activity, the shared responsibility between the agencies involved and an overlap or merging of roles. An overlap or a merging of roles indicated that boundaries between the agencies had become blurred, and in the main this was felt to have been beneficial. However, others felt that maintaining distinct roles was crucial in allowing individual agencies to make a valuable and unique contribution to multi-agency working.

♦ A wide range of roles and responsibilities was felt to be involved in multi-agency working and those identified suggested that a complex hierarchy of roles and responsibilities may exist, for example, at the level of the initiative itself, at an interagency level and at the level of individual agencies. Professionals working in collaboration with other agencies therefore have to balance differing roles and responsibilities at all these different levels.

Impact

♦ A wide range of direct benefits of working in a multi-agency way was identified for children and their families. These centred on three main areas: improved services, direct outcomes and prevention. Improved access to services was commonly highlighted, as well as an improvement in children's educational attainment and their access to education. This points to the contribution that other agencies can make to children's education.

♦ For the agencies involved, the advantages of multi-agency work centred on offering them a broader perspective, a better understanding of the issues, and increased understanding of, and improved interactions with, other agencies. However, whilst it was sometimes felt to raise their profile, it was also commonly reported to create increased demands and pressures on individual agencies.

♦ For the individual professionals involved, on the one hand, working with professionals from other backgrounds was rewarding and stimulating. On the other, it often led to increased work or pressure. They commonly reported that their work alongside other professionals gave them a broad perspective and raised their awareness of the operation of other agencies.

Challenges

♦ The challenges identified in association with multi-agency working were numerous and reflected the complexities involved when professionals engage in collaborative ventures. The issues involved, however, centred broadly around the areas of funding and resources, roles and responsibilities, competing priorities, communication, professional and agency cultures and management.

♦ Perhaps not surprisingly, issues around funding were the most often cited challenges, not only generally, but also in the early stages of development of projects. Challenges involved conflicts over funding within and between agencies, a general lack of funding for multi-agency work and concerns about sustainability. This was the case regardless of the type of multi-agency activity. Other types of resources were also an issue: multi-agency work being cited in some cases to be particularly demanding of staff, time and accommodation, compared to a single agency approach.

♦ Communication was identified as a challenge at all levels of working, although different interpretations of the problem were evident at strategic and operational level. Communication was most commonly reported as a difficulty within coordinator-led initiatives, where those involved were more disparate, and least in operational teams where close working may have ironed out such problems.

♦ Conflicting professional and agency cultures surfaced as a challenge and particularly by those at strategic level.

♦ Many of the same issues were highlighted as difficulties in the early stages of development of multi-agency initiatives. However, particular common challenges at this initial stage included funding, time, different policies and procedures, finding accommodation, the appointment of staff, changes in personnel, ensuring agency commitment and in particular involving Health.

Skills and key factors

♦ The key factors essential for successful multi-agency working were wide-ranging and varied. They involved not only setting up effective systems and procedures, such as for communication and involving the relevant people; ensuring adequate resources in terms of funding, staffing and time; and establishing common aims from the outset, but also the more personal qualities of the professionals involved, such as their commitment and drive.

♦ Commitment to and a willingness to be involved in multi-agency working, whatever the type, was felt to be key to effective collaboration. What emerged was the importance of those involved wanting to be involved and having a belief in multi-agency working, rather than being directed to engage in it.

♦ A number of other key factors identified – understanding the roles and responsibilities of other agencies; the need for common aims, and communication and information sharing, leadership or drive at strategic level – were found to involve a number of underlying facets. Two essential ingredients of the leadership role, for example, included having a vision and tenacity.

♦ Sharing and access to funding and resources were deemed the most important single factor in overcoming challenges, since challenges were often focused in this area. Pooled budgets, joint funding and the identification and the use of alternative resources to enhance multi-agency work were discussed in this respect.

♦ Interviewees also described a range of different 'skills' they felt were beneficial for multi-agency working. Communication skills, including listening, negotiating and compromising, stood out as important generally, although some skills were felt to be more important within specific models of multi-agency working.

Concluding comments

This study of multi-agency activity has highlighted once again the complexity and also potential of 'joining up' services. It has revealed the investment needed, in terms of finance, time and staff resources to develop new ways of working and interagency collaboration. Indeed, the attitudinal shift required in successful initiatives is an important finding. The kinds of challenges inherent in all joint service activity have been clearly laid out and, along with key factors in effective practice, should provide a useful checklist to reassure professionals (at both policy and practitioner level) that multi-agency working is not easy or easily achieved.

Equally, the study has revealed a new and 'hybrid' professional type who has personal experience and knowledge of other agencies, including, importantly, these services' cultures, structures, discourse and priorities. This understanding would seem to be a vital *sine qua non* for successful interagency collaboration. It may be that such familiarity needs to be offered to many others during initial training and in continuing professional development.

Finally, the models of multi-agency working offered in this report intimate the enormous variation in initiatives and practice that are operating under the nomenclature of 'multi-agency'. This suggests there might be value in refining descriptors and vocabulary associated with interagency activity to advance general awareness and understanding of its processes and outcomes.

INTRODUCTION

The research documented in this report set out to examine the range of multi-agency activity within LEAs and what makes it successful. It was commissioned by the Local Government Association (LGA) research programme and was conducted between April 2000 and September 2001. The aims of the research were to:

♦ identify and audit a range of different examples of coordinated and multi-agency activity between Health and/or Social Services and LEA providers

♦ adumbrate key factors in the perceived success of these collaborations and, equally, any inhibiting factors

♦ provide an in-depth and evaluative review of the impact of such joint working on the practice of professionals and their service.

An initial audit of multi-agency activity was conducted in Phase One of the project (telephone interviews with senior managers in 117 LEAs), and 221 multi-agency initiatives were identified. These findings were outlined in a report called *Multi-agency Working: An Audit of Activity*. The present report, based on the data collected in Phases Two and Three of the project, extends further the initial areas of investigation.

The aims of **Phase Two** of the study were, in particular, to examine:

♦ the aims of multi-agency working and how a coordinated approach furthered the aims and policies of the LEA, Health and Social Services

♦ the roles and responsibilities of different agencies

♦ how common aims, complementary roles and effective communication were established

♦ the challenges that were encountered and how these were overcome

♦ the impact on services, agency professionals and the target group

♦ the skills required and key factors in the success of multi-agency working.

Following the telephone interviews in Phase One, a sample of 30 initiatives was chosen to reflect a range of target groups or focuses and different agency involvement, as well as different contexts, i.e. different types and sizes of LEA. Detailed information on the sample is provided at the end of Chapter 1. Selection also took into account the stage of development that multi-agency working had reached. Within the 30 initiatives, face-to-face interviews were conducted with personnel from the LEA, Health and Social Services, where relevant. Interviews were conducted with both strategic-level and operational-level personnel within the services involved.

The aims of **Phase Three** of the study were, in particular, to examine in more depth:

♦ the links between strategic- and operational-level multi-agency working

♦ the relationships between the agencies involved and where links were considered to be working particularly well or not so well

♦ funding and cost-effectiveness of the project

♦ evaluation of the project and its outcomes.

In Phase Three, therefore, in-depth case studies of six of the identified initiatives were undertaken. These initiatives were selected for their distinctive service delivery in terms of the types of multi-agency activity identified in Phase Two of the project and their perceived effectiveness, as well as being selected to cover a range of working practices and target groups. Case studies involved telephone interviews with professional client groups (i.e. those in receipt of multi-agency services) and more in-depth interviews with key personnel, as well as detailed observation of interagency collaborative activity. Documentation on the impact, perceived effectiveness and cost-effectiveness of working practices was also collected.

LITERATURE REVIEW

Introduction

This chapter describes some of the current literature addressing multi-agency working. The review was intended to explore issues relating to collaborative and multi-agency working primarily between Education, Social Services and Health. However, a lot of the literature focused on a particular case or project, or a particular area of work. The rationale for multi-agency work, different types and models of multi-agency working and the factors which may impede or facilitate its effectiveness are considered.

The rationale for multi-agency working

In 1998, Payne put forward an argument for multi-agency working within local authorities: '... *the case for treating social problems in a holistic fashion is overwhelming. People know, in a simple everyday fashion, that crime, poverty, low achievement at school, bad housing and so on are connected*' (Payne, 1998, p.12).

Given this basic rationale, it is perhaps unsurprising that much of the literature relating to multi-agency working espouses its benefits – both in specific and broad general terms. Recent Government strategies have also supported the belief in multi-agency working. The Children Act (GB. Parliament. HoC, 1989), Quality Protects legislation and documents such as *Working Together to Safeguard Children* (DoH. HO and DfEE, 1999) have drawn attention to the importance of agencies working together in this way. This report states that:

> *Promoting children's well-being and safeguarding them from significant harm depends crucially upon effective information sharing, collaboration and understanding between agencies and professionals. Constructive relationships between workers need to be supported by a strong lead from elected or appointed authority members, and the commitment of chief officers* (pp.2–3).

However, Delaney (1994) cites various authors who suggest other reasons why agencies may choose to collaborate. These include: increased efficiency in the face of declining resources and minimisation of client frustration when using the service (Whetten, 1982), and pre-existing networks or collaboration (Rogers and Whetten, 1982; Zapka *et al.*, 1992).

Models and examples of multi-agency working

Given the range of reasons why agencies may wish to collaborate, this section looks at examples of their collaboration and models of how this may be organised in practice. Much of the available literature about multi-agency working describes it in the context of a single project or initiative where agencies had come together to address a specific issue or concern – there has been very little in the way of debate about the broad models or types of multi-agency working. Therefore, models of multi-agency working are a key focus for this study. However, an Audit Commission report, *A Fruitful Partnership: Effective Partnership Working* (Audit Commission, 1998) introduces several different types of partnership working – ranging from large-scale strategic partnerships, to small, local community partnerships. Within this range, four different models are described:

♦ Formation of a separate legal entity – where the agencies come together to form a new organisation with an identity separate from that of any of the partners. The new organisation employs its own staff and is particularly suited to large partnerships. This type of partnership may be able to achieve more than the individual partner agencies, and there is a limited risk of one agency being dominant.

♦ Formation of a virtual organisation – where a separate organisation is formed, but without generating a new legal identity. One agency is responsible for employing the staff and managing resources for the new organisation. This type of organisation avoids some of the problems of setting up a new, independent legal entity, but there is a risk that the agency responsible for managing the partnership becomes dominant.

♦ Co-locating staff from partner organisations – where staff from partner organisations are co-located to work together, but are still employed by their own agency. The only difference between this and a virtual organisation is staff belief – in a virtual organisation, they see themselves as working for the organisation. If they are simply co-located, they retain their membership of their own agency, whilst working towards a common goal. Decisions are still implemented by the group.

♦ Steering groups without dedicated resources – this is the simplest, least formal model of multi-agency working, where partners come together as a steering group, but the group does not have its own resources and thus decisions are implemented through the individual partners' own agencies.

Within the literature, others discuss different types and examples of partnership working and the difficulties encountered. Some of these are now discussed.

A project designed to raise educational achievement through general school improvement, described by Easen (1998) was founded on a notion of partnership – specifically between the central project and the schools. It was based on '*a growing recognition, internationally as well as nationally, that deep-rooted problems with both economic and social dimensions require a multi-agency approach based on communities*' (Easen, op. cit., p.1). It was a three-year project involving 22 local schools and their local communities.

Throughout the three years of the project, the partnership faced many problems. Despite the fact that *'partnership was seen as the cornerstone'* of the project, *'conflict between the partners significantly weakened the design and implementation of the project. Communication between the different parties involved ... became strained and insufficient dialogue hindered progress'* (Easen, op. cit., p.5). As a result, there were difficulties in determining a shared understanding of the aims and objectives of the project, and thus problems of setting targets for evaluation. Easen's conclusion was that partnership working is a learning experience for those involved and that *'success will depend on the personal and interpersonal qualities of the individuals who represent the partnership organisations as much as, if not more so than, the expertises they represent'* (Easen, op. cit., p.12).

Machell (1999) views the situation slightly differently, citing Fullan's use of complexity theory, suggesting that *'creative solutions arise out of interaction under conditions of uncertainty, diversity and instability'* (Fullan, 1999, quoted in Machell, 1999, p.2). Machell suggests that this type of creative problem solving is the key to addressing the issue of disaffection amongst young people, and that it can effectively result from the presence of the conflicting views of the different agencies involved in a multi-agency collaboration. Thus, within this model the strength of multi-agency activity lies specifically in the diversity of opinions and ideas represented within the partnership, rather than its ability to bring the opinions of participants to some common viewpoint.

In terms of school exclusion, Normington and Kyriacou (1994) suggest that: *'The records maintained by schools and agencies differ markedly, and none reflects the full extent of the pupils' problems nor gives a clear picture of the multi-disciplinary work occurring. In effect, each agency seems to have only a partial view of the case'* (p.14). This clearly identifies a common problem faced by partnerships – that of information sharing.

The authors go on to describe a possible solution to this problem – the case conference approach to tackling school exclusion – where all the agencies meet together to discuss specific cases. However, this is not without its own difficulties. They describe the argument put forward by Cline (1989) suggesting that a good case conference requires *'the professionals involved to monitor the proceedings carefully and make effective contributions, rather than allowing one dominant voice to carry the day'*. They go on to state that *'unfortunately power relationships and role responsibilities can inhibit this'* (p.14). This would seem to support Fullan's argument that partnerships are at their most effective when all opposing voices around the table can be heard.

Similarly, case conferences often take place in order to resolve child protection issues. Harris (1999) considers how such multi-professional panels make decisions about the action to be taken, and illustrates the same potential pitfall – that professionals defer to the leader of the group for a decision, rather than risk conflict between the agencies represented within the group. His suggestion is that, in this circumstance, multi-professional decision making does not lead to the most effective decisions being reached – again, supporting Fullan's notion that conflicting views can produce the most creative solutions.

Angele *et al.* (1997) wrote about policies and practices in the field of special educational needs. Their stance was that: '*Currently, limited solutions appear to exist at a case management level, with professionals and practitioners finding ways to work together on stopgap measures in the absence of effective formal structures*' (p.13). Their suggestion was that local authorities could take a corporate decision and insist that Social Services and Education work more closely together on this issue, although it was recognised that they had no power to influence Health in the same manner.

Looking specifically at Health, an audit of alliances between Health Promotion and Education showed that '*health promotion specialists are extremely active in both the initiation and management of collaborative initiatives, with 98 per cent of health promotion units having alliances in place with the education sector*' (Scriven, 1995, p.176). However, the health promoters who were interviewed as part of the research felt that the momentum for this collaboration came from the health professionals involved, and that the schools and the LEA played a more passive role.

Bloxham (1996) also describes a particular instance of multi-agency working in the field of young people's sexual health. Her key finding was that '*shared aims and mutual respect among the participants can be achieved by slowly nurtured relationships growing from a clear personal incentive to collaborate*' (p.389). However, she goes on to describe that '*this strong interpersonal network was linked with a lack of cross-agency planning at a management level*' (p.389), thus concluding that '*the challenge is to combine a strategic approach without losing the genuine commitment of participating staff*' (p.389). A key issue therefore is the mechanism by which strategic and operational levels are linked together.

Factors facilitating or impeding multi-agency working

Throughout the literature, a wide range of factors was suggested to play a part in determining the effectiveness of multi-agency working and collaboration. Many of the articles already cited provide their own lists of the factors that, in their view, play a part, and these are discussed in the remainder of this section. Factors commonly cited included:

- ◆ agency differences
- ◆ local authority structures and boundaries
- ◆ staffing arrangements and time investment
- ◆ individuals' and agencies' expectations and priorities

♦ agencies' aims and objectives

♦ budgets and finances

♦ confidentiality and information-sharing protocols

♦ the need for development of a common language

♦ joint training.

A major factor which was identified as having an influence on multi-agency working was the differences between the agencies involved. These differences manifested themselves in a number of different ways – different boundaries and authority organisation, different working conditions and expectations, interagency rivalries, different viewpoints and priorities and different working methods and roles. These differences resulted in the increased importance of finding a common language.

A survey of 'healthy alliances' conducted by Scriven (1995) suggested that a major factor influencing alliances between Education and NHS health promotion units was the changing structures of local authorities. In this case, it was particularly identified in terms of the increase in local management of schools (rather than central management from the LEA). Maychell and Bradley (1991) put forward a similar viewpoint, that *the way in which individual jobs or whole services are organised can obviously affect the way in which people work and the opportunities created for interagency cooperation*' (p.15).

They go on to raise several specific problems relating to the staffing arrangements, and time investment required for successful multi-agency working:

♦ identifying the right people to be involved in the collaboration

♦ persuading the people who need to be involved that multi-agency working is important and worth the time investment

♦ for senior professionals involved in multi-agency steering groups, finding mutually convenient times to meet in the midst of their demanding workloads

♦ maintaining multi-agency work and relationships despite staff changes – the links need to be embedded and built into job descriptions, with good record keeping to facilitate staff changeovers.

They also note that lack of time is a common excuse for agencies to avoid participation in multi-agency collaboration, although actual reasons may involve many of the other factors mentioned.

Authority boundaries were also an important issue – where the boundaries of the agencies involved in the collaboration were coterminous, this was thought to be of immense benefit. Maychell and Bradley (1991) note, with reference to a special needs initiative, that *'a further problem was that the Health Authority and local authority boundaries were not the same; thus the Social Services Department was only in communication with one of the three health authorities which dealt with its clients'* (pp.16-17). They similarly explained that the individuals involved had different expectations of their work and working conditions, different training and different line management and organisational structures. They suggest that *'developing interagency initiatives and new work patterns can seem to pose a threat to individual workers or groups of workers, particularly if in the process 'their' clients become the responsibility of other professionals'* (p.38).

Concerns were also expressed about the impact of agencies having different priorities and views – both at an agency level and at an individual professional level. Easen (1998) describes how a school improvement project suffered as a result of this type of issue:

> *Most of the problems which ran through the implementation ... stemmed from the fundamentally polarised views of the key partners which surfaced repeatedly at each level. The tensions and conflicts which bedevilled implementation are one consequence of this polarisation which, once it was locked into the strategy, had been difficult to shift* (pp.6–7).

A similar case was put forward by Normington and Kyriacou (1994), where problems were mainly found to stem from *'the mix of role perceptions and expectations the different agencies have about themselves and each other, coupled with under-resourcing of staff and time to deal with their case-loads'* (p.12).

A related theme is that of shared aims and objectives. There were two ways in which shared aims and objectives were found to influence multi-agency working. One was the extent to which the different agencies already had similar aims and objectives (Bloxham, 1996), and the second was the extent to which each agency had a shared vision, and shared ownership of the aims and objectives of a particular multi-agency project or activity (Bloxham, 1996; Cable, 1997; Easen, 1998; Maychell and Bradley, 1991). Maychell and Bradley also suggest that overcoming differences in aims and objectives requires joint strategic planning and appropriate policy documentation: *'Without the support of a joint policy which bridges the boundaries between the various statutory and voluntary bodies individuals' attempts to establish links across agencies are inevitably limited'* (p.11).

This variation in agencies' cultures and working practices has been shown to lead to rivalry between the different agencies, which often manifests itself in terms of defending agency boundaries. This is clearly seen in the literature relating to budgets and funding, but also in terms of sharing information.

Several authors referred to budgets and finances as factors influencing agencies' ability to work together. Both Capey (1997) and Scriven (1995) referred to agencies' inflexible funding arrangements, which made working together difficult. However, they also suggested that agencies may use this situation as an excuse for protecting their own funds.

Sharing information and confidentiality policies were often seen as factors militating against multi-agency working. While the authors who made such comments generally respected the need for confidentiality for client groups, some concerns were expressed that this was being enforced specifically to protect agency responsibilities and defend boundaries. The point is clearly made by Maychell and Bradley (1991), who state that

> *Obviously professionals have responsibility for maintaining confidentiality and clients have a right to this. Sometimes, however, workers suspect that information of a non-confidential nature is being withheld as a means of retaining a degree of control/authority. Careful negotiation over what really is, and is not, necessary seems to be important* (p.39).

One way in which it has been suggested that these agency differences can be overcome, and a common language developed, is through joint training. Scrine (1989) writes that '... *no progress will be made in interdisciplinary understanding until, as well as practice experience of working in multidisciplinary settings, there are opportunities for shared academic teaching in professional education*' (p.161). Hallett and Stevenson (1980) have also supported this view, suggesting that joint training is the only way to instil a true sense of multi-agency working.

Similarly Bloxham (1996), drawing on the views of various authors (Butterfoss *et al.*, 1992; Hornby, 1993; Cole, 1995), notes that '*it is not surprising that training, and particularly shared training, is associated with good interagency work as it provides a key opportunity to clarify aims and values*' (p.391). Thus, two of the key factors discussed within this section as potential problems for multi-agency working may be addressed by joint training.

Conclusion

It is clear that there are a large number of different rationales for multi-agency working, and a similarly wide range of issues or problems to which it could be applied. However, the literature revealed relatively few different models or types of multi-agency activity. Those that were identified focused on:

♦   new collaborative organisations

♦   co-location of agency staff

♦   steering groups

♦   case conferences.

The literature also described a large number of factors which could influence the success, or otherwise, of multi-agency collaboration, including:

♦   differences between authorities and agencies

♦   finding a common language

- ◆ joint training
- ◆ staffing and time commitments
- ◆ good organisation and communication
- ◆ shared aims and objectives
- ◆ information sharing and confidentiality
- ◆ budgets and financing.

From the body of literature relating to multi-agency working, it is clear that any new research would be valuable and timely given the emphasis currently placed on 'joined-up thinking'.

Within the available literature, a wide range of factors was identified as having an impact on the effectiveness of collaboration. However, in many cases, articles focused on very clearly defined multi-agency projects, such as the school and community improvement project described by Easen (1998), or within particular fields of work, such as special needs.

There is clearly an important opportunity for research which looks more broadly at models and the processes of multi-agency working independently of its setting or focus. It would also be apposite to revisit the area of factors influencing multi-agency working in more depth, with comparison across the types of collaboration and spheres of work.

1. DIFFERENT TYPES OF MULTI-AGENCY ACTIVITY

1.1 Introduction

This section of the report introduces the different models of multi-agency activity that were encountered within the study. Initiatives were classified according to the type of multi-agency activity involved, centring on the main purpose or aim of joint working. However, this did not preclude initiatives having elements of the other types of multi-agency working that are now described. Five models of multi-agency activity were identified:

♦ decision-making groups

♦ consultation and training

♦ centre-based delivery

♦ coordinated delivery

♦ operational-team delivery.

Decision-making groups and coordinated delivery were the most frequent types of multi-agency activity encountered within the sample, whilst operational-team delivery was the least frequently encountered. The different models of joint working will now be described. A summary of the initiatives, their target groups, the agencies involved and the types and sizes of LEAs is provided at the end of this chapter.

1.2 Decision-making groups

The main purpose of the multi-agency activity in the initiatives classified within this group was to provide a forum whereby professionals from different agencies could meet to discuss issues and to make decisions. Diagrammatic representation of this type of activity is presented in Figure 1.1, and illustrative examples of two decision-making groups are shown in Illustrations 1 and 2 on the following page. Decision making tended to be focused at a strategic level, but was also expected to impact indirectly on service delivery at operational level. A two-way exchange of information (represented by the arrows) was evident, in that professionals brought to the group knowledge and a view from their own agency to feed into the decision-making process, but also took away issues from the discussions to feed back to others within their own agency.

Figure 1.1   Decision -making groups

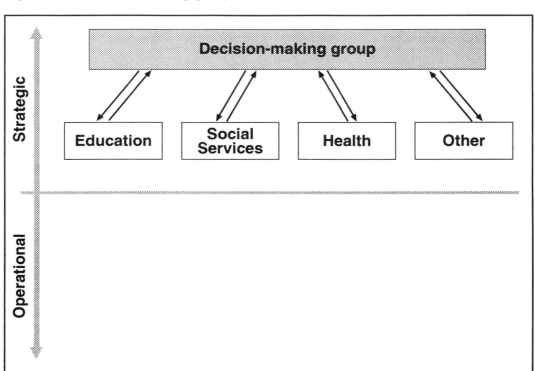

Nine initiatives were classified as decision-making groups, and their focus or target groups were as follows (the number of initiatives in each target group is shown in brackets):

♦   strategic planning, i.e. focused on all children's services (3)

♦   children in public care (2)

♦   children and young people with mental health problems (1)

♦   children at risk, i.e. those involved in prostitution (1)

♦   children with complex needs (1)

♦   disaffected pupils (1).

Thus, as well as having a broad agenda, decision-making strategic groups existed with a number of specific focuses. Six out of the nine initiatives in this group involved all three of the main agencies, with the remainder being initiatives developed between Education and Social Services. Thus, according to the sample, it appeared that Education rarely engaged solely with Health for the purpose of decision making, perhaps indicating the ease with which local authority services can engage with each other compared to developing links outside of the council with Health Trusts and Health Authorities. Six of the nine LEAs involved were new authorities, and four of these were new city authorities, suggesting that joint decision-making processes may be facilitated by significant structural changes within an authority, such as local reorganisation.

Examples of decision-making groups

Illustration 1

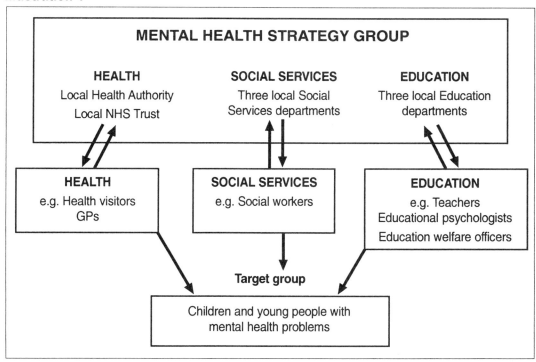

Illustration 2

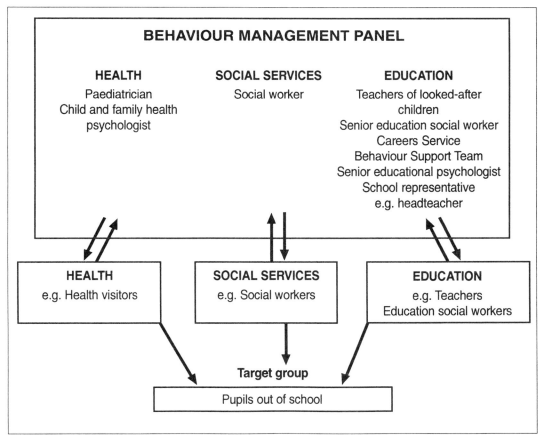

1.3 Consultation and training

Within initiatives classified as consultation and training, the main purpose of the multi-agency activity was for the professionals from one agency to enhance the expertise of those of another by providing consultation and/or training for them. This usually took place at operational level. Figure 1.2 shows a diagrammatic representation of this type of initiative, and illustrative examples of consultation and training are shown in Illustrations 3 and 4 on the following page. Whilst, perhaps inevitably, within this type of activity there was a two-way exchange of knowledge and understanding (as indicated by the arrows), one agency was generally considered the provider and the other the receiver.

Figure 1.2   Consultation and training

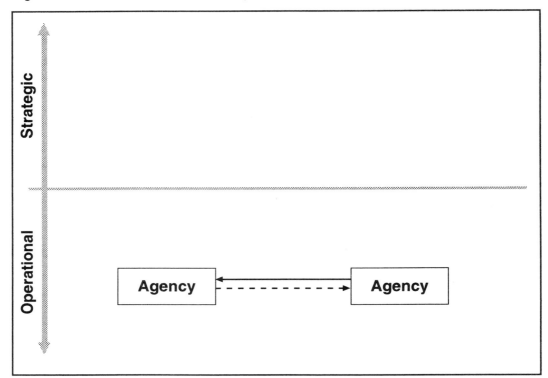

Five initiatives were classified within this category, and their focus or target groups were as follows:

- children with speech and language difficulties (2)

- children and families with mental health problems (1)

- children in public care (1)

- children with emotional and behavioural difficulties (1).

Examples of consultation and training initiatives

Illustration 3

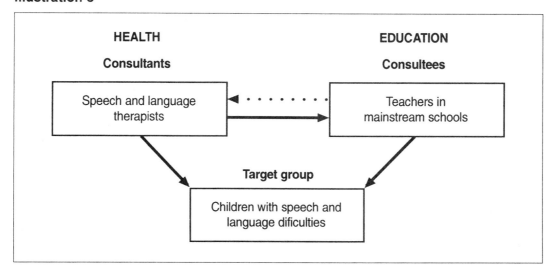

Illustration 4

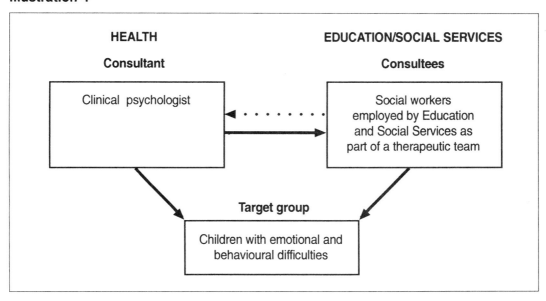

Interestingly, four out of the five initiatives within this group involved health professionals in a consultation and training role with educational professionals and were focused on children with particular health difficulties. This may indicate a significant emphasis on the role of health professionals in passing on their expertise to other professionals, as opposed to engaging with Education in joint service delivery. To some extent this may be a result of a lack of resources within Health, such as speech and language therapists, as it means that they are able to reach more children in this way. Three out of the five initiatives were found within new authorities, two with a city and one with a regional focus.

1.4   Centre-based delivery

The main purpose of the multi-agency activity in centre-based initiatives was to gather a range of expertise together in one place in order to deliver a more coordinated and comprehensive service. Figure 1.3 presents a diagrammatic representation of this type of initiative, and illustrative examples of centre-based initiatives are provided in Illustrations 5 and 6 on the following page. By locating professionals from different agencies in a central base (represented by the box), whilst they may not jointly deliver services to clients, exchange of information, ideas and discussion between agencies was facilitated (as indicated by the arrows). They were thus aware of each other's role and were able to deliver a more coordinated approach. In addition, access to agencies by clients was facilitated.

Figure 1.3   Centre-based delivery

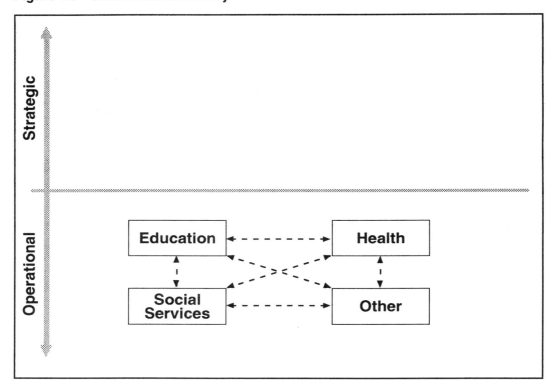

Four initiatives were classified as examples of centre-based multi-agency activity, and their focus or target groups were as follows:

◆ counselling and advice for young people (2)

◆ children in need (1)

◆ pre-school children with complex needs (1).

Two initiatives involved Education and Health, whilst one involved all three agencies and the other involved professionals from a range of backgrounds but all employed by a voluntary agency. It is perhaps worth noting that another initiative with a centre-based delivery element (although classified as an operational team) also had significant voluntary sector involvement. This may indicate a role for the voluntary sector in

Examples of centre-based delivery

Illustration 5

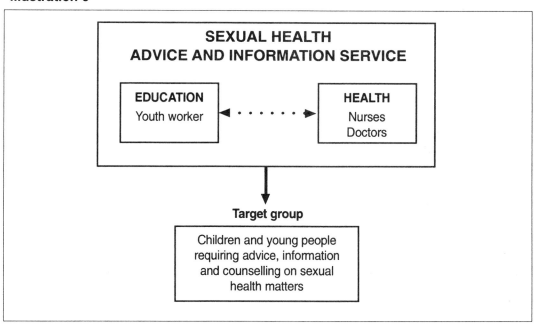

Illustration 6

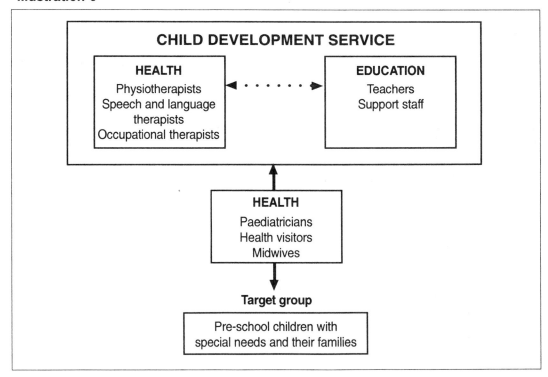

coordinating a range of agency resources within centre-based services (this is discussed further in the chapter on roles and responsibilities). Centre-based initiatives were located within two large, one medium-sized and one small LEA and within different types of LEA: one London borough, one county, one metropolitan and one new city authority.

1.5   Coordinated delivery

In a similar way to centre-based delivery, the main aim of multi-agency coordinated delivery was to draw together a number of agencies involved in the delivery of services so that a more coordinated and cohesive response to need could be adopted. This was typically achieved by the appointment of a coordinator with responsibility for pulling together previously disparate services. This type of multi-agency service delivery is diagrammatically represented in Figure 1.4, and illustrative examples of two different coordinator-led initiatives are shown in Illustrations 7 and 8. Whilst the coordinator might be seen as operating between operational and strategic level, delivery by the agency professionals was at operational level. Within this model, professionals from different agencies often had limited contact with each other, but they received information and gained understanding of other agencies through links with the coordinator (as indicated by the two-way arrows).

Figure 1.4   Coordinated delivery

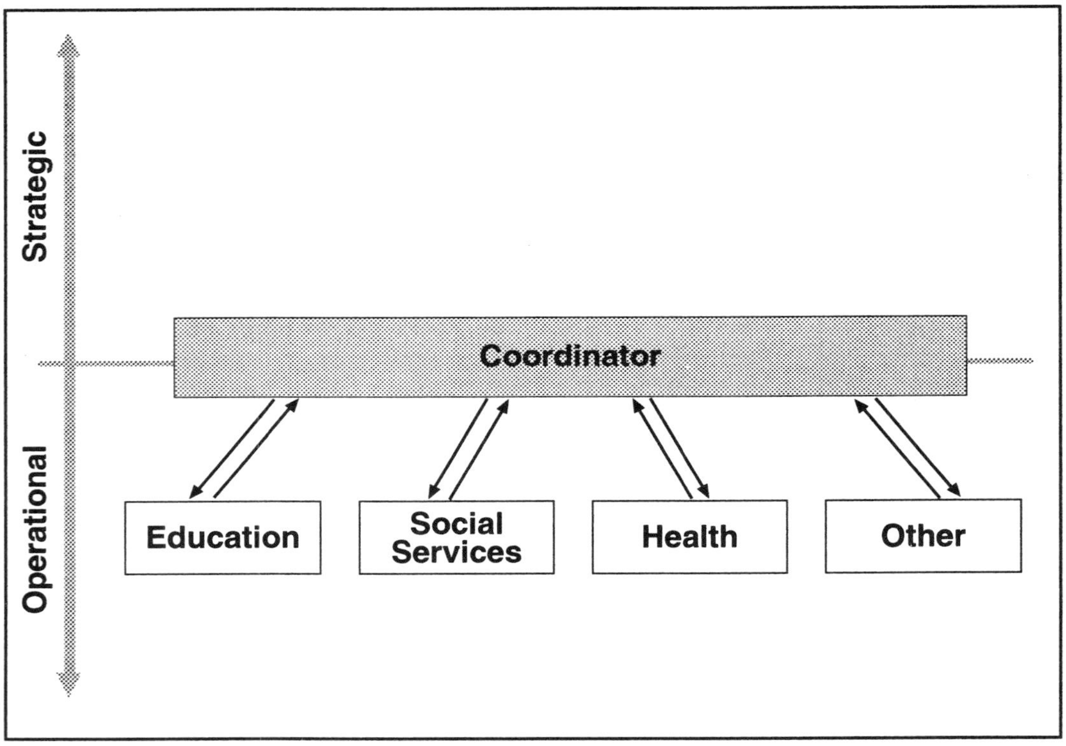

Nine initiatives were classified as mainly offering a coordinated multi-agency approach, and their focus or target groups were as follows:

♦   children's health (3)

♦   early years (3)

♦   children in public care (1)

♦   children with autism (1)

♦   disaffected pupils (1).

Examples of coordinated delivery

Illustration 7

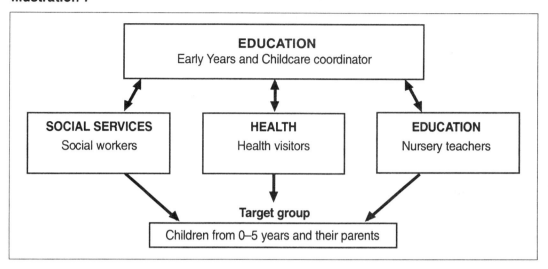

Illustration 8

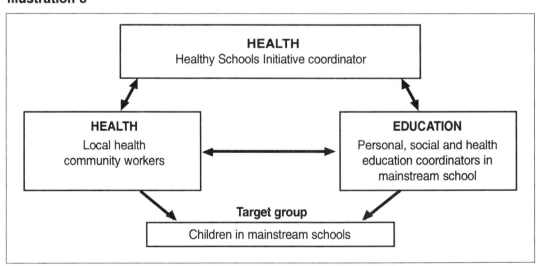

Equal numbers of initiatives involving all three of the main agencies, Education and Social Services, and Education and Health were found within this group. However, this seemed to reflect the focus or target group. These initiatives were generally large-scale projects with coordinators often expected to pull together the work of a large number of professional groups, and eight of the nine initiatives were operating within medium-sized or large LEAs. For these authorities, therefore, this perhaps offered a way of coordinating a range of widespread services so that a more cohesive multi-agency approach was established. Six of the nine initiatives were housed within medium-sized new city authorities or London boroughs.

1.6   Operational-team delivery

The aim of initiatives within this category was for professionals from different agencies to work together on a day-to-day basis and to form a cohesive multi-agency team that delivered services directly to clients. Diagrammatic representation of this type of initiative is provided in Figure 1.5, and illustrative examples of operational teams are presented on the following page in Illustrations 9 and 10. The professionals involved in operational teams worked in close proximity and worked together to deliver services to clients. Thus, a two-way exchange of knowledge, ideas and skills took place between all those involved (as indicated by the arrows), and roles and responsibilities were often less distinct than in other models.

Figure 1.5   Operational-team delivery

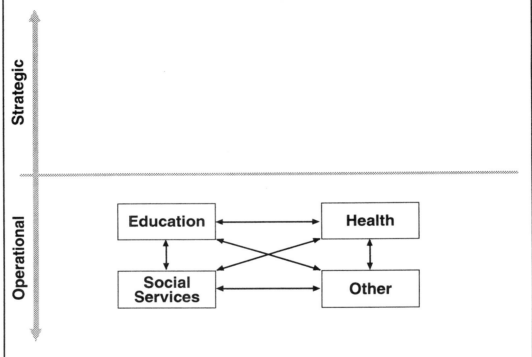

Only three initiatives were identified within this category, and the scarcity of this type of multi-agency activity within the sample may indicate the difficulties inherent with this type of approach, such as maintaining agency boundaries. This issue is discussed further in a later chapter on challenges. The target groups for these initiatives were as follows:

◆   children with disabilities (1)

◆   children in public care (1)

◆   children and families with mental health problems (1).

Two initiatives involved all three agencies, whilst one involved Education and Social Services only. Two out of the three initiatives within this group were located within large county authorities, the other within a medium-sized new city LEA.

Examples of operational-team delivery

Illustration 9

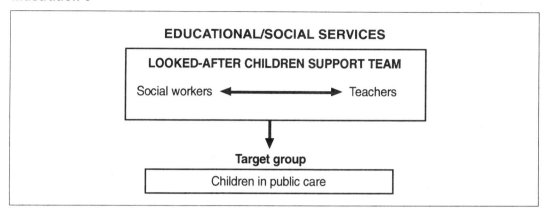

Illustration 10

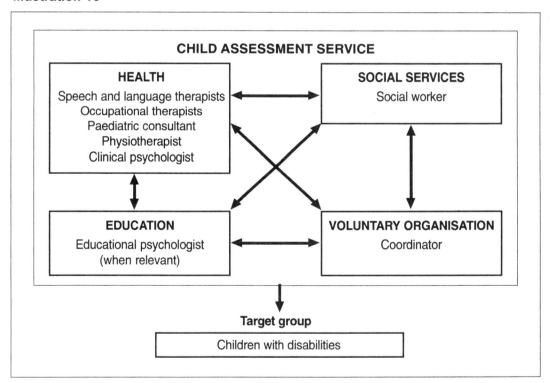

A summary of the 30 initiatives, which are grouped together under the type of multi-agency activity and which includes the target group or focus, the agencies involved and the type and size of LEA, is now provided in Table 1.

Table 1. **Summary of the initiatives**

Target group/focus	Agencies involved	LEA
Decision-making groups		
Mental health strategy steering group	Education, Social Services and Health	Large new region
Joint officers planning group	Education and Social Services	Large county
Strategic planning meeting	Education and Social Services	Small Welsh
Steering group focused on prostitution	Education, Social Services, Health and a voluntary agency	Medium new city
Looked-after children strategic planning group	Education, Social Services and Health	Medium new city
Strategic planning team	Education, Social Services and Health	Medium new city
Joint strategy group focused on children with complex needs	Education, Social Services and Health	Small new city
Looked-after children planning group	Education and Social Services	Large metropolitan
Behaviour management panel	Education, Social Services and Health	Large new region
Consultation and training		
Children with speech and language difficulties	Education and Health	Medium London borough
Children and families with mental health problems	Education and Health	Large new region
Children with speech and language difficulties	Education and Health	Small new city
Children with emotional and behavioural problems	Education, Social Services and Health	Small new city
Children in public care	Education and Social Services	Large metropolitan
Centre-based delivery		
Counselling and advice centre	Voluntary agency	Small London borough
Children in need	Education, Social Services and Health	Large county
Counselling and advice centre	Education and Health	Large metropolitan
Pre-school children with complex needs	Education and Health	Medium new city
Coordinator-led delivery		
Autism development worker	Education, Social Services and Health	Medium new city
Children in public care	Education and Social Services	Medium new city
Disaffected pupils	Education and Social Services	Medium new city
Early years	Education and Social Services	Medium London borough
Early years	Education, Social Services and Health	Small Welsh
Healthy Schools Initiative	Education and Health	Large county
Joint Health Promotion Service	Education and Health	Medium London borough
Healthy Schools Initiative	Education and Health	Large metropolitan
Early years	Education, Social Services and Health	Medium new city
Operational-team delivery		
Assessment of children with learning disabilities	Education, Social Services and Health	Large county
Children and families with mental health problems	Education, Social Services and Health	Medium new city
Children in public care	Education and Social Services	Large new region

Key points

♦ Five different models of multi-agency activity were evident within the sample: decision-making groups; consultation and training; centre-based delivery; coordinated delivery; and operational-team delivery. Thus, some models focused on direct delivery to a range of target groups, whilst in others, the primary aim or purpose was decision making or providing consultation and training to other professionals.

♦ The most common models of multi-agency activity found within the sample were examples of decision-making groups and coordinated delivery, whilst operational teams were the least evident.

♦ Agencies came together for different reasons and, for each of the different models of multi-agency activity, the proximity and degree of engagement between the professionals from different agencies varied.

ΓIONALE AND DEVELOPMENT

2.1 Introduction

This section of the report covers the rationale and aims behind the multi-agency initiatives and the processes involved in their development. Firstly, the rationales behind the different initiatives are detailed and then, linked to this, the aims and objectives of multi-agency activity are discussed. Finally, the processes involved in the development of multi-agency activity are illuminated, together with the stages of development that the initiatives were at, followed by a brief look at the difficulties encountered within the early stages (since these are discussed in more depth in Chapter 6, which is devoted to challenges).

2.2. Rationale behind multi-agency activity

Strategic- and operational-level staff were asked to articulate their understanding of the history of the particular initiative in which they were involved and, as part of this, they were asked to explain the rationale behind it. Not all interviewees felt able to do this because they had joined the initiative at a later stage and therefore had not been involved from its inception.

Whilst some types of multi-agency activity, namely decision-making groups and coordinator-led initiatives, were reportedly set up for a variety of reasons, other types appeared to be linked with particular rationale and, where this was the case, this is indicated in the text.

The main rationale or impetus for the development of the various initiatives, as outlined by interviewees (with the number of initiatives in which they were identified in brackets), included:

- to meet the needs of a specific target group (8)
- to offer a more effective/comprehensive service (8)
- a specific desire for multi-agency working (7)
- a response to review/research (3)
- to address gaps in provision (2)
- a response to Government trends/initiatives (2).

Illustrative examples of the three most frequently cited rationales for the development of multi-agency initiatives are shown below.

Examples of the main rationales behind multi-agency initiatives

To meet the needs of a specific target group	*I quickly realised, when I came into Education, and learnt from my colleagues here, that really you can't underestimate the value of education, for everybody, but particularly for disadvantaged groups, and especially for the poorest performing group, which was children in care. I started thinking, 'What should we be doing for those kids?'* (education access manager). *I have to say that we were overjoyed at the thought of it because we had been making noises about the need for more speech therapy and particularly the lack of, well I'd say the desperate cases of children with statements requiring speech therapy and still not receiving it. And also how obvious it was becoming that a lot of children needed this input, because the Literacy Hour in school, the teaching of phonics, has opened up a chasm of need, because when you are teaching phonics, children cannot hear and speak the phonics you are trying to teach them, so it's making it more obvious* (headteacher).
To offer a more effective or comprehensive service	*A recognition that the work needed to be brought together in a coordinated and an integrated way because our interests coincided. It seemed a natural progression really that we should put together an Early Years and Childcare Team which drew from all the different aspects of the council departments and Health, those people that needed to work very closely together* (assistant director, Education). *There was an existing initiative ... a drop-in coffee bar type place. As young people came in they brought problems with them so they started to provide information. Sexual health issues were coming up and the Health Authority got involved. We've expanded, developed outreach around sexual health and brought youth groups in ... basically providing a quality service of advice and information* (senior youth worker).
A specific desire for multi-agency working	*[It was] in early '98 the arrival of the new local authority chief executive, which had been preceded a year or so before by the arrival of the new Health Authority chief executive. The two people realised that things were not working well and had not worked well between the two major statutory partners and decided to establish the [strategy group] which was established in early 1998* (deputy director, Health). *It was driven by members who wanted an example of the two agencies working together well in one geographical area on behalf of the county council* (chief educational psychologist).

The above table shows that one of the main rationales for developing a multi-agency initiative was believed to be to meet the needs of a specific target group (i.e. children in public care, children with speech and language difficulties, autistic children, those at risk of exclusion and those affected by mental health problems). Three of the five initiatives focused on consultation and training were set up with this aim, two focusing on children with speech and language difficulties and one for children in public care. Two coordinator-led initiatives that were initiated to meet the needs of specific target groups – children with autism and children in public care – had both been influenced by parents. Interviewees in one, for example, referred to '*a strong parental lobby*'.

Another of the main rationales for developing a multi-agency initiative was believed to be to offer a more effective and/or comprehensive service. The latter was noted particularly in initiatives involving all three agencies. Three out of the four centre-based initiatives (two focused on providing counselling and advice for young people and one focused on pre-school complex needs) had been set up with this rationale in mind, as were three out of the nine decision-making groups (one focused on all children's services, one on children with complex needs and one on disaffection, and each involving all three agencies).

The next most common rationale offered was an acknowledged desire for greater multi-agency working, often because relationships between the various agencies had been poor in the past (see Chapter 3). Multi-agency initiatives were seen as a means of sharing knowledge, skills and experience in order to integrate and thus improve provision: '*It took a while but began to blossom into a much more helpful strategic view.*' Two out of the three initiatives identified as operational-team delivery arose from a desire for increased multi-agency working. One, focused on children with disabilities and involving a team of health workers and social workers with some educational input, developed from an operational-level push for multi-agency assessment, which was also influenced by parental desire for a '*one-stop shop*' approach to assessment. The other project to arise from a desire for increased multi-agency working focused on children in public care and was influenced by a review of multi-agency links and resources. Two strategic decision-making groups, both involving Education and Social Services, also arose from a specific desire for increased multi-agency working.

Three initiatives were set up in response to reviews of current practice and/ or to national research which, in some cases, had acted as a '*powerful*' stimulus to draw attention to weaknesses in existing provision. One of the four initiatives providing centre-based multi-agency support, focused on children in need, had, for example, been set up in response to a joint development review. Two of the nine coordinator-led initiatives, both involving Education and Social Services (one focused on children in public care and one on disaffection), were set up in response to previous research.

Finally, two initiatives (both decision-making groups involving all three agencies) were set up in order to address identified gaps in provision. One was focused on mental health and one on young people involved in prostitution. Two others (both coordinator-led initiatives involving

MULTI-AGE...

Education and Health) were set up in response to Gc
initiatives, perhaps reflecting a desire at national level f(
to work together more.

Other factors, such as the personal commitment or int
work with a similar focus, parental pressure and, in parน.ս...,
government reorganisation were highlighted by interviewees as having an
influence on the development of the initiatives. The latter was often seen
as an opportunity to review what was in place and what needed to happen
in order to move forward: '*a chance to do things differently and better from
how it had been before*'.

2.3 Aims

Interviewees were asked about the aims and objectives of the multi-agency
initiatives in which they were involved. Analysis showed that there was
significant agreement between professionals from different agencies within
the same initiative about the broad aims. Not surprisingly, the aims were
often closely related to the rationale for the initial development of initiatives
(as discussed in the previous section), and commensurate with this, a variety
of aims were also evident. Some differences between the aims, as expressed
by different professional groups, did emerge, whilst more significant
differences between the aims in different types of multi-agency activity
were evident. Firstly, therefore, the overall aims are discussed, and this is
followed by discussion of the aims linked with different types of multi-
agency activity.

2.3.1 Overall aims

The most common aims, as expressed by interviewees, were as follows
(the numbers of initiatives within which they were highlighted are given in
brackets):

◆   to improve services (9)

◆   to raise educational achievement (9)

◆   to improve/explore joint working (9)

◆   to identify/meet the needs of the target group (8)

◆   early identification/intervention (7)

◆   to provide support for young people (7)

◆   to promote social inclusion (7)

◆   a holistic approach (7)

◆   to improve opportunities/life chances for children (7)

◆   to coordinate services (6)

◆   to improve outcomes for children and families (6)

◆   information sharing (6)

◆   to raise awareness/understanding of other agencies (6).

Illustrative examples of some of the aims of multi-agency initiatives are provided over the page. Although a number of different aims were identified, these appeared to be focused at three levels:

♦ improving services

♦ improving outcomes for children and families

♦ improving multi-agency working.

Not surprisingly, these are linked to the areas of impact interviewees identified, which are discussed in Chapter 5. Following the illustrations, therefore, the aims are discussed broadly within these three areas.

Examples of the aims of multi-agency initiatives

To improve services	*To try and work as a children's service. To try and work as a seamless children's service, despite the fact that we're actually two departments of one council and another authority* (assistant director, Education).
	To actually try and provide the most appropriate service to the child and preferably to the parent and to the school, and to ensure that we were not overlooking factors that might be relevant to the behaviour and just assuming that it was an education problem (consultant paediatrician).
	Clearly, the overall aim is to provide a better service for young people – that's the bottom line, isn't it? (deputy headteacher).
To raise educational achievement	*For raising achievement, the ethos of the school and health of individual children and their families is important and that it is interlinked and as important as literacy and numeracy and ICT* (director of education).
	To enable every child to benefit from education, basically, and to deal with any problems that are preventing them from benefiting from education. (education access manager).
To improve/ explore joint working	*To look at better ways of working in a multi-agency way – forward planning, developing links with other agencies and so on* (consultant paediatrician).
	Mental health is everybody's business. It's something which is shared ... so our overall aims are to make that ... to make mental health understood and shared by all organisations (strategy manager, Health).
	To look at developing a multi-agency approach, as I have said, looking at working together and providing support for these children because obviously it affects their education, affects their health and Social Services are involved as well. So, it's about looking at a multi-agency approach to addressing those in the long term. So, hopefully getting the agencies to take on that responsibility (Social Services manager).

To identify/meet the needs of the target group	*It is about working with children whose parents have a mental health problem, and identifying their needs, and how they can be supported in a multi-agency setting* (principal officer for the education of LAC).
Early identification and intervention	*To work with schools to identify early young children across a whole range of areas, you know, physical disabilities, learning disabilities, mental health, social skills, and to help them at an early age in an environment that was safe and that they felt secure in* (children's manager for mental health). *The greater coordination of services in order to more readily identify children's mental health needs at an earlier stage in their onset and to provide a range of services and resources to meet a range of mental health needs in a much more integrated way across the key providers* (children's services planning manager, Social Services).
To provide support for young people	*To provide a safe place and confidential setting where young people can have their problems met and be listened to and respected, and help them to work through what is going on in their lives* (psychotherapist, voluntary agency).
A holistic approach	*It's a case of the young people that we work with have special educational needs and that essentially does relate to their psychiatric needs. It relates to their social needs. So, it's really very important that we are more fully aware of any sort of support that can be given to them and of the holistic needs of the child really* (education social worker).
To coordinate services	*To try and provide a more coordinated response to need – a joined-up assessment – so that families could be assessed once rather than lots of different times, and then access whatever services they needed* (children's services manager, Education).

Improving services

In just under a third of all the initiatives, multi-agency working was adopted as a means of improving services, and this was also one of the primary rationales presented for the initial development of initiatives discussed previously. The coordination of services, for example, was raised as an aim within a fifth of all the initiatives and, furthermore, some interviewees also felt that the aim of multi-agency initiatives was the development of fully integrated services. Though highlighted by interviewees from all three agencies, almost all of these service-focused aims, perhaps not surprisingly, were cited by strategic-level personnel. Other aims focused on service improvement included improved assessment, saving money and establishing one point of access to services.

Improving outcomes for children and families

Improving educational attainment, perhaps not surprisingly given the LEA focus of the research, was also highlighted within just under a third of all initiatives. This might suggest that, by working with other agencies and using their expertise, educational outcomes and targets can be achieved. In initiatives where educational achievement was considered a major focus, professionals from all agencies cited this as an aim. This was also the case where the promotion of social inclusion was cited as an aim (in almost a quarter of all the initiatives). In fact, six of the 13 interviewees referring to social inclusion (all from different initiatives) were from Health, indicating commitment to a joint agenda. In contrast, where there was a major focus on joint working to improve the general health of children, educational professionals tended to focus solely on educational outcomes when describing the aims. Educational professionals, however, formed the largest group of interviewees identifying a focus on a holistic approach, i.e. addressing the social, emotional and physical needs of children as well as their educational needs, identified as an aim in over a fifth of all the initiatives. In addition, early identification and intervention were also highlighted in almost a quarter of all the initiatives. By using the skills of a range of professionals, therefore, it was deemed possible to intervene early and, in this way, improve the outcomes for children and their families.

Improving multi-agency working

Whilst two of the most common aims were to improve services and to raise the educational achievement of children, an inherent and equally common aim was to improve or explore multi-agency working, thus focusing on the process of joint working as well as outcomes. A specific desire for multi-agency working was also described as one of the main rationales for the development of initiatives. Similarly, information sharing between the agencies and raising awareness and understanding of other agencies were also common aims, both raised within a fifth of all the initiatives, though information sharing was not raised at all by Social Services professionals. In addition, the promotion of a shared responsibility between the agencies was also highlighted in just under a fifth. However, only Health and Social Services representatives, almost all at strategic level, raised the issue of shared responsibility between agencies. It could be suggested that this might indicate some desire on the part of those within Education to retain their independence and autonomy. The focus on shared responsibility was illustrated by the following comment from a health manager:

> *Our overall aims are to make mental health understood and shared by all organisations. Our big aim at response line one is to make ground floor staff – primary care staff, teachers, social workers, health professionals, voluntary staff – aware that we are talking about mental health which everybody has and not mental illness and to make everyone aware that they have a part to play in it ... that the vast majority of mental health problems that are worked with are worked with by them* (children's strategy manager, Health).

2.3.2 Aims of different types of multi-agency activity

Some aims, such as the coordination of services, early identification and intervention, identifying and addressing the needs of children and developing a shared responsibility between the agencies, featured in nearly all, if not all, the different types of multi-agency activity. A three-pronged approach, aimed at services, clients and agencies, was therefore present whatever the type. Many aims, however, were closely related to the type of multi-agency activity undertaken. Specific aims relating to the different types of multi-agency activity are therefore discussed next, beginning with decision-making groups.

Decision-making groups

As well as focusing on some of the aims shared by all types of multi-agency activity, one of the most common aims of multi-agency decision-making groups was to ensure the efficient use of funding and resources. It was felt that, by making decisions collaboratively, costs could be shared between the agencies and limited resources used in the most efficient way. In some cases, joint decision making had meant, for example, that needs were met locally rather than having to access expensive specialist services from outside the area. One assistant director within Social Services described the motivation for joint working as a result of the need to cut costs:

> *From memory, it was where cases – by and large, you were looking at residential placements that were high cost – required funding. My memory of it was that the initial impetus for the group was simply looking at cases where you wanted to share funding. I think it moved on from that, though ... trying to work out a way of spreading the budget expenditure* (assistant director, Social Services).

Strategic decision-making groups, not surprisingly, were also the main focus for the development of integrated services and for establishing joint priorities, as indicated by the joint Education and Social Services project manager within one initiative: '*For example, Education paid £500 to each school for each looked-after child. This tackles a number of objectives where the priorities overlap and so means that one agency is tackling both agencies' priorities*' (project manager, Education and Social Services). An assistant director of Education involved in another decision-making group stressed the focus on joint priorities because of the range of factors that influenced outcomes: '*So, it's no use the* [Primary Care Trust] *trying to convince people not to smoke at 55 so they don't get cancer, if nothing is going on in schools, or going on in parenting groups, or raising awareness about it.*'

The mutual benefit of the joint decision-making process for agency practice was also highlighted:

> [It is] *very much about sharing the complexities of the work, I think, because they are clearly the ways that Education work. Social Services can learn from that in terms of promoting children's*

best interests, and I think a lot of what we do in Social Services is of benefit to Education. For instance, something like how Education deal with complaints ... Social Services is perceived as having a good complaints system, so there has been some sharing of how to do that, and I think traditionally we are very good at working with parents and I think that, certainly at strategic level, we have got much more awareness and we are more in touch with parents than perhaps Education are (team manager, Social Services).

The role of the voluntary sector in helping other agencies to establish aims and objectives in multi-agency projects was also raised by one interviewee from within a decision-making group.

Consultation and training

In contrast to decision-making groups, two of the main aims of initiatives classified as consultation and training focused on broadening the focus of the work so that more children received access to expertise, and on improving collaboration and joint working between agencies. Thus, providing consultation and training was seen as a way of reaching more children where there were limited numbers of staff with the required expertise, as with speech and language therapists from Health. One headteacher, for example, referred to the work of speech and language therapists within his/her school and described how the aims were much broader than s/he had initially thought:

> *Speech therapy was the initial term that was used but I think that was probably due to a lack of understanding on my part ... about the wider, broader issues relating to speech therapy, not just about pronunciation but actually about language and communication difficulties ... so the aims and objectives were much wider than we originally thought, and it opened up a whole new spectrum in terms of the children that it might reach* (headteacher).

Concomitant with this, the danger of the consultant agency being seen by others to shirk their responsibilities was also raised (see Chapter 6 on challenges, where this is discussed in more depth). One Health professional stressed that, whilst engaged in both consultation and direct work with children, the former was more important, but s/he was reticent to suggest that the educational professionals with whom they worked would agree.

Centre-based delivery

Overwhelmingly the most common aim of centre-based initiatives was identified as providing one point of access to services, or, as many interviewees from all different agencies put it, a '*one-stop shop*'. Thus, professional expertise was brought together in one place, and this ensured a highly accessible service for clients, as one educational professional pointed out: '*It provides a focal point for parents of children with complex needs ... which means that parents can gain access to professionals quite*

RATIONALE AND DEVELOPMENT

quickly.' Other key features of centre-based delivery, as well as providing support for children (particularly noted was a safe environment), included support for parents, early identification and intervention, acting as an information point and providing a joint assessment process. One consultant paediatrician, for example, described the aims of a child development centre as:

> *Defining the holistic needs of a child who appears to have needs over and above that of their peers. So, it's looking at their educational needs, health needs and social needs in a context and making a plan around an individual child. And then it's looking at the early educational placement for those children pre-school, and providing an educational plan and dovetailing in with that the therapeutic interventions that are required* (consultant paediatrician).

Coordinated delivery

In contrast to other types of multi-agency activity, the emerging aims of multi-agency coordinated delivery included a focus on involving parents in education and improving home–school relations, as well as raising educational achievement, improving the life chances of children and promoting social inclusion. Health, as well as education, professionals highlighted the support and involvement of parents in education and the focus on home–school relations as aims. Another feature of the aims of a coordinated delivery was the focus on joint planning and the incorporation of the views of all agencies into a broad, strategic framework – an element raised by strategic-level interviewees from all agencies. A health manager, for example, described the aims as: '*having a bigger vision rather than piecemeal ... resource according to need rather than who shouted the loudest or which department had a bit of turf they were trying to protect*' (senior manager, Health). One Social Services manager, however, referred to the difficulties involved in implementing such a plan:

> *Do you make that a universal and broad plan, which I think is what people would wish, which then is so much an espousal of what people want that it would be virtually impossible to achieve an enactment of it, or do you recognise that a children's services plan really should be looking at targeting particular issues around mental health, teenage pregnancy, social exclusion, disability, looked-after children?* (acting group manager, Social Services).

Operational-team delivery

Although there was significant agreement amongst professionals from different agencies about the aims of all initiatives, this was most evident within initiatives focused on operational-team delivery. This is perhaps not surprising given the close working and the nature of engagement between professionals required in this type of approach. Recognition of the links between social, health and educational needs, for example, was more evident within the dialogue of professionals involved in such initiatives, as illustrated by a district manager for Social Services:

When I was a social worker, education was almost a marginal activity. 'Oh, yes, we're into social care' and, 'Oh, yes, there is education'. I have shifted that through my experience and I think that it should be part of the [team] ethos as well – that it isn't a marginal activity, it is actually central and it's probably more important that a child has a stable educational placement than a care placement because school is normal (district manager, Social Services).

Other aims in operational teams, although each only raised within one initiative, included similar aims to those found in centre-based delivery, such as providing a one-stop shop for parents and developing a joint assessment process. An interviewee from a voluntary organisation, for example, described the aims of one initiative as: *'trying to make sure that parents felt that they could go through one door and come out through the other with having seen everybody that they needed to see'* (director of centre, voluntary agency). A joint assessment process was felt to result in the child's holistic needs being met and in a better understanding for parents within another initiative:

I guess, in simple terms, trying to run things in parallel rather than in series. So, rather than the health diagnosis and then maybe Social Services involved and then Education involvement, trying to pull that, draw that together, so that, as parents and children moved through the process, they were being talked to from all three agencies and getting a better understanding of the agencies' perspective and processes and seeing how, for example, social care decisions might impact on education, the learning processes for the children, and, as I said, the social workers weren't just caring but they were thinking about educating as well (head of Children's Services Development Team, Education).

Within one multi-agency operational team focused on mental health, there appeared to be a more definite agreed aim to promote understanding between the agencies involved and to influence the attitudes of professionals from other agencies, as this was highlighted by individuals from all three agencies:

I think the long-term aim of the project has to be around the agencies developing their understanding, developing systems, processes, ways of working, so that communication can carry on, that working together can carry on, that expertise that's been gained by the [initiative] that we can take on board and hopefully complete ... continue to improve our services and meet the needs of this group of people (services manager, Social Services).

Some focus about the thinking, about how mental health or mental illness is thought about in school and thought about in education, because it's clear there are many negatives around it and this remains the case to this day. So, some thoughts about that – there would be an opportunity to explore that as well (clinical coordinator, specialist mental health team).

Trying to influence Health to consider the needs of young people at the same time as they were formulating care plans for adults. Adult services and children services work separately, and it was trying to get the adult service to take into account the needs of the child in the work that they were doing with the parents or carers (acting head of SEN Support Service).

The main rationale for the development of multi-agency initiatives and their aims and objectives having been discussed, the processes involved in their development are now examined.

2.4   Processes involved in development

When interviewees were asked to describe the way in which the initiatives had been developed, their accounts understandably varied according to the amount of involvement they had had in the process. From their responses, a number of key aspects of the developmental process emerged. The analysis showed that neither the agencies involved in the initiatives, nor the type of multi-agency activity undertaken appeared to feature significantly as key variables. However, some points of interest did emerge, and these are illuminated where relevant.

The key processes referred to, in rank order (with the number of initiatives in brackets), were:

♦   establishment of strategic-level meetings/steering groups (9)

♦   appointment of key staff (7)

♦   submission of a bid for funding (4)

♦   consultation with interested parties (4)

♦   adjustment/development of current provision (4)

♦   relocation of agencies on to one site (4)

♦   establishment of operational-level implementation groups (3)

♦   examination of good practice elsewhere (2)

♦   policy development (1)

♦   establishment of a small project that was then extended county-wide (1).

Illustrations of these processes as they occurred in different types of initiative are provided at the end of this section, and these show in more detail the progression of events in setting up some of the multi-agency projects.

The most commonly identified process involved in the development of multi-agency activity was the setting up of multi-agency strategic-level meetings or steering groups, mentioned as a significant part of the process by interviewees within nine of the 30 initiatives. For example, where previous relationships between agencies had historically been poor, two multi-agency decision-making groups had involved the introduction of structured meetings in order to broker work strategically. Interestingly, both initiatives involved Education and Social Services, two agencies in which interviewees reported conflicts around differing priorities emerging. In one of these initiatives, there had been initial difficulties with members not wanting to work together until two people had been appointed with a specific brief '*to make it work*'.

The next most common process described was the appointment of key staff, a feature particularly of initiatives within the category of consultation and training. Four of the five initiatives within this category, reportedly, involved the appointment of key staff. Two joint Education and Health initiatives focused on children with speech and language difficulties had both involved the appointment of therapists to work in target schools, so that more children could be seen in school rather than having to go out to attend clinics (see Initiative 3 at the end of this section). An initiative focused on children in public care had involved the appointment of a key person: '*someone of enough status to be able to communicate with heads and schools*'. This was felt to be necessary because it was in schools that the targets set to raise the achievements of this group of pupils would be met. An initiative focusing on disaffection, in particular children who had been abused, was set up to provide therapeutic services in a more effective, multi-agency way. This was achieved by funding extra social workers to form a therapeutic team (see Initiative 4 at the end of this section).

The submission of a bid for funding was mentioned in relation to four of the 30 initiatives, and this was noted most often in initiatives where all three agencies were involved. The two decision-making initiatives set up to meet the needs of children in public care, for example, both involved the submission of successful bids for funding, which then facilitated the appointment of the appropriate staff.

In four cases, consultation with interested parties was a significant feature. In a consultation and training initiative focused on mental health, which arose from a specific desire for multi-agency working and involved Health professionals providing training and expertise to Education staff, meetings were held initially to consult interested parties about their needs and how those needs should be addressed. Two coordinator-led initiatives had also involved consultation with interested parties. One, an early intervention project aimed at early years, had begun with parental consultations and had involved looking at a previous project to see what had been achieved previously through a multi-agency approach. It was set up as a way of engaging parents more in their children's education by building up a partnership between parents and schools. The other, a Healthy Schools Initiative set up in response to Government policy, had begun with a conference for schools and other agencies to assess the level of interest and the direction to follow (see Initiative 7 at the end of this section). Finally, another Healthy Schools Initiative had involved reviewing and revising a current scheme in order to involve all its schools within the target time.

Adjustment or development of current provision was also mentioned as part of the development process, at least within four initiatives, and predominantly within decision-making groups involving all three agencies. The three decision-making groups set up in order to develop a more effective and comprehensive service, perhaps unsurprisingly, involved adjusting and developing current provision. One of the three decision-making groups set up in this way, which was focused on strategic planning for all children's services, had extended current planning and implementation groups to ensure equity of representation. Similarly, another, focused on disaffection, had recognised that by ensuring broader representation and widening its remit, it could be more effective (see Initiative 1 at the end of this section). The third, focused on children with complex needs, had moved from agreeing outcomes or making recommendations towards a more strategic and policy-led approach.

In four cases, the relocation of agencies on to one site had played a significant part in the process of development of the project. Perhaps unsurprisingly, the development of centre-based initiatives, the purpose of which was to deliver a coordinated service by gathering together a range of expertise, was most likely to involve the relocation of agencies on to one site. In all three cases, it was felt that bringing everything together on to a single site would be far more effective, offering, as noted previously, what was described in two cases as 'a one-stop shop' (see Initiatives 5 and 6 at the end of this section). One operational-team initiative, focused on children with disabilities, also involved the relocation of the agencies involved on to one site. Interviewees described it as being 'opportunistic' to some extent, in that the premises became available at the time Health was looking to relocate some of its paediatricians.

The establishment of operational-level implementation groups was a key process in three initiatives, all of which were coordinator led. Five of the nine coordinator-led initiatives involved the development of strategic groups, with, in three cases, the subsequent introduction of operational-level implementation groups. The two set up in response to a review and/or research (one focused on children in public care and one on disaffection), and one focused on children's health that arose from a specific desire for multi-agency working, all involved the development of a steering group to decide the parameters of the project and secure funding, and then the introduction of multi-agency implementation groups, or teams, to carry out the work (see Initiative 8 at the end of this section). Another initiative that arose from a desire for increased multi-agency working and one set up in order to offer a more effective, comprehensive service, both of which focused on early years, involved the creation of an Early Years Partnership. For the latter initiative, the development of an Early Years and Childcare Team had seemed 'the logical progression' from their Partnership, which had then, in effect, acted as a steering group for the team.

Other points raised included the examination of good practice conducted elsewhere, policy development and the establishment, in the first instance, of a local project which then went county-wide. One initiative involving operational-team delivery and focused on children in public care was influenced by a review of multi-agency links and resources. This led to an initial project focused on implementing draft guidance and then to the formation of a county-wide team dedicated to the education of this vulnerable group of young people (see Initiative 10 at the end of this section).

Illustrations of the processes involved in establishing multi-agency initiatives are now presented, followed by a consideration of what interviewees had to say about the stages of development the different initiatives had reached.

Decision-making groups

Initiative 1
A behaviour management panel involving professionals from all three agencies who met to address specific cases as well as more general issues relating to disaffection.

Rationale
To offer a more effective/comprehensive service.

Development
The LEA already had a number of out-of-school panels, which were disparate and not well planned. It was recognised that they could be made more effective by having a broader remit and wider representation.

One panel had a Social Services representative, and this panel appeared to work more effectively and had a better relationship with schools than others. It was therefore felt that this model could be extended to other parts of the county. The introduction of IT also meant that much more comprehensive information could be made available to the panel.

Although Education was the principal provider, it was recognised that extra support was needed. A range of agencies was therefore identified and invited to the meetings. It took more than a year to get things moving but the panel has now become embedded in the structures of each of the organisations involved.

Initiative 2
A mental health strategy and related child behaviour intervention initiatives involving all three agencies.

Rationale
To address gaps in services at an early intervention level.

Development
Dating back to the early '90s, it took five years to put the strategy together, but this was spurred on by the Health Advisory Service (HAS) report.

By 1997, a strategy document had been written covering key target areas. A strategy manager and a number of implementation managers were then employed so that people had dedicated time for the work.

Potential funding through the Mental Health Grant became available in early 1998, so the implementation came later. There was a natural break between planning and developing the strategy and then implementing it, which, it was felt, allowed for new people with new enthusiasm to become engaged in the initiative.

Consultation and training

Initiative 3

A school-based service for non-statemented children with speech and language difficulties and involving joint commissioning between Health and Education.

Rationale

To meet the needs of a specific target group.

Development

An initial baseline assessment was carried out to assess the relationship between the agencies and how the service was working. Health and Education discussed and defined a service specification. They conducted a literature search and produced a draft document, which then went to wide consultation.

Once the funding was agreed, the new money from Education allowed children without a statement to be seen in schools, whereas previously they had been seen in clinics.

A number of therapists were employed, and they contacted schools to develop links and to gather information. They were responsible for coordinating the service. They developed service criteria and undertook a screening programme. They then set up the necessary systems, and recruited and inducted new staff.

Initiative 4

A therapeutic team made up of social workers from Education and Social Services who received consultation and support from a clinical psychologist. This initiative therefore involved all three agencies.

Rationale

To offer a more effective/comprehensive service.

Development

Before going unitary, the authority used to purchase therapeutic services from another LEA. This was not satisfactory, as children had to travel long distances, so different ways of delivering a local service were examined.

At the same time, Education was looking at the role of their specialist social workers who had previously been employed as part of the Educational Psychology Service. Social Services and Education decided to look at how these services could join together.

Initially, this was achieved by giving social workers some dedicated time to support the social workers from Education, but this did not work as they could not ring-fence the time with such heavy caseloads. So Quality Protects money was used to recruit 1.5 social workers to join with the education social workers to form the therapeutic team.

Centre-based delivery

Initiative 5
A project involving all three agencies focused on providing a better service for children in need.

Rationale
A response to review/research.

Development
This initiative evolved from a joint development review. It was considered a good idea to bring a multi-agency team together into the same building so three staff, one from each agency, were seconded to a team with the brief to look at ways of improving joint working and to develop joint initiatives.

The original idea was for the team to work with schools to prevent young people from being excluded and from becoming offenders.

However, the idea was '*hijacked*' politically and became a type of 'bolt-on' initiative to Social Services rather than a new team. There was no preparatory work done to see what people's expectations were or how it was going to work. So for the first two years the team was pretty chaotic and was not operating as expected. There was general dissatisfaction because the team did not work in schools and initially there was an increase in referrals to child mental health. In addition, because it had not started off as a unique entity, when any difficulties arose, team members tended to retreat to their own agency.

Since then, however, the team has started to work more with schools and, in the last couple of years, it has started to operate more as a team.

Initiative 6
A children's centre for pre-school children with complex needs, based within a hospital and involving Education and Health.

Rationale
To offer a more effective/comprehensive service.

Development
The children's centre was set up jointly some time ago, before reorganisation, by a consultant paediatrician and a specialist educational psychologist working for the previous authority. They recognised that it would be more effective to bring together services for pre-school children with complex difficulties on one single site with combined assessment and intervention.

Education provided the staffing; Health the accommodation. The centre has grown and developed since then and moved to better accommodation, although still within the hospital.

The centre started with one teacher and one nursery nurse, and it now has an acting headteacher, two other teachers, five nursery nurses, input from speech and language therapists, physiotherapists, educational psychologists and community nurses, plus an outreach service offering advice for children in mainstream.

It is now considered very much part of the established pattern of working and integral to the Special Needs Service.

However, with the drive towards inclusion, the question was raised as to whether providing services on a single site is best or whether they should be looking to develop more provision within the community itself.

Coordinator-led delivery

Initiative 7
A Healthy Schools Initiative involving Education and Health.

Rationale
A response to Government trends/initiatives.

Development
This initiative was the authority's response to a new Government initiative. Two hundred people from schools and other agencies attended a conference, which set out where the authority wanted to go, and who was willing to be involved.

This led to 85 expressions of interest from individual schools, 26 of which joined in the first phase. The initiative had three phases: it was currently in Phase One; 25–30 more schools were expected to join in Phase Two in September 2001; and the rest were expected to join in Phase Three in September 2002.

Initially there was a narrow steering group, which proved inadequate. An operational worker was recruited in September 2000 to work with schools on their action plans. When schools signed up, they were given training and a lot of time was being spent on preparing for accreditation.

Initiative 8
An educational psychologist coordinating multi-agency activity to cater for the needs of children in public care.

Rationale
A response to review/research.

Development
Reports in the mid-'90s (*Children Like Us*, 1994; the Utting Report, 1997) acted as a powerful stimulus to draw attention to the plight of children in public care and their disadvantaged position in terms of educational opportunities and outcomes, and their health needs. This, together with a conference outlining what other authorities were doing in this area, created a recognition that these children should become a priority for the authority.

The project was set up in collaboration with the National Children's Bureau (NCB). Funding from the Joint Consultative Committee (JCC) allowed for a consultant from the NCB to work with them for 18 months.

Initially, a multi-agency steering group of senior managers was set up and, under that, a multi-agency implementation group was established. The remit of the Steering Group was to set out the parameters of the project, secure funding and support, and to set the tasks for the implementation group.

The implementation group consisted of people from the voluntary sector, Health, Education and Social Services. Their brief was to conduct an audit of children in public care and then to build up services in response to identified need. This phase ended with the publication of the NCB report.

The Steering Group was replaced by a Quality Protects Steering Group, which now has oversight of the project and it is largely driven by Social Services.

The implementation group has also dissolved to some extent. Presently, an educational psychologist, who works two days a week on the project, is responsible for the educational needs of children in public care, whilst Social Services provides for their care needs. Social Services involvement has been more problematic at strategic level since the Quality Protects manager left.

41

Operational-team delivery

Initiative 9
A mental health project involving all three agencies.

Rationale
To meet the needs of a specific target group.

Development
Education was invited to join Social Services and Health to discuss funding for this project because it had to be a three-way bid. Discussions took place around a proposal for providing services from a multi-agency perspective for meeting the needs of young people who may have been affected by mental health problems. They decided to focus on meeting the needs of young people whose parents suffer from mental health problems. They agreed Education's involvement and that Health would provide the premises.

A proposal was sent in and was accepted immediately. It was described as the only project in the country that actually satisfied all the criteria.

The project got off to a very good start, as all the agencies involved were very positive, but when the project leader fell ill, this undermined it before it was established and this led to further staffing problems.

The health building was not forthcoming and, in the absence of a project leader, it was overseen by educationalists which, it was felt, skewed the project. There were no health workers even though the focus was on mental health. The first 12 months was a struggle and the initiative twice failed to appoint a project leader.

Since a project leader has been appointed, the initiative has been much more focused. A multi-agency conference was organised involving all the agencies, including the voluntary sector, which put the project 'on the map'.

Initiative 10
A team involving Education and Social Services focused on the education of children in public care.

Rationale
A specific desire for multi-agency working.

Development
This initiative was originally driven by members, who wanted more multi-agency working. The council, through a branch review, looked at multi-agency links and mapped out resources. Immediately they began to see how many children the agencies had in common and where the links were.

At the same time, joint work was going on through the Joint Agency Committee for Looked-after Children (JACLAC) and Quality Protects. Models were put forward and the work of other authorities examined.

A project was set up focusing on implementing the draft guidance for the education of children in public care in a small area to look at the 'ripple' effects. This was monitored and led to the formation of a county-wide team focusing on the education of children in public care, which is how the guidance is now delivered.

2.5 Stages of development

Interviewees were asked about the stage of development at which they considered the multi-agency initiative they were involved in to be. Interviewees were presented with options ranging from an initial proposal or idea to well-established delivery. In 18 out of the 30 initiatives, interviewees from different agencies and at different levels agreed about the stage of development. Decision-making groups, however, were poorly represented, and in only three out of the nine initiatives in this group was there general agreement amongst professionals about the stage of development, in contrast to the majority of initiatives in other types of multi-agency activity. Professionals working at operational and strategic levels also sometimes disagreed, and this appeared to stem in part from the different rationales professionals used to assess the stage of development. Their opinions about the stages of development are detailed in Research Vignette 1 on the following page, whilst the rationales for their responses are now discussed.

Table 2.1 shows the most common rationales interviewees offered when considering the stage of development of multi-agency activity. They have been ranked according to the number of interviewees who cited them, although the number of initiatives in which these interviewees were involved has also been presented

Table 2.1   Rationales offered for the stage of development

Rationale	Initiatives (N=30)		Interviewees (N=139)	
	No.	%	No.	%
Length of time	21	70	31	22
Framework or plan in place	12	40	15	11
Review or evaluation	10	33	13	9
Commitment of those involved	10	33	11	8
Surviving changes of personnel	8	27	11	8
Remaining issues/obstacles to be overcome	7	23	11	8
Appointment/permanency of key personnel	6	20	9	7
Number and range of initiatives or services	4	13	5	4

A multiple-response question; therefore, percentages may not sum to 100
Source: *Interviews in Phase Two of the NFER study, 2001*

The most frequently cited factor in relation to the stage of development was the length of time the project had been running. Personnel from all three agencies and all different types of multi-agency activity offered this as a rationale (see Illustrations 1 and 2 at the end of this section).

The second most common rationale for established practice cited by interviewees was having a framework, model or plan in place that had been agreed by all the agencies involved (see Illustration 1 at the end of this section). Seven out of the 15 interviewees citing this as a rationale were involved in decision-making groups, and five were from initiatives classified as coordinated delivery, suggesting that this is an especially important indicator in this type of multi-agency activity. The following quotes illustrate how establishing an overall model or framework, or incorporating multi-agency working into strategic plans, was considered to be an important aspect of joint working becoming embedded in practice:

Research Vignette 1   Stages of development

All initiatives were considered to be either well established, just starting to deliver, or somewhere between these two options. Fifty-five interviewees, referring to 24 of the 30 initiatives, stated that initiatives were well established, whilst 30 interviewees, referring to 14 of the 30 initiatives, stated that they were in their early stages. Eleven interviewees felt that seven initiatives, three of which were focused on multi-agency consultation and training, were between these two phases. Fourteen interviewees, referring to seven different initiatives, all except one of which were either decision-making groups or concerned with coordinated delivery, felt that different levels of their initiative were at different stages of development. This probably reflects the breadth of these types of multi-agency activity, which frequently involved a vast range of projects or interventions.

In 17 of the 30 initiatives, however, 29 interviewees indicated that they considered the joint work they were involved in to be still developing or evolving, and this was particularly the case in initiatives classified as decision-making groups (seven), coordinated delivery (six), and centre-based delivery (three). In addition, ten interviewees, five of whom were involved in coordinated multi-agency working, commented on the fast rate of expansion. Thus, rapid development and growth appeared to be a particular feature of multi-agency coordinated delivery. A Healthy Schools Initiative, for example, was described by the health coordinator as '*growing and developing*', and one early years project was described by a health worker as '*burgeoning* and *moving onwards and upwards*'. Within another early years project, the assistant director for Education commented on the rapid growth of the project and highlighted the importance of managing this appropriately to ensure that multi-agency working remained effective: '*managing that is something we need to keep a clear grip on, to make sure that it remains integrated and coordinated and that is doesn't actually lose its capacity to deliver high-quality provision and services because of the pace of change*' (assistant director, Education).

Seven interviewees referred to setbacks that had meant that joint working was not at the stage they expected at the time of interviewing. These overlapped with the issues raised when interviewees were asked about the difficulties in the early stages, the responses to which are discussed in Chapter 6 on challenges. Difficulties concerning illness of key staff and lack of resources or staffing were noted. Thus, despite the appointment of key staff being considered one of the key processes in the development of multi-agency initiatives and also a significant factor in their establishment, difficulties with this were highlighted. One educational professional referred specifically to the difficulties of getting Health's commitment, whilst, in contrast, one health representative in a different project felt that there had been a lack of consultation with Health in the early stages, although this was since felt to have been overcome. Consultation with all those involved was also considered a key part of the setting-up process. Similarly, whilst gaining the commitment of other agencies was felt to be a key factor in the establishment of projects, this was also noted as a difficulty in the early stages, and involving Health specifically was mentioned.

In the early days, we were dependent on people making things happen, at least agreeing to things happening, and now I think we are ... it's dependent on people keeping on signing up to the idea that it's something that they need to keep on with the philosophy really, and that when the chips go down on money and all the rest of it, that the idea and the model is one that people still hold hard to (director of voluntary agency).

We are contained within the Education Development Plan. We have our own section in the Education, Youth and Leisure Service Plan. We are within the Best Value Review process and we are within the Health Authority's service and financial frameworks and a central part to things like national service frameworks for coronary heart disease and mental health and to implement the provincial part of the NHS plan, and so on. So, I would say, where we are, we are a core part of the response to a number of strategic documents coming out of the Government (head of health promotion, Health).

Whether the multi-agency initiative had been reviewed or evaluated was also referred to by 13 interviewees. In contrast to having a framework or plan in place, this was mentioned more by interviewees involved in service delivery, and interviewees from centre-based, coordinated and operational-team delivery were all represented within this group.

Eleven interviewees suggested that the commitment of individuals from the different agencies to the project was a good indicator of how far it had progressed. Of these 11, all except one were involved in multi-agency decision-making groups and coordinated delivery, suggesting that commitment to these types of multi-agency activity was important to establish, and all of those citing this as a rationale were from either Education or Social Services. Commitment, for some interviewees, meant that tasks were undertaken and information was fed back to others: '*People put their name to things and come back and say what they have done so that is a measure of how well established it is*' (deputy unit manager, Social Services). Alternatively, for others, funding availability and support from key strategic personnel were important in terms of commitment. Thus, in one early years project, for example, the fact that the money for the project was to come from the base education budget was seen as an important sign of commitment:

We've made a quantum leap in the last year from a [local] *children's project that was cobbled together from bits and pieces of funding from all over the place that was always a bit uncertain, to actually, through working closely with Social Services, putting forward a service development bid that was hugely supported by the chair of the education committee personally...He's been key to getting the project established under the funding in the base budget and sufficient funding to become a borough-wide project* (head of education, planning and communication).

Similarly, having pooled budgets or joint funding was also seen as an indication that a project was well established. The argument for pooled budgets as a clear indication of the maturity of joint working was clearly expressed by one strategic manager who had the benefit of working jointly for Health and Social Services:

> *My notion of adulthood for this group is one that has devolved responsibility for making the best decision about that child to whatever group or process is appropriate, that is no longer having to have an argument about how much of the funding should come from Health, how much of the funding should come from Social Services and how much of the funding should come from Education ... One of my colleagues once said to me 'When a child's having lunch, is he having his health needs met, his educational needs met or his social care needs met?' It points up the stupidness of the question – he's clearly having all three needs met* (assistant director of Social Services and head of Children's Services for Health).

Eleven interviewees stated that being able to survive changes of personnel was an important criterion for established multi-agency working, as indicated by this example: '*A key person retired and we have been able to make the transition and keep it moving so it is now embedded, since Health saw it necessary to ensure that someone continued to come*' (head of the SEN Support Service). Six of those who cited this were from decision-making groups, suggesting that consistency of staff is particularly important in the joint decision-making process. One education worker felt that the multi-agency team they were involved in was always having to cope with staff changes, such that they were '*always having to build up new relationships*', although, as the team became established it was felt that they could continue to deliver services despite this. Similarly, a member of a multi-agency operational team felt that, as they had become more established and ground rules had been developed, the quality of service had been maintained despite staff changes.

The appointment and permanency of key staff were also felt by many interviewees to be indicative of a well-established multi-agency project, especially where coordinated delivery was involved, with six out of the 11 interviewees involved in this type of multi-agency activity citing this. This may reflect the key role that the coordinator plays in this type of joint working. For one project coordinator from Education, for example, complications with the funding for posts and getting commitment from all the agencies involved had been a particular problem in establishing the project:

> *In the whole group dynamics of things, we seem to have been permanently storming ever since we started because it's got a complicated set-up of how we got the money for posts, and there was a bit of confusion last time, last year, about whether or not the education welfare workers and the educational psychologist,*

who is only three hours a week, would be part of us or not, which was to do with funding and being stretched this way and that way and all over the place. Lots of multi-agency initiatives expect different departments to get involved but they still have got to do their statutory stuff, so it was a practical issue and a funding issue (project coordinator, Education).

In addition, where interviewees felt there were problems or issues still to sort out between the agencies, multi-agency working was not considered to have reached the well-established stage (see Illustrations 3 and 4 at the end of this section). For example, in one initiative focused on the assessment of children with disabilities, whilst Social Services and Health professionals considered that the team was well established, remaining difficulties around integrating a joint assessment process with the formal assessment process within Education led Educational professionals to feel that the project was still in its early stages.

Illustrations of how rationales varied between agencies or between strategic- and operational-level staff are presented in Illustrations 1–4.

Illustration 1

In one initiative, focused on health promotion, and an example of coordinated delivery, Health professionals at strategic level felt that the initiative had now been incorporated into both Education and Health plans and frameworks and therefore considered it to be '*embedded*'. In contrast, an educational professional working at operational level felt that, although they had learnt a great deal, from their perspective, in terms of delivery, the project was just completing its pilot year and was between just starting to deliver and well established.

Illustration 2

In another initiative, focused on children with disabilities and an example of operational-team delivery, Social Services and voluntary sector personnel felt that the project was well established as the service had been operating for a number of years, people were signed up to the principles and it had survived changes in key staff. However, for Education, there were still issues to be addressed about how the initiative fitted within educational structures and frameworks, so, as far as they were concerned, it was only at the stage where it was almost ready to deliver.

Illustration 3

In an initiative focused on children in public care and an example of a decision-making group, whilst Social Services and voluntary sector strategic-level staff felt that there were still unresolved issues, they agreed with education strategic-level staff that the initiative was still very much expanding and developing. In contrast, a ground-level worker within Social Services considered the project to be well established because '*everyone knows about it*'.

Illustration 4

In an initiative focused on children with complex needs and an example of a decision-making group, the Social Services/Health strategic representative felt that the initiative had progressed because it had moved from dealing with individual cases to policy development, although s/he stated that s/he felt that the group was in '*adolescence*' and would only become fully mature when agencies had pooled budgets and no longer argued about money. The strategic-level education representative also felt that the group had matured, but there was still a lot of '*baggage*' around and no definite model to follow for multi-agency working. In contrast, the education operational interviewee felt that, in terms of delivery, policies, protocols and clear responsibilities were established, and the Social Services operational representative also felt that, whilst there were staff changes, the group was well established.

Key points

♦ Although a variety of rationales and aims for multi-agency working were presented, the aims centred on three main areas: improving services, improving outcomes for children and families, and improving multi-agency working.

♦ Aims in these three broad areas were common to all types of multi-agency activity, but more specific aims within different types were also identified. Decision-making groups, for example, focused on ensuring joint priorities and ensuring effective use of funding and resources; consultation and training focused on collaborative working and ensuring more children accessed services; centre-based and operational-team delivery focused on providing one point of access for children and parents; coordinated delivery focused on improving home–school relations, joint planning and bringing all the views of one agency into a broad strategic framework.

♦ A number of key processes involved in setting up multi-agency initiatives were identified, particularly the establishment of multi-agency steering groups or management groups and the appointment of key staff. Whilst the appointment of key staff was common in consultation and training initiatives, the relocation of agencies on to one site was key in centre-based delivery.

♦ All the multi-agency initiatives studied were considered to be either well established, just starting to deliver or in between these two options. Whilst many interviewees commented that projects were still evolving, rapid growth and development were a key feature of coordinator-led initiatives, which therefore required close monitoring.

♦ Where discrepancies in views about the stage of development were in evidence, this tended to be due to the different rationales on which judgement about establishment was formulated. Differences emerged, for example, where one agency felt there were still issues to be addressed or where there were different perspectives at strategic and operational level. These may provide some useful pointers to the progression of multi-agency work in the future.

♦ Whilst the appointment of key staff, gaining the commitment of agencies and consultation with relevant agencies were felt to be key processes in development, difficulties in these areas in the early stages were also reported. These are discussed in more depth in Chapter 6 on challenges.

3. PROFESSIONAL AND AGENCY INVOLVEMENT

3.1 Introduction

This chapter examines the professional background of those involved in the multi-agency initiatives under study and how they came to be involved, as well as the LEA multi-agency context and how the agencies came to be involved. Firstly, it focuses on the individuals and considers their different professional backgrounds, the implications of these backgrounds and how professionals came to be involved. Secondly, it focuses on the agencies, and explores the relationships between agencies and the multi-agency working that existed in the local authorities prior to the formation of initiatives, as well as how the agencies came to be involved.

3.2 Professional backgrounds

The professional backgrounds of individuals were examined under three main themes: the agencies they had worked for in the past, their qualifications and training, and the roles they had previously assumed.

3.2.1 Previous agency employment

The description of their professional background given by the interviewees was examined first in terms of all the agencies that they had previously worked for. Perhaps unsurprisingly, given the education focus of the initiatives examined and the number of Education professionals within the sample, over half of the interviewees involved stated that they had worked previously in a local authority Education department or setting. Just over a third (35 per cent) had previously worked in Social Services, and just under a third (29 per cent) in Health. Only 12 per cent of the interviewees stated that they had worked in the voluntary sector at any time during their career.

However, more important than the range of agencies worked in by interviewees were the numbers of interviewees who had worked in more than one agency during their career. In total, 52 interviewees (38 per cent) described having worked in multiple agencies during their career. Specific examples included: 21 per cent of Education professionals who had worked for Social Services; 18 per cent of those currently working for Social Services who had worked for Education, 20 per cent of those currently working within Health who had previously worked for Education, and 18 per cent of those currently working for Social Services who described previous work in the voluntary sector. However, as might be expected, the more common occurrence was for people to have assumed different roles whilst working for the same agency. There was very little difference in this pattern between strategic- and operational-level staff.

3.2.2 Qualifications and training of those involved

When asked about their professional background, interviewees were also asked about the qualifications that they had gained. Analysis showed that those involved in the multi-agency projects under study had a wide range of qualifications, including professional qualifications and training, such as teaching qualifications, social work training, or nursing qualifications, as well as a range of academic qualifications, such as degrees, (in a variety of subjects) and postgraduate qualifications, e.g. master's degrees and diplomas. Their professional training and qualifications are discussed first, before their academic qualifications.

Professional training and qualifications

Where individuals cited professional training and qualifications they had undertaken, these included, in rank order (with the number of interviewees in brackets):

- teacher training or a teaching qualification (49)
- social work training or qualification (34)
- nursing training or qualification (15)
- management qualification (7).

Over a third of those involved in the multi-agency initiatives under study had a teaching qualification and had undergone teacher training. All the initiatives, except three, which were focused on prostitution, counselling and information for young people (both involving youth workers) and abused children, had a professional with a teaching qualification involved, reflecting the educational focus of the study. All except eight of the 49 interviewees with a teaching qualification presently worked within Education. Six individuals worked within Social Services, their involvement being at strategic rather than operational level and in decision-making groups rather than other types of multi-agency activity (three focused on children in public care). Of the two health employees with education-related qualifications, one now worked as a health coordinator within the health education field and the other, who had undergone educational psychology training, worked as a clinical psychologist involved in providing consultation and training to education and Social Services social workers working with abused children.

Almost a quarter of all the professionals interviewed had undergone social work training, although only seven specifically stated that they had a certificate in social work and only four a diploma. Interestingly, four out of the seven who had a certificate were involved in decision-making groups. Social workers were involved in almost three-quarters of all the initiatives, all types of activity and with all target groups except children with speech and language difficulties. Only five out of the 34 interviewees with social work training were now working for other agencies: four worked for Education in initiatives focused on children in public care, children in need and disaffection, whilst the sole health worker with social work training was a qualified nursery nurse working in an early years project.

Fifteen interviewees in total stated that they had a nursing qualification. All except four of these were presently working within Health. All of those with a nursing qualification were working within initiatives classified as delivery, i.e. not decision-making groups or consultation and training, and six out of the 11 were involved in coordinator-led projects, suggesting that these workers tended to be involved at operational level rather than having any strategic responsibilities. Five out of the 15 with nursing qualifications had also at some time worked in other agencies. Three, two of whom were nursery nurses, were now employed by Social Services in projects focused on autism, early years and mental health. One, also a nursery nurse, was employed by Education in another project focused on early years.

Seven interviewees mentioned having some form of management qualification or training. Not surprisingly, all worked at strategic level, but no Health professionals were represented. All except one of those with a management qualification were involved in decision-making groups or coordinated delivery, suggesting perhaps the importance of this type of qualification in these types of work, although this would appear to be contrary to findings concerning the lack of management roles undertaken within coordinator-led delivery (see Chapter 4).

The next most frequently mentioned professional training cited by interviewees was educational psychology training (6), followed by medical training (3) and psychiatry (3). Of the six interviewees who had been involved in educational psychology training, all except one, who was from Health and now offering consultation and training to social workers from Education and Social Services, were employed by Education. The three with medical training were involved in initiatives focused on disaffection, children's health and complex needs, whilst the three with psychiatric training, not surprisingly, were involved in two initiatives focused on mental health and one on counselling for young people.

Thus, although a significant number of interviewees indicated that they had experience in working within other agencies, the number of those with dual qualifications would appear to have been very limited. This suggests that a number of professionals who have crossed agency boundaries have been appointed on the basis of their experience of work in a particular field and the skills developed 'on the job' rather than having professional qualifications for the type of work.

Academic qualifications

Many interviewees indicated that, as well as professional qualifications and training, they had undertaken a variety of academic qualifications. The most common included 36 interviewees who had undertaken a first degree and 22 interviewees who had undertaken a master's degree.

Over a quarter of all those interviewed, representing over two-thirds of all the projects, had a first degree. These included individuals from all three agencies working at both operational and strategic level and within all types of initiative. A broad range of degree subjects was evident, but overwhelmingly, the most frequently mentioned was psychology, whilst others included English, drama and economics. This is perhaps not surprising since psychology would seem to be a subject that is relevant to working with children across agencies. Sixteen out of the 36 who had a first degree had also had experience of working in agencies other than the one they were presently employed by.

Twenty-two interviewees, representing over half of all the initiatives (of all different types), stated that they had a master's degree. Over half of these were from Education, and more Health than Social Services staff were included. Compared with those who had first degrees, only a small proportion (six of the 22) had worked within other agencies. Master's degrees, like first degrees, encompassed a range of subjects, including business, counselling and social studies. Those with master's degrees were involved with the whole range of target groups.

3.2.3 Previous roles undertaken

Given the wide range of qualifications and training undertaken by interviewees, it is perhaps not surprising that the different roles that interviewees had assumed during their careers were many and varied. These included, in rank order (with the number of interviewees in brackets):

♦ education-related roles (e.g. teacher, youth worker, educational psychologist, education welfare officer, education adviser, school inspector) (66)

♦ social worker (34)

♦ operational-level manager (34)

♦ health-related roles (e.g. nurse, health visitor, qualified doctor, speech and language therapist, psychiatrist, psychotherapist, nursery nurse and psychologist) (33)

♦ strategic-level manager (24)

♦ administrator (11)

♦ counsellor (5).

Education-related roles

Nearly half (66) of the professionals involved in the multi-agency initiatives within this study had previously worked in education-related arenas. Of these, 45 had previously worked as teachers, 13 of whom specifically referred to a role within special educational needs, two to an earlier teaching role within a residential care setting, and one to a responsibility for child protection. More than three-quarters (35) of those who referred to having been a teacher were currently working within Education in initiatives covering all five models of multi-agency activity. Of the other ten, six were currently working in Social Services and were mainly involved in decision-making groups, two were currently working within Health in coordinator-led initiatives focusing on children's health, and two were currently working for the voluntary sector in the same centre-based initiative offering counselling and advice to young people.

The role of youth worker was highlighted by six interviewees, four of whom were currently working within Education, two within the same decision-making group focused on prostitution and two within the same centre-based initiative offering counselling and advice to young people. Of the other two interviewees who referred to having been a youth worker, one was currently employed by Social Services in an operational team focused on children with disabilities, while the other was working within the voluntary sector in another centre-based initiative offering counselling and advice to young people. Five interviewees, all currently employed in strategic roles within Education, had previously worked as educational psychologists. All but one of these now occupied the role of principal educational psychologist and were involved in all models of multi-agency activity, except for consultation and training. Four interviewees referred to having worked previously as education welfare officers (EWOs), two of whom were currently working in Social Services in the same operational team focused on children with disabilities. The other two referring to the role of EWO were currently working in Education, one in a centre-based initiative focused on children in need and one in a coordinator-led initiative focused on disaffection. Finally, three interviewees, all currently employed by Education, referred to previous work as an education adviser, while three, again all currently employed by Education, referred to having worked as a school inspector.

Social worker

Nearly a quarter (34) of all the professionals interviewed commented that they had previously been employed as social workers (although not all were qualified). Fourteen of these specified having worked in a residential care setting, and six of referred to a responsibility for child protection. Twenty-three of those referring to a social worker role were currently employed in Social Services, with over half of these (14) currently involved in decision-making groups, and predominantly at strategic level. Of the other 11 interviewees referring to a social work role, nine were currently employed within Education and two within the voluntary sector. No professionals currently working in Health referred to having been a social worker.

Operational-level manager

Nearly a quarter (34) of those interviewed also specified some sort of operational-level management role. Of these, 22 were currently employed within Social Services, all of whom had undertaken this management role as part of a career as a social worker, for example, as a team manager. Six of the other 12 interviewees referring to an operational-level management role were currently employed by Health, five of whom had previously managed teams of health professionals and one had been a project manager whilst working within the voluntary sector. Five of the remaining six interviewees were currently working in Education; two of these had adopted management roles whilst teaching, two whilst working as a social worker, and one had taken on responsibility for a team of administrative staff. The last of the interviewees referring to an operational-level management role was currently working within the voluntary sector but had taken on this responsibility as part of his/her career as a social worker.

Health-related roles

Within this category, one-third of the interviewees (11), all currently employed within Health, referred to having worked as a nurse, with two specifically referring to a focus on mental health and one to paediatric training. Six, again all currently employed by Health, referred to having worked as a health visitor – five of these had previously worked as nurses. Four interviewees, all currently employed within Health, had worked as qualified doctors, three specifying the role of paediatrician and two of general practitioner (GP). Another four had worked as speech and language therapists and were currently employed by Health, three in initiatives offering consultation and training, and one in a centre-based initiative focusing on pre-school children with complex needs. Three current health professionals referred to having worked as a psychiatrist, two of whom were now consultants. Two interviewees, one currently employed by Health and one by Social Services, had previously worked as psychotherapists. Two other interviewees referred to having worked as nursery nurses. One of these was currently working in Social Services and one in Education, and both were involved in coordinator-led initiatives focusing on autism and early years respectively. Finally, one interviewee, currently working in Health in an initiative providing consultation and training, had previously worked as a clinical psychologist. All types of multi-agency activity were represented amongst the above accounts, although decision-making groups were in the minority.

Strategic-level manager

A role as a strategic-level manager was mentioned by 24 of the professionals interviewed. It should be noted that some of these interviewees indicated that this was a responsibility they had only taken on recently and presently still held within their current position. Almost half of the 24 interviewees (11) were currently employed at strategic level within Social Services and had, in the main, adopted this role during their career as a social worker, for example, as a service manager or planning officer. Seven interviewees who had assumed a strategic-level management role were from Education and had worked, or were working as, for example, an assistant director or head of service. Five interviewees were currently working in Health, in either decision-making groups or coordinator-led initiatives, and had previously worked, or were currently working as, for example, directors or joint commissioning managers. Finally, one interviewee currently employed within the voluntary sector had previously worked as a planning manager and service manager during a career as a social worker within Social Services.

Administrator

Of the 11 professionals who referred to previous administrative roles, seven (four of whom had also previously worked as teachers) were currently working in Education. Two interviewees currently working in Social Services within the same operational team delivering services to children with disabilities had previously worked in an administrative capacity, one within their own agency and one within Education. Two professionals currently working at a strategic level within Health (one in a coordinator-led initiative and the other in one offering consultation and training) also referred to a role as an administrator, one while previously working within Health and one while previously within the voluntary sector.

Counsellor

Finally, five interviewees commented that they had previously undertaken a counselling role. Two of these were currently working within the voluntary sector on the same initiative, one within Education, one within Social Services and one within Health. All but one of the interviewees were involved in centre-based initiatives offering, perhaps unsurprisingly, counselling and advice to young people or support for children in need. The remaining interviewee was involved in a coordinator-led initiative focused on disaffection.

3.2.4 The implications of different professional backgrounds

Having described their different backgrounds, interviewees were then asked to reflect on the implications that their background had for the multi-agency work in which they were currently involved. As may be expected, given the wide variety of different backgrounds of those now involved in the broad spectrum of multi-agency working, a considerable number of different implications were mentioned. Interviewees also often referred to multiple implications of their backgrounds.

In some instances, interviewees did not elaborate on the implications of their backgrounds specifically for multi-agency working, but described in more general terms the formative nature of their past experiences. However, over 80 per cent of interviewees did describe their prior experiences as being relevant to their current multi-agency context, and within these remarks some common themes were clearly apparent. Only two interviewees remarked specifically that their background had no implications for the multi-agency work in which they were currently involved.

Interviewees described the implications of the following (the numbers of interviewees are given in brackets):

♦ prior multi-agency work or liaison (63)

♦ prior employment in other agencies (25)

♦ prior work in a single agency (17)

♦ training (5).

Prior multi-agency work or liaison

Nearly half of all interviewees described having been involved in multi-agency working, liaison or consultation in the past. However, a fifth of these interviewees did not provide any additional elaboration as to how this had impacted on their current work.

Of those who gave more detailed explanations of their multi-agency background, a common theme was that multi-agency working or liaison was vital to the type of work in which they were engaged; thus professionals working together was simply a regular feature of their work. Three comments were made to the effect that all work involving Social Services should involve other agencies, and a further two that all work with children should involve multiple professions in order to address the child's needs holistically. Specific fields of work which were cited by more than one interviewee as being reliant on multi-agency work in this way included (with the numbers of interviewees citing them in brackets):

♦   special needs (6)

♦   educational psychology/child psychiatry (5)

♦   disaffected or disadvantaged children (4)

♦   children in public care (3)

♦   health promotion/health improvement (3)

♦   speech and language therapy (2)

♦   health visiting (2)

♦   school nursing (2)

♦   project commissioning (2).

Work with children in the broad area of special needs (including speech and language therapy) is an area which interviewees felt to be heavily reliant on multi-agency work. This meant that many of those who had worked in the field during their career had had prior experience of this way of working. As one interviewee explained:

> *When we're looking at children with special educational needs that has implications for both the health side and the social side, so over the last 30 years I've been working very closely with both Health and Social Services, involved in both assessment and provision for the children we've been jointly working with* (senior education officer for looked-after children).

An assistant director of Education had a similar view: '*Where you have children with complex needs, the solution doesn't rest with one agency because you can't compartmentalise children. The answers lie in multi-agency work.*'

These quotes show how children with special needs and complex problems needed a range of professionals to help overcome them. Educational psychology and psychiatry were similar cases, although they seemed to rely much more on information sharing and liaison between agencies, rather than direct multi-agency work with the child themselves.

Work with disadvantaged and disaffected children, including those in the care of the local authority, was a similar case, where interviewees described the need to address the child's needs holistically. In the specific case of children in public care, one interviewee explained that this amounted to 'corporate parenting', where the different agencies all accepted their responsibility for the well-being of the child, rather than all the responsibility falling on Social Services, although s/he said:

> There are certain people in Education that have the old fashioned view that children who are looked after are the responsibility of Social Services. We have a long way to go with some people ... in terms of understanding the principle of corporate parenting (head of the Special Educational Needs Support Service).

According to interviewees, a range of child health roles also required close cooperation between agencies. Health promotion and school nursing were felt to have clear links with education – with individuals from Health working directly in schools. In addition, health promotion and home visiting were felt to link with both education and Social Services aspects.

Ten individuals remarked that their commitment to multi-agency working as a concept had increased as a result of their previous involvement in this way of working, or through liaison with other agencies. Previous experience of residential social work seemed to be a particularly influential occupation in terms of increasing interviewees' belief in the value of agencies working together. Again, there appeared to be an acknowledgement that complex problems cannot be dealt with by agencies in isolation, and eight of these interviewees described seeing the practical benefits of working together, for example:

> I think it must be incredibly hard for families to have to keep repeating what it is they're looking for from a service time and time again, and the fact that a multi-agency initiative exists, it just makes it so much easier for children and families and young people to have a coordinated, collaborative approach (school health manager).

> In the course of doing a number of jobs, both as an educational psychologist, as a teacher, and working in various other things, like a high security children's place, and working with adults in prisons, my entire experience has always persuaded me that professionals can never work on their own. You have to have support and perspectives from other people (principal educational psychologist).

Additionally, six interviewees explained that they had previously been involved in types of multi-agency working that they felt were particularly good examples, and which most had then tried to implement in their current post.

Nine interviewees raised the issue of having developed specific knowledge or skills from previous multi-agency working or liaison (although it is interesting to note that this was mentioned more frequently, and in more detail, by interviewees who had actually been employed within other agencies, rather than simply working/liaising with other agencies). These comments included references to recognising the differences between the agencies, understanding structures, protocols and legislation, understanding the difficulties faced by other agencies, and developing particular knowledge or skills in working in the field.

Prior employment in other agencies

Approximately one-fifth of all interviewees described the importance they attached to prior work in other agencies for their current multi-agency activity. A wide variety of reasons and benefits of this prior work were given.

The most commonly cited benefit of having worked in other agencies was the development of a working knowledge of their structure, culture and working methods. For example, as one interviewee noted:

> *I've worked in both Social Services and Education. In fact, I've also worked in the Health Service, because part of the time I was in Social Services I was based in a hospital. So I've got a reasonably good idea of what goes on in each of those areas ... People who have worked just in this agency ... they have to work hard to broaden their vision. It is just about understanding where other people are coming from* (Education access manager).

Another interviewee, a teacher who had been seconded to work within Social Services, explained that a lack of understanding of how another agency worked could be a barrier to multi-agency working (this is discussed in more detail in Chapter 6 on challenges). S/he had developed an understanding of Social Services through his/her secondment, and during the time had also shared his/her knowledge of Education with those from Social Services. In addition to understanding the structure, culture and working methods utilised within different agencies, several interviewees also explained that they had learnt about different individuals' roles and could thus empathise with the pressures faced by others during their work: '*If you know about the stresses that people in Social Services are under, it helps you to understand* [empathise] *when they make a mistake, and you don't go for the jugular*' (Education access manager). There was a similar sense of empathy and understanding of the more general pressures faced by whole agencies.

Another common advantage of work in other agencies was the professional credibility that ensued. Interviewees from all agencies, both strategic and operational, described how their past work in other agencies meant they could work with individuals from that agency on a more level footing than they would otherwise have been able to do. Examples included five people, from Health, Social Services, and the Youth Service, who found their own teaching background gave them credibility when working in schools. Another interviewee, currently working within Education, explained that his/her prior work at a high security hospital meant s/he could engage health professionals more easily in the multi-agency project s/he was establishing because s/he had gained their respect through being able to understand their technical language.

Several interviewees described how their general commitment to multi-agency working had been established, or increased, as a result of their experiences working within other agencies. There seemed to be a particular link between Social Services and Education in this instance – all of the five comments coming from these agencies. The central theme of these comments was the recognition, through having worked in both agencies, that Social Services and Education needed to work closely together in order to treat children in a holistic manner. One interviewee was clear:

I fervently believe that one has to look at the whole child and you can't just look at the education perspective. You have to look at the whole child ... I think working in the boys' community home [Social Services, residential care] *was really the first time that it became evident, and that was much more the link between Social Services and Education* (head of Children's Services, Education).

Other benefits mentioned less frequently than those described above included: the development of background knowledge, drawing on experiences in other agencies when managing a multi-agency team, networking, i.e. knowing a lot of different people within different agencies, and not becoming entrenched in a single way of working or looking at things.

Prior work within a single agency

Just over one-tenth of interviewees made references to the implications of their previous work within a single agency. This manifested itself in two key ways – the ability to contribute to a multi-agency group from a position of knowledge or status within their own agency, and for those currently at strategic level who had had an operational background within the same agency, a sense of empathy for, and credibility with those now working at the front line.

Six interviewees, all working at strategic level, from Education, Health and Social Services, described their contribution to multi-agency working in terms of providing an experienced perspective from their agency. For example, an interviewee from Health explained how his/her background as a paediatrician allowed him/her to contribute to a multi-agency project:

I think a panel that's actually dealing with behaviour and trying to support children and families and teachers and so on, has to have a health input, it has to have clinical input [his/her role] *... I think it was the combination of having a paediatrician who had the liaison links with specific parts of the Health Service, and sometimes was able to talk doctor-to-doctor, which is sometimes a barrier for non-doctors* (consultant community paediatrician).

Another described how his/her role as a headteacher allowed him/her to contribute to a strategy group from the perspective of understanding the needs of schools and young people. Yet another explained that working for Social Services meant s/he had a clear understanding of Social Services' remit, and thus what areas of the multi-agency work they could get involved with, and in what practical ways.

Interviewees who had undertaken a range of different jobs within the same agency often made references to how this helped them with multi-agency working. Some of these were similar to those made by interviewees who had experienced work within different agencies – particularly relating to the development of credibility with and empathy for others. Five interviewees currently working within Education described how having been a classroom teacher gave them credibility with other classroom teachers. One headteacher was specifically asked to be involved in a multi-agency project because it was thought it would add weight to the project with other schools. All but one of these references came from individuals who were now engaged in strategic roles, and implied that an operational background allowed them to empathise with those currently at operational level where their strategic decisions would impact.

Training

Eight interviewees made reference to their training as influencing their current multi-agency working. Over half of these comments suggested that various types of training involved consideration of multi-agency working, and this was often linked to the previously described issue of some areas of work relying on professionals working effectively together. These included psychology (and particularly educational psychology) and child psychiatry. As one of the educational psychologists said:

> *Through training and experience you become used to working with people in other agencies and the usual barriers tend not to be so prominent around educational psychologists because the day-to-day work is about supporting children in a multi-agency context. You could not possibly do your job as an educational psychologist if you did not meet regularly with all the practitioners involved around an individual child. It is embedded firmly in my philosophy* (chief educational psychologist).

Other comments about the relevance of training included: references to the way in which health visitors are taught to use jargon-free language (thus facilitating multi-agency discourse), and how having completed training in a different area of work could lend credibility even where an individual had not gone on to employment within that field.

3.3   How professionals came to be involved

When asked how they personally came to be involved in the initiative, interviewees offered a variety of different explanations. Little difference between strategic- and operational-level responses was identified, and where there were differences, these are noted. The responses are shown in rank order in Table 3.1.

Table 3.1   Reasons for professionals' involvement in initiatives

Reason for involvement	Interviewees	
	No.	% (N=139)
On taking up their current post	33	24
Invited to participate	21	15
Involved from the beginning as a key player	17	12
Because of their current position/area of responsibility	15	11
Involved previously in similar work	12	9
Personal interest	9	6
Through a change in workload/commitments	8	6
Involved in initial bid/securing the contract for the work	4	3
As the instigator	3	2
Seconded or responsibility delegated	2	1
No response	15	11

Percentages have been rounded to the nearest whole number, and therefore may not sum to 100
Source: *Interviews in Phase Two of the NFER study, 2001*

As Table 3.1 shows, interviewees offered a range of different reasons for becoming involved in the initiatives. These appeared to fall into three main categories, although there was some crossover between these. The categories were:

♦   reasons related to their specific position

♦   an invitation to become involved

♦   personal reasons.

3.3.1 Reasons related to current position

The most frequently cited way in which interviewees had become involved in the initiatives was on taking up their current post (identified by almost a quarter of the interviewees), especially where strategic-level positions were concerned. They had either applied for a specific post within an initiative or had found that responsibility for it was part of the role they had taken on. Fifteen interviewees had become involved in initiatives because their current position or area of responsibility meant that the logical step had been to include them. For example, one interviewee had been involved in an initial audit of current arrangements for children in public care and felt therefore that they had been the '*natural*' choice for involvement in a project designed to improve services for this group of young people.

Eight interviewees referred to a change in their current workload or commitments, which had meant that they now had the time to devote to working in this area of work, for example:

Very often, when there are new initiatives and it looks as though somebody from our service might be involved in those initiatives, it often comes at a time when we are looking to expand or reduce in size. Whenever that happens, there has to be some readjustment to individual or professional responsibilities and workloads. The person who had been doing it no longer wanted to continue, felt that [s/he] needed to move on to something else. We held some discussion about what the job might involve at the same time as we were discussing other areas for development. ... I can't say I jumped at the chance because I was quite anxious about it, it's a new area for me. I did volunteer to do it and I do think that helps (educational psychologist).

Two interviewees highlighted being seconded to the initiative or having responsibility for it delegated to them.

3.3.2 Invited to participate

The second most common reason for involvement, cited by 21 interviewees, was because they had been invited to participate, often because of their experience and/or skills in working with the particular target group concerned. Interestingly, nearly half of the interviewees who gave this response were involved in initiatives where Health professionals were offering consultation and training to Education professionals. The majority of these interviewees were operational-level professionals within Education, several of whom reported seeing it as a welcome opportunity, one that was '*too good to miss*'.

In a similar vein, 12 interviewees became involved because they had previously worked in the same, or a similar, area of work and were considered to have the necessary experience to take on the work, for example:

[I became involved] *from my experience and involvement and years of working on special needs and dealing with the most complex children, and from a school point of view, knowing how you knit it into the pastoral point of view* (head of the Special Needs Service, Education).

3.3.3 Personal reasons

Seventeen interviewees commented that they had been involved as an individual from the beginning of the initiative, both in establishing it and in shaping the way in which it subsequently developed. Perhaps not surprisingly, the majority of interviewees proffering this response were strategic-level personnel. Nine interviewees specifically referred to their personal interest in the type of work, six of whom were from Education, mainly within initiatives involving their own agency working with Social Services, and particularly where children in public care were the focus.

This was the case, for example, for an education project worker involved in a project on disaffection who stated that: '*I was interested in the idea ... and when the project was being got together, I was keen to apply to be part of the team. I was very excited by the project.*'

Four interviewees had become involved in the initiatives through developing the initial bid or in securing the contract for the work; while three commented that it had been their idea originally and they had '*made it happen essentially*'.

Having examined professional backgrounds and involvement, we move on to examine the agency context within which initiatives were set up in different authorities and how the agencies became involved.

3.4 Extent of multi-agency activity prior to the initiatives

The interim report, which examined the first phase of data collection, identified 'good working relationships' as being a key factor in the success of multi-agency initiatives, according to Phase One interviewees. Prior networks and relationships were also identified in previous studies (see Literature Review) as being an important rationale for collaboration. For this reason, it was thought important to determine the working relationships and multi-agency working which existed in the local authority prior to the establishment of the initiative being studied, to see whether there was any consistency across the authorities where exemplary multi-agency working was taking place. Interviewees were asked to describe the general extent of multi-agency activity in the authority prior to this initiative being formed, and then to describe the nature of relationships between the main agencies – Education, Social Services, Health, and the voluntary sector.

When asked about the extent of multi-agency activity prior to the initiatives under study, just over a tenth of interviewees (19) indicated that multi-agency working generally had been '*limited*' or '*poor*' previously, whilst in contrast, a similar number (17) indicated that it had been '*extensive*' or '*good*' beforehand. Fourteen interviewees felt unable to comment as they had no experience of previous multi-agency work in the authority. Others talked more specifically about the focus or limitations of previous work or about the factors which had been influential in initiating more multi-agency activity in their authority, and these are discussed next.

3.4.1 The limitations of previous multi-agency work

Of those who felt that interagency work had been limited or poor generally (including one who felt there had been none at all), all but one worked at strategic level or across the strategic–operational interface and all except one was from Education or Health. Comments included, for example: '*everyone tended to keep to themselves*' or that they '*only talk to each other to hurl insults across the battlements*'. Interviewees reported that services were not coordinated or cohesively planned and were seen as fragmented by service users, that there was no communication between agencies about decisions, that areas of overlap were not acknowledged or that agencies were suspicious of each other, for example:

> *It would appear to me that mostly Education and Social Services make their own decisions. They inform Health when they want something, and then they moan when we can't deliver it* (children's strategy manager, Health).

> *Education had a healthy suspicion of Social Services. Some overlaps of work were not acknowledged at all. For example, teachers worked in community homes and education workers and care workers in residential schools with little reference to each other* (joint strategy manager, Education and Social Services).

Others were more specific about the focus of any previous collaborations. Many interviewees (numbers given in brackets) intimated that previous multi-agency working had been '*patchy*' or '*ad hoc*' because it was:

♦ focused on specific initiatives or specific areas of work (36)

♦ dependent on individuals (22)

♦ inhibited by specific obstacles (12)

♦ focused on case work (11)

♦ focused on liaison (10)

♦ historically determined (2).

Focused on specific initiatives or areas of work

Over a quarter of all interviewees indicated that, within their authority, multi-agency working had previously been focused on specific initiatives or specific areas of work. This appeared to be the case, whatever type of multi-agency activity they were now involved in, but it was identified more by those at strategic level, who had an overview, than those working at operational level. A very wide range of fields was reported to have been the focus for previous work, and those cited by more than one interviewee included, in rank order:

♦ children in public care (9)

♦ child protection (9)

♦ mental health (4)

♦ children with disabilities (3)

♦ drugs education (3)

♦ sexual health (3)

♦ special educational needs (3)

♦ youth offending teams (3)

♦ early years (2)

♦ complex needs/specialist placements (2)

♦ housing (2).

With regard to the two most common areas, interviewees reported, for example, that there was strategic commitment to multi-agency work for children in public care, and they mentioned Government drivers, such as Quality Protects and the Social Services Inspectorate report. This reportedly had led to cross-service delivery and shared budgets, sometimes not yet tackled in other fields. In contrast, multi-agency work within child protection, according to interviewees, went back a long way and was considered to be well-established practice.

Dependent on individuals

Over a tenth of all interviewees stated that previous multi-agency work had been dependent on individuals or had been taking place in localised areas, and this meant that it was variable and that there was no consistency across the authority:

> *Yes, I think individual people had good relationships with specific teachers or specific headteachers or connected well with particular schools, but there was certainly no coordination ... so it was just a bit void, I think, particularly around strategy and joint working ... and managed to survive because of individual relationships* (senior family therapist, Health).

> *My perspective was that there was a lot of good work went on on the ground, between people who knew each other, got on well, and who made the effort because they believed in it. But we had a long way to go in coordinating that, and actually planning strategically for it to happen* (principal education officer).

Interviewees frequently stated that there were '*pockets*' of multi-agency work but that it was not '*coordinated*' or '*joined up*'. They felt that previously there had been little attempt to plan strategically, to develop a coherent policy, or to coordinate multi-agency work in any way and that there were no structures supporting multi-agency work at strategic level:

> [There was] *nothing bringing people together that meant that they had to share their visions, philosophies or backgrounds and ways they communicated and the structures they worked in the way this project has* (chief educational psychologist).

> *To some extent joint work, but we would work to different policy agendas, different legal frameworks, different priorities and, in many cases, with the same children and young people and providing services which overlapped, but we worked as if were in separate boxes* (group manager, Social Services).

Seven interviewees stated that multi-agency work was now more formalised, whereas before it had been conducted on an informal basis, and this meant that it was less dependent on personal relationships and that there was now more strategic-level support.

Inhibited by specific obstacles

Twelve interviewees, as part of their response, indicated that a variety of obstacles had hindered previous multi-agency work. Many of these were the same as those issues raised by interviewees when asked about the challenges of multi-agency working, and they are discussed in more depth in Chapter 6. These included:

♦ lack of appropriate structures

♦ high staff turnover and staff shortages

♦ different agency priorities

♦ inconsistent management arrangements

♦ budget demarcations

♦ getting the relevant people together

♦ lack of understanding of each other's roles

♦ protection of roles

♦ lack of commitment

♦ local politics

♦ lack of physical space

♦ lack of coterminous boundaries

♦ lack of resources.

Focused on case work

Eleven interviewees stated that multi-agency work undertaken previously had been case led. Whilst raised by seven education workers, this was only raised by three individuals from Health and one from Social Services. Like those who stated that multi-agency work was person led, these interviewees also commented that the focus on individual cases meant that there was limited, or no, strategic thinking beyond this:

> It tended to be much more operationally than strategic. There were reasonable relationships between different people and different agencies, at the level of working with a particular child, for instance ... what there wasn't was the ability to look at producing linked programmes at any kind of strategic level (head of Behaviour Support Service, Education).

Limited to liaison

Ten interviewees indicated that multi-agency work previously had been limited to liaison only, that it was therefore focused on information exchange and communication rather than 'true collaboration', or 'actually working together on aims and targets', or 'properly commissioned'. Where this was the case, it was felt that there was no way agencies could gain the depth of understanding that could be gained from genuine joint working. As one social worker put it: 'Perhaps it's the difference between having a route to exchange information, which is what we had, to having a real understanding of the roles and actually what people can do'. In many cases, the initiatives now engaged in were therefore felt to be a significant move forward. Where a specialist service had been established, for example, it was reported that there had always been multi-agency procedures, but that this was felt to be 'a step into joint working'. The establishment of cohesive services was also felt to be advancement over liaison and communication:

Generally, across the county, multi-agency working was far more to do with better liaison, better communication, making sure we all knew what the other was doing, and the shift in terms of the [project] team has been actually bringing people together so that they are working together and coordinating their services in a far more cohesive way (Children's Services manager, Social Services).

Significantly, for one interviewee, the initiative they were involved in had moved beyond any previous work since there was now a requirement for him/her to be accountable to two agencies:

Well, before it began it was different in that unlike now, we weren't accountable to two different bodies, so we hadn't had any previous experience of that. So that has taken some getting used to, particularly in terms of the agendas set by each of them, particularly in terms of reporting our results to say the Department of Health who may have different data collection strategies that may not necessarily be compatible with those of the Department of Education (education support team member, Social Services).

Whilst a number of interviewees suggested that multi-agency work had previously been focused on liaison only, one interviewee felt that convincing professionals that more than just liaison was involved in genuine multi-agency work was a significant obstacle to be overcome.

Historically determined

Two interviewees suggested that previous multi-agency working had been historically determined and therefore lacked strategic planning. One interviewee emphasised how the present project was different in that someone had been specifically identified to establish a strategic plan:

My experience of multi-agency work within this service, and maybe other services, is that sometimes it's been very ad hoc. It has existed, but either it's existed because there are historical linkages or it's case-by-case linkage. What impressed me about this approach is that it came from someone specifically identified to address multi-agency coordinating and there was a strategy, if you like. It was more than just operational and something that grew out of that. I think that was the difference for me (clinical nurse).

In summary, however, despite the limitations outlined, six interviewees described multi-agency work generally within their authority as '*improving*' and that it had been given more emphasis recently. Others, who spoke more specifically, also suggested that there was an increasing trend towards joint working. These interviewees felt that there was a commitment to examining children's needs more holistically and not just to view problems as a single-agency responsibility, or that professionals were becoming increasingly confident at multi-agency work:

I think there is a movement ... people are trying to now feel a lot more committed to looking at the child more holistically, and the more questions that are asked from each service, the more other services are aware about how they are viewing the situation of this young person, that you can't just say this is an educational problem, that it's a group problem (looked-after children support teacher, Social Services).

I think it has moved on quite significantly since then as people gained more confidence in multi-agency working. It became easier and more fluid (educational psychologist).

However, contrary to this trend, one interviewee felt that multi-agency working had been good, but was now becoming more limited because of the pressures on professionals at the present time, noting many of the obstacles to joint working previously mentioned:

Times have changed politically, demands change, budgets change and structures change and, in effect, from my personal perspective, I would say that a lot of that interagency contact, never mind working, has pretty much gone to pot ... there's a whole variety of reasons – staff shortages, small teams, pressures of work, trying to focus on your own priorities and agendas, the provision of figures to justify what you are meant to be doing, and so on. I think it's part of the political climate which we are in which has resulted, in my opinion, in less satisfactory interagency collaboration (education welfare officer).

3.4.2 Influential factors in the development of previous multi-agency work

Where interviewees reported that multi-agency working was extensive or good, some indicated that there were appropriate structures in place, such as shared systems and protocols, or that there were good relationships between agencies generally. Other interviewees who spoke positively about previous multi-agency working within their authority suggested that it had been:

♦ influenced by a specific event

♦ focused on their particular area of work

♦ located at strategic level.

Influenced by a specific event

Where multi-agency working was reported to be good, over a tenth of interviewees indicated that a specific event in their authority's history had been influential in this respect. Those who saw multi-agency working as event instigated commonly worked at strategic level and came more from Social Services rather than Education or Health. Events referred to by more than one interviewee, in rank order, included:

♦   local government reorganisation (13)

♦   establishment of a multi-agency strategic group (12)

♦   appointment of key personnel (4)

♦   a change of government (3).

Overwhelmingly, the specific event most frequently referred to was local government reorganisation, raised by 13 interviewees. This was reported by one interviewee to be '*the catalyst*' for multi-agency working in their authority, prior to which there were not the structures in place: '*there wasn't really a platform or a structure for joint working to flourish*'. A small authority, as was often the case following reorganisation, was felt to facilitate joint working because personnel knew each other better and because they were closer to the decision making. Following reorganisation, a review of services was often undertaken, the dynamics in an authority were reported to change and multi-agency working often became more of a priority. The opportunities that this presented were illustrated by the following comments:

We had to review and audit our interagency systems and reform them. For the first time, the unitary authority had responsibility for Social Services and Education, so internally, as a borough council, we had to review our interfaces of how we worked together. In some ways it was an advantage having a new beginning because we were able to review what was in place, what was working well, what needed to happen and to particularly identify some of the tensions around working with agencies who still have a wider focus ... who still cover a number of boroughs, and our own internal interfaces with other departments in the council and then new interfaces that we've had to form over the last few years (director, Social Services).

From day one there was a clear intention to make sure there was a good working relationship between Education and Social Services, which wasn't always the case under the previous county structure. The fact that both departments have got their headquarters here in the same building makes a difference. I have regular contact with a counterpart assistant director in Education. We have got a good positive working relationship at an individual level and I think that knocks on then through the organisation (assistant director, Social Services).

The fact that a new authority had no previous history was also mentioned:

It was a completely new authority, no history of its own, so surely we could create our own set up, and I think there was a lot of energy about at that time that was used to good effect and a number of projects were set up that were genuinely, from their inception, planned on a multi-agency basis ... They not only had benefits in terms of the individual bits of work that were set up, it also pulled managers into a planning arena where we started having a more personal relationship with each other, which was great and I think it has served us well (educational psychologist).

Twelve interviewees referred to the establishment of a key multi-agency group, often focused on children and young people generally, as being influential and a key point in facilitating joint working. This again emphasises the importance of the establishment of a multi-agency strategy or management group as part of the development process of multi-agency working as discussed in the previous chapter. The majority of those who mentioned this, not surprisingly, worked at strategic level. Five were from Health and four from Social Services, so few were from Education. Multi-agency groups were reportedly set up to discuss joint working issues and to address the different viewpoints of agencies, although one interviewee stated that they had been involved in setting up such a group purely to focus on joint finance projects.

Focused on their particular area of work

Ten interviewees, perhaps understandably, when asked about previous multi-agency work, focused on their specific area of work and stressed that multi-agency working had always been perceived as an essential part of their role or was essential in order to address the needs of their specific target group. These areas overlapped with those mentioned when individuals were asked about the implications of their previous work, and this again gives some indication of the areas where professionals considered multi-agency work to be imperative. Those who mentioned this included: those working with children with disabilities, behaviour problems, speech and language difficulties and with children in need; those working in the fields of health promotion, early years and child protection; as well as those working in the roles of education social worker, paediatrician and as a family resource worker.

Comments indicated, for example, that multi-agency working was often imperative because of the complex nature of children's difficulties, because the focus on the family meant that a range of agencies might be involved, or because professionals were legally required to engage in consultation with others:

> *I think, because of the nature of the children that we work with ... their whole lives are complex and there are difficulties throughout, then multi-agency working is a feature of it. It just has to be because of the nature of the difficulties they bring* (multi-disciplinary coordinator, Behaviour Support Service).

> *From an education social worker point of view it's absolutely essential that one works in a multi-agency way because of the needs of the young people and of their families ... and that ultimately means contacting any agencies involved to support that family and child and I would act as a link between all of those agencies and Education and I think that's the essential point* (education social worker).

> *I think that the essence of paediatrics is that you work in a multi-agency way. We are in fact governed by statutes of law to work together with Social Services and Education – the Children Act,*

71

the Education Act, the Disability Act, etc. – so there are statutes that actually oblige us to look at things together (consultant paediatrician).

One interviewee, from Health, suggested that, within the field of speech and language therapy, they had always worked in a multi-agency way because communication problems pervaded all aspects of children's lives and this meant that the majority of their work was conducted outside of health premises, making contact with professionals from other agencies, as well as parents, inevitable:

> *We have always worked in day nurseries, in children's homes, in hospital settings, in schools ... so we have always been involved in multi-agency working and I think it is clear that communication doesn't just happen in a vacuum, it is not just something you work on and then the child goes home and then that's it. Obviously, everybody involved with that child, from the parents to their carers and so on, has to be involved in order for there to be any change in a child's communication so we are automatically out there working with everybody else who is involved with the child* (manager, Speech and Language Therapy Service)

In addition, another interviewee felt that public health was high profile in their LEA; therefore, any multi-agency work that promoted this was encouraged.

Located at strategic level

Six interviewees, who all worked at strategic level, specifically stated that multi-agency collaboration was particularly good or established at strategic level, in some cases, compared to operational level. They talked about pooled budgets being '*a reality*' rather than having to go through extensive procedures and genuine joint planning rather than '*you tell us and we'll tell you and we'll do our own thing*'. One interviewee reported that they were '*struggling to translate this down to operational level*' because of a lack of equivalent-level personnel in different organisations.

During the interviews, interviewees were also asked to describe the relationships between their agency and the other agencies within the local authority. The comments that they made about the specific relationships between Education and Social Services, Education and Health and between Health and Social Services are presented in Research Vignette 2. Having examined the context and nature of multi-agency relationships prior to the establishment of the initiatives, how the agencies came to be involved will now be discussed.

Research Vignette 2   Previous multi-agency relations

In response to a question asking about the state of interagency working relationships between each of the three different agencies prior to the current initiative, interviewees expressed a range of viewpoints. Both positive and negative accounts emerged. Many of the negative views and supporting anecdotes replicated the kinds of challenges of multi-agency working outlined in Chapter 6, such as lack of understanding of other professional cultures, different priorities for the different agencies and tensions over resources. Similarly, those interviewees who felt that interagency relations had previously been positive went on to highlight factors such as coterminous boundaries and local reorganisation; well-established cooperation at operational-level; sharing of sites; or the benefit of imperatives like child protection legislation. Despite such overlap, analysis of this discourse provided some distinct and valuable insights into historical differences and affinities between the three agencies.

Descriptors of problematic relations with Health often referred to a lack of understanding of that agency's structures and its *'provider and purchaser culture'*. Those structures in turn meant that partnership working often had been perceived as difficult due to an inability to *'commit finances'* at interagency meetings: *'they didn't ever bring funding to the table'*. Another common description of working relations between Health and the other agencies surfaced in terms like *'distant'*, *'a lack of communication'* and *'arm's length'*. The view that in some parts of the Health Service, *'separate treatment models'* or *'the medicalisation of problems'* interfered with joint activity also surfaced.

When previous problematic relations between Social Services and Education were discussed, the descriptors showed some slight variation. Here, as well as terms like *'distant'*, there were notably more references to apparent estrangement: the terms *'hostile'*, *'antagonistic'*, *'adversarial'*, *'confrontational'*, *'distrust'* *'suspicious'*, *'wary'* and *'tense'* all surfaced among the sample. Many of these clearly related to funding and where the onus of responsibility lay for certain groups of young people. Lack of understanding of *'roles'* (rather than structures *per se*) emerged from education-located interviewees about Social Services, and there was comment about the *'transience'* of social workers at operational level affecting interagency relationships. Not knowing *'the territory'* of Education, and again previous lack of clarity about the roles of certain education-related agencies, such as the Education Welfare Service and the Youth Service, were highlighted by some Social Services interviewees. Finally, comment was made that Social Services and Health were *'similar cultures'* in that both were familiar with *'externalising services and being commissioning bodies'*.

Overall, across each agency, there were a number of examples of references to the different priorities of the three agencies and how those could, in the past, affect relations. *'There is a fundamental difference in what we do'* was how one Social Services interviewee explained the existence of previous tensions. Summarising those different agency agendas, the perception that the clients of Education and Social Services *'can drop down the agenda of Health'* surfaced, while Education in turn was seen to not focus enough on *'the social relationships and emotional well-being'* of a vulnerable minority of children who were the remit of Social Services. The lack of availability of specialist support for clients (due to financial or staff shortages) emerged as an issue about both Social Services and Health, with references to *'a blame culture'* and *'scapegoating'* between agencies. Underestimating the significance of educational achievement for young people was also raised about these services.

Where anecdotes and accounts of previous positive interagency relationships were cited, as already noted, these tended to refer to operational level, or to a '*case-by-case*' or '*individual client*' basis. Terms like '*ad hoc*' or '*informal*' also recurred. Sometimes specific multi-agency initiatives or posts were nominated as examples of positive interagency working (e.g. for looked-after and autistic children and within school health teams). Other interviewees offered examples of pockets of 'good' strategic-level relationships (e.g. '*at the second tier only*' or '*between directors, but just building middle structures*'). Sometimes strategic 'joined-up' activity, such as the sharing of targets, dual protocols, joint planning and commissioning, was also cited as exemplifying previous positive relations.

Overall, the perspectives offered clearly spanned a wide variation in the period being recalled, as well as differences in status and agency experience. Nevertheless, the sample's collective memory perhaps, above all, demonstrates the baseline from which current interagency activity has developed.

3.5   How agencies came to be involved

As with the question about the rationale for the development of the initiative (see Chapter 2), some interviewees had little or no knowledge of how their particular agency had become involved, having joined the initiative after it had been established. Overall, a similar range of reasons was presented as for professional involvement, and again factors both within and external to agencies were cited.

Table 3.2   Reasons for agencies' involvement in initiatives

	Interviewees	
Reason for involvement	**No.**	**% (N=139)**
An understanding that they should be involved, a key player	35	25
Invited to participate	16	12
External influences (e.g. reorganisation/restructuring, reviews or statutory guidance)	15	11
Recognition of the need for more work between the agencies	12	9
As the instigating agency	11	8
Discussion between the agencies	9	6
Submission of bid/winning tender	4	3
Through a key person in their agency	4	3
Agency's own desire to be involved	1	0
Brought in later	1	0
No response	31	22

Percentages have been rounded to the nearest whole number, and therefore may not sum to 100
Source: *Interviews in Phase Two of the NFER study, 2001*

Table 3.2 shows the most commonly cited ways in which those interviewees who proffered an answer believed their agency had become involved in the various initiatives.

A number of the reasons offered reflect some of the ways in which individuals identified that they had become involved, in that this was related to their role, or they were invited to participate, or that they were the instigator, or had a personal desire to be involved.

It is clear from Table 3.2 that the most common reason for agencies becoming involved in the initiatives (cited by a quarter of the interviewees) was because they were believed to be a key player, usually because of previous work with the target group.

> *It didn't necessarily have to be education welfare, but in practice, in terms of working face-to-face with young people and children, the two departments within the Education Department, if you like, who do the face-to-face work on a daily basis, it's education welfare and education psychology, so I would suppose that it seemed logical in discussions with our colleagues at the top of the pile, within our directorate, that education welfare should have been chosen* (education welfare officer).

As a result, the majority of these agencies had been involved from the inception of the initiative. Most of the interviewees who gave this response were from either Education or Social Services and occupied strategic-level positions.

The second most commonly given reason for involvement, offered by 16 interviewees, was because their agency had been invited to participate, usually by the instigating agency. For example, in one initiative, both Social Services and Health had been invited by Education to join a behaviour management panel in order to offer a more effective service through a multi-agency approach:

> *The new grouping is because we are a service that are responsible for the education plans of looked-after children ... you are always going to have some of those children, a small proportion, who are involved with the Behaviour Support Service and this initiative, ... and I think it is important that that continues ... It is about working together, so that when you are identifying and assessing and evaluating, people work together in that respect in collating and collaborating with information* (team coordinator, Social Services).

The next most commonly given reason involved external influences. Fifteen interviewees referred to either government reorganisation, which had provided greater opportunities for multi-agency working, reviews of interagency links, statutory guidance, such as Quality Protects, or the restructuring of existing services to ensure that the key people were involved:

'*We felt that* [the structure] *needed to be revamped to make sure we had the right representation on the groups at the right levels*' (assistant director, Education).

Twelve interviewees (most of whom had either strategic responsibility or both strategic- and operational-level responsibilities) referred to a recognition of the need for more multi-agency work. This was either because historically interagency relationships had been poor, or because this was felt to be the best approach in order to meet the needs of the particular target groups.

> *It came about with the previous head of Children's Services and the previous assistant director for Education and they decided things were so bad between the two agencies that they would start up a group. It started as a workshop and it really got people together ...* (head of Children's Services, Social Services).

> *Up until the summer of '97, there wasn't really a strategic partnership ... So they came together and said 'OK, what we need to do is work in partnership to improve health in the borough. What are the issues?' And one of the things that came up was the need for a specialist health promotion service* (head of health promotion).

Eleven interviewees explained that theirs had been the instigating agency and thus had been responsible for bringing other agencies on board and then driving the initiative forward. The next most common reason for agency involvement, cited by nine interviewees, was discussion between the core agencies, often at multi-agency group meetings, around providing multi-agency services to the target groups concerned. Perhaps not surprisingly, the majority of interviewees giving this response occupied strategic-level positions. Submitting a successful bid for the work was given as the reason for their agency becoming involved by four interviewees. Similarly, four interviewees commented that the 'vision' or idea for the initiative had come from a key person within their agency who had then started things off.

> *It was set up very largely at the inspiration of the head of the Children's Service and it was articulated in a fairly academic but quite powerful way and was developed by the Children's Service* (strategic director for learning and development).

Finally, the agency's own desire to be involved in the initiative, and being brought in later in an advisory capacity, were each mentioned by one interviewee.

Key points

- The background to the multi-agency initiatives clearly varied enormously – both in terms of the personal backgrounds of those involved and the context of agency relationships within the authority. Interviewees also described a range of ways in which both individual professionals and agencies became involved in multi-agency work.

- Interviewees described their own backgrounds in terms of having a wide range of training and qualifications, and a wide range of roles within a variety of different agencies. What was interesting was that over a third of those involved in the initiatives under study had worked in multiple agencies during their career, perhaps indicating this as a beneficial experience for multi-agency working.

- Interviewees also identified a range of different ways that their background impacted on their present work. This included involvement in previous multi-agency working; experience of different agencies or roles; having been a practitioner (before becoming a manager); and the training they had received.

- Similarly, the background contexts of the different authorities clearly varied considerably in terms of interviewees' perceptions of the general multi-agency activity and relationships that existed prior to the initiative, as well as their perceptions of the relationships between specific agencies.

- Limitations to previous multi-agency work were described. Prior work had often focused on specific initiatives, was focused on individual cases, was dependent on individuals, or involved liaison rather than true collaborative working.

- Influential factors in the development of prior multi-agency activity included specific events, particularly local government reorganisation, and the focus on a particular area of work. There were many comments about how multi-agency work was essential in particular fields, and this suggests that specific areas or target groups, such as children in public care and children with behavioural problems, lend themselves more to joint working.

- As with professional involvement, the motivation for agency involvement again varied, ranging from multi-agency work generally being considered to be part of the role and responsibility of the agency to a genuine desire to instigate and be proactive in developing multi-agency practice.

4. ROLES AND RESPONSIBILITIES

4.1 Introduction

This section of the report covers the roles and responsibilities taken on by different agencies within the multi-agency initiatives. Firstly, how roles and responsibilities were initially determined is discussed, followed by an examination of the roles taken on by individuals from different agencies and the roles and responsibilities of other agencies as described by interviewees.

4.2 Determination of roles and responsibilities

Interviewees were asked to identify the way in which the roles and responsibilities of agencies and individuals had been determined within the initiative. Once again, several interviewees had no knowledge of this, not having been involved in the developmental stages of the initiative. Others chose to talk in more descriptive terms about the roles and responsibilities themselves, rather than the manner in which they had been determined. Twenty interviewees stated that roles and responsibilities had simply evolved over time, and a further 14 interviewees specifically stated that nothing definite had been determined, thus pointing to the unformed manner in which many of the multi-agency projects under study may have begun. Interviewees spoke in the main about things happening naturally as issues arose: '*I don't think anything was written in tablets of stone*'. Interviewees referred to this being done '*by chance rather than by design*', and by '*a cutting up of the cake*'. Three interviewees, two of whom were Health professionals from the same initiative, were critical of this approach, as staff had sometimes been left not fully understanding the extent of their, or of others', responsibilities. It was noted that a clearer remit setting out the roles and responsibilities of all involved in the initiative would have been helpful.

Where interviewees did make reference to the way in which the roles and responsibilities of the different agencies involved were determined, in rank order (with number of interviewees shown in brackets), interviewees indicated that they had been:

♦ discussed jointly (20)

♦ determined according to expertise/experience (14)

♦ decided at strategic level (14)

♦ laid out in the specification (8)

♦ determined by need (4).

Twenty interviewees noted that roles and responsibilities had been decided as a result of initial discussion between the different agencies, although more than half the interviewees noting this were strategic-level professionals. Several interviewees went on to stress that this did not mean that things were not changed later in the light of experience, but '*it definitely helped thrashing those things out at the beginning*'. Equally, one interviewee believed that, had there been more time allowed for this initial discussion, some of the problems with meeting targets that they had encountered at a later stage may well have been avoided.

The skills and experience of the professionals involved had been the main factor in determining roles and responsibilities for 14 interviewees. In some cases, people who were already working in a similar field were allocated certain roles, but where new appointments were made, this was often on the basis of individual expertise rather than agency background. Interestingly, in contrast to this, within two initiatives, an interviewee from each stated that, within multi-agency working, personal qualities were considered more important than professional expertise or training. Thus, they had been appointed to specific roles on that basis and considered profession secondarily, for example:

> *People have been chosen to work with the project because of their personal qualities. So that's been that they are very respectful, that they work in partnership with people rather than working on people ... most of the people involved have had that kind of enabling role and where people have come in and tried to be very rigidly in their own profession and been bound by that, they haven't been very effective. If they've had the flexibility to work in a holistic partnership way, they've been very good* (early years coordinator, Education).

This approach is evident in the references to the skills required for multi-agency working in the final chapter, where personal skills were emphasised as particularly important.

According to another 14 interviewees, roles and responsibilities were decided at strategic level and then information was cascaded down to the initiatives. In the main, this had worked effectively. However, two interviewees were critical of this approach, claiming that because roles had been negotiated at a strategic level, they had not transferred well to a more operational level, with some staff having little understanding of what they were supposed to do.

Finally, for eight interviewees, the roles and responsibilities had in fact been clearly laid out '*in black and white*' in the specification for the initiative, while four interviewees commented that roles had been clearly defined by the needs that had been apparent, each agency then providing their particular expertise.

Having discussed the way in which roles were determined, we focus now on the roles and responsibilities taken on by different professionals and different agencies. Interviewees were asked about their own role within the initiative and about the roles and responsibilities of other agencies. Firstly, what they considered to be their own role is discussed, and this is followed by their views on the roles of other agencies.

4.3 Roles and responsibilities: a general overview

Interviewees were asked about the roles and responsibilities of the different agencies involved in the initiatives and more specifically about their own role. Most interviewees talked generally about roles and responsibilities, rather than specifically about individual agencies and their roles. The main features with regard to agency roles and responsibilities in the multi-agency projects under study, according to interviewees, were:

♦ the multi-agency steering group (32)

♦ a shared responsibility or equal partners (11)

♦ overlap or merging of roles (9).

4.3.1 The multi-agency steering group

Interviewees most frequently referred to agency representation on a steering or management group when asked about their own and the role of other agencies. In over three-quarters of the initiatives, they indicated that there was a multi-agency steering or management group at strategic level at which all the agencies involved were represented. Joint agency responsibility for the overall management of initiatives in this way was therefore evident in the majority of cases and across all types of multi-agency working. The importance of having all the agencies engaged at strategic level was stressed. Thus, within an initiative focused on speech and language difficulties, whilst Health were seen as the main deliverers and provided the bulk of the funding, it was felt vital to have Education involved at strategic level since most of the work was done in schools. Education was therefore considered to have a *'strong role in defining the service and how the speech and language therapists worked with staff in education and in monitoring'*.

Having said this, within four initiatives, lack of Health involvement in such a group was noted by Education personnel. In two cases, one a strategic decision-making group and the other a coordinator-led early years project, this was reported to have been deliberate. In one, the aim was to keep the project *'very focused internally'* for the first year until all the staff were in place. In the other, the head of Children's Services for Education stated: *'At one level we regard ourselves as the County Council and there is a bit of us not washing our dirty linen because we still do have disagreements about things, about us washing certain things in public or in front of Health.'* In another initiative focused on children in public care, it was felt that, whilst Health was involved in setting the initiative up, interest had waned as a lot of the activity was *'geared around education issues'* and Health therefore did not see it as a priority. This was reportedly to do with '*competing priorities and people trying to juggle their time*' and there being '*more biting performance indicators for this area within Education*'. The issue of competing priorities for agencies is discussed in more depth in Chapter 6 on challenges. In the remaining initiative, despite a focus on mental health, Health support at strategic level reportedly '*just did not happen*'.

When asked about their own role, representing their agency on a multi-agency steering group or management group was the role that interviewees most frequently cited. Unsurprisingly, those involved were mainly strategic-level personnel, and the need for them to take on such a role appeared to be central to any form of multi-agency work. Within such a group, where stated, it was reported that each agency took on a similar role in that they brought an agency perspective to the group, whilst at the same time taking back information of relevance to feed back to others within their own agency. According to interviewees, for example, it involved ensuring that professionals from other agencies were aware of the constraints on one's own agency and the way in which the agency operated, so that realistic expectations were placed upon it, as indicated by this Social Services manager:

> *I was sitting as a representative from Social Services, really, so that people understood what resource shortfalls there were within the area, how the areas work, who you would go to. I would give them names of who to speak to within that Social Services office, so I was like a link* (coordinator for a team of teachers within Social Services).

4.3.2 Shared roles and responsibilities

When asked generally about roles and responsibilities, 17 interviewees from over a third of all the initiatives emphasised the shared responsibility for the project between the agencies involved. In six initiatives, five of which were decision-making groups, direct reference was made to a shared responsibility between the agencies, although this was highlighted only by Education and Social Services staff. Similarly, in another five initiatives, the agencies involved were described by interviewees as '*equal partners*', again suggesting a shared responsibility. 'Partnership' was a term used by Education and Health personnel only, not by Social Services staff, and mainly when referring to multi-agency work that involved consultation and training and coordinator-led initiatives, perhaps suggesting that more of a true partnership approach was likely in such cases.

In contrast, however, a few interviewees referred to the reluctance of other agencies to become involved in multi-agency work and to share responsibilities. Within two initiatives, for example, Education was described as a reluctant partner by both Health and Social Services staff and to be in some way resistant to joint working, whilst in another, Health was described as a reluctant partner by Education personnel. Education resistance was described particularly in relation to schools and was reportedly due to Government requirements and the need to focus on statutory duties and targets. In the case of Health, resistance was felt to be due to lack of Government guidance concerning children in public care with a focus on health.

4.3.3 Overlapping/merging roles

Eleven interviewees from just under a third of all the initiatives intimated an overlap or even a merging of the roles of different agencies within their project. Seven interviewees from seven different initiatives, for example, considered there to be an inevitable overlap of roles between the agencies because of the overlap in needs of the target group, an issue highlighted mainly by Education staff. In one Social Services/Education initiative, for example, it was reported that roles at strategic level were '*complementary*' and that '*the usual divides between what we were doing got blurred in a way that was productive ... and our roles might interchange a bit*'. Moreover, a merging of roles was indicated within four initiatives, two of which were operational teams, suggesting this as an issue where professionals worked in close proximity. Whilst an educational operational representative in an initiative focused on children in public care felt that some distinct roles were necessary, s/he emphasised also the need to cross boundaries:

> *My mindset is not 'that bit is Social Services, that bit is Education' – I think it is very important that we start to blur those edges, and that everybody has a responsibility for the education of that child. Now, in terms of Education, we have some very particular roles, but the carer does as well, and there may well be, particularly when it comes to training, there may well be roles where we cross over. So, I would like to think that we are coming together and blurring the edges of our work, rather than providing divisions between us* (head of Educational Needs Support Service).

In contrast, there were two initiatives within which distinct roles were considered important by some interviewees. Where roles were clear, this was felt to lead to agencies being able to make a unique contribution to multi-agency working. In one initiative, for example, whilst there had been an initial '*vision*' of merging roles and an original aim that '*at some stage you wouldn't be able to tell who was a social worker and who was an education welfare officer and who was a school nurse*', a Social Services manager reported that this had not been realistic, since: '*Whilst there is overlap between the various professions, there is still a large amount of core business that relies on the skills, knowledge, qualifications, whatever, of those individual professionals.*' Thus, a clear difference between the different specialisms emerged, and a shared understanding of the overlaps and the boundaries was emphasised:

> *I think we have a shared understanding that children's needs are complex, some of them are health, some of them are social, some of them are educational and there are bound to be overlaps. If*

you use the term psychological need or emotional well-being, all of those three ingredients are necessary to achieve that one thing, but I think we are clear: Health deal with health, Education deal with education and we deal with the social side (Social Services manager).

Linked to the issue of merging roles, in two initiatives, individuals from different agency backgrounds were located or employed within one agency. In such cases, there was evidence of attempts to verbalise to some extent the merging of roles by calling all workers, regardless of background, 'project workers'. In one operational team, for example, the head of SENSS described individuals, despite different backgrounds, as *'first and foremost* [X] *project personnel'*. This is exemplified too by the following comment:

We have got an identity as members of this team so I wouldn't describe any of our roles as being social worker or an Education role or a youth worker; we are a [project] *role … One of the areas of developing a multi-agency team has to be, as I view it, how to take all of these skills from our different and diverse backgrounds; and, through use of those skills, how to enhance the overall skill and abilities of the team. But we need to do that without being an education welfare officer specialist on the team and without being a social worker specialist on the team. Finally, how we share those skills is an area for development … and give them a name* (education welfare officer).

Such comments point to the possibility of conflicting roles for those working in a multi-agency environment where their responsibilities to their agency may conflict with, and have to be secondary to, the overall requirements imposed on them by their roles and responsibilities within the project. This issue is discussed in more depth in the chapter on challenges. More specific roles and responsibilities pertinent to multi-agency working are now discussed.

4.4   The range of roles and responsibilities

When asked about their own role, interviewee responses suggested a wide range of roles and responsibilities that involvement in multi-agency working could entail. Those identified indicate that a complex mixture of roles and responsibilities existed within the multi-agency initiatives under study. There appeared to be a hierarchical model involving roles and responsibilities at three different levels:

♦   at the level of the *initiative*, i.e. roles and responsibilities connected broadly with the initiative, such as planning and management of the initiative and budget management

♦   at an *interagency* level, i.e. roles concerning interaction between agencies, such as information exchange and giving advice and support to professionals from other agencies

◆   at the level of the individual *agency*, i.e. responsibilities connected solely with their own agency, such as managing their own agency contribution and ensuring agency appropriateness.

The most often cited role was that of representing one's own agency on a management or steering group (identified by 28 interviewees), as discussed in the previous section. Other roles they undertook, as described by interviewees, included, in rank order (with the number of interviewees in brackets):

◆   management/development of the initiative (21)

◆   providing training, advice and support to others (18)

◆   information exchange and dissemination (15)

◆   direct work with children and families (14)

◆   management of staff (14)

◆   ensuring agency appropriateness (12)

◆   planning and implementing the initiative (11)

◆   budget or funding management (11)

◆   managing/leading the contribution of one's own agency (9)

◆   initiation of the project (9)

◆   coordination, i.e. bringing together agencies/ensuring partnerships (9)

◆   providing an agency perspective (6).

The specific roles that were most commonly highlighted are now discussed. However, as the hierarchy suggests, professionals are rarely engaged in only one role at any one time, and a complex interaction of roles is therefore most often likely. This means that professionals engaged in multi-agency work have to take account of their roles and responsibilities at all these levels. Interviewees described some roles that might be taken on by any, or all, of the agencies involved or were a joint responsibility, and others that were taken on by specific agencies because they were generally considered to be within their remit. This is discussed within each of the identified roles.

Management of initiatives

Despite the existence of multi-agency steering or management groups, the overall day-to-day management of the multi-agency initiatives was often stated to be the responsibility of a single agency. Within six of the 30 initiatives (with a range of target groups), this was cited as being the role of Education, whilst in four (with a children in need or children in public care focus), it was the responsibility of Social Services. The lead agency therefore appeared to be related to the target group or focus of initiatives. In no cases in this sample did interviewees describe Health as taking the lead.

When asked about their own role, 21 interviewees, some from each of the three main agencies, stated that they had responsibility for management and/or development of the initiative, implying a single-agency project management role. However, four of these interviewees also went on to clarify that management was actually the joint responsibility of all the agencies involved or that they undertook this role jointly with a counterpart from another agency, and one interviewee was jointly employed by Education and Social Services. In contrast, nine interviewees stated specifically that they led or managed their own agency's contribution to the initiative. Where single-agency project management involved staff managing professionals from different agencies, this is discussed later under staff management.

Providing training, advice and support to others

Whilst all three agencies were often equally involved in delivery and in liaising with other professionals from their own agency, Health reportedly had a particular role in offering consultation and advice to professionals from other agencies, and this was evident in seven out of the 30 initiatives.

When individuals were asked about their own role, 18 interviewees referred to providing training, advice and support to others, rather than, or as well as, direct delivery to clients, and of these 18, five were from Health, ten were from Education and only three from Social Services. Within the multi-agency projects under study, therefore, Education and Health staff appeared to play a key role in offering training, advice and support to others, whilst Social Services staff played a more limited role in this. Whilst some of these individuals cited that they offered training and support to all agencies around issues related to the target group, some also noted that they only offered advice and support to those within their own agency. Some noted that they did this in conjunction with professionals from other agencies.

Information exchange or dissemination

Information exchange or dissemination was the third most commonly identified role and one which was undertaken by individuals at both strategic and operational level. Information exchange was mentioned as a key role by interviewees from all types of multi-agency activity except centre-based delivery, but was particularly noted within operational teams since it was highlighted within all three initiatives within this group. A two-way exchange of information appeared to occur, and this concerned information relevant to both individual cases and developmental issues. This two-way exchange of information is exemplified by the following comments from a Health representative:

> *While on the panel I am able to comment about particular issues that maybe need to be addressed for the pupils that are being discussed and I am also able to take back information to colleagues after the meetings if there are any particular unmet health needs that need pursuing* (consultant community paediatrician).

Direct work with children and families

Involvement in direct work with children and their families was cited by a tenth of interviewees from over a third of all the initiatives, and again interviewees citing this included those from all three agencies. Perhaps not surprisingly, this was a role identified only by those working at operational level or at the operational–strategic interface. It was only mentioned by one person involved in a decision-making group, but otherwise was highlighted within all types of delivery, as well as in initiatives focused on consultation and training. Thus face-to-face work with clients was an essential operational role within all types of multi-agency work except decision-making groups.

Staff management

When asked about their own role, staff management was the fifth most frequently identified responsibility. In some cases, managers from one agency were expected to be responsible for staff from other agencies. This, however, raises the question of the legality of professionals from one agency being managed by personnel from another and the need for professionals to retain line management within their own agency for their professional development, so, in effect, having two managers. Difficulties, for example, were expressed in one case where Social Services, despite having lead responsibility, had limited influence over the professionals involved in a project, who were still line managed within their own agency. In addition, the strategic health manager involved was uncertain whether the Social Services lead was the right decision because s/he felt that the team was perceived as a Social Services team with people added on, rather than one that was shared equally. This might present an argument for starting a multi-agency team from scratch rather than with staff already aligned to one agency. In contrast, in other cases within the sample, particularly where multi-agency professionals were brought together by a coordinator or by location in a centre, the line management responsibility for professionals was usually retained through their own agency. Within coordinator-led and centre-based multi-agency working, therefore, there appeared to be less need for someone with overall management responsibility, perhaps because the key role was one of coordination as opposed to staff management.

Ensuring agency appropriateness

A single-agency dimension to multi-agency working was the need for professionals to ensure that multi-agency work was congruous with the aims of their own agency, and was therefore appropriate to be involved in. For 12 interviewees, this was felt to be a significant role that they undertook. This was identified by some of those working at strategic and some at operational level, although, interestingly, mainly by Education personnel. It appeared to be a key issue for Education staff particularly where they were in receipt of consultation and training from another agency and for staff from all agencies where they were involved in operational teams. This might imply a danger that the remit of a single agency may be lost or submerged when professionals work together in close proximity. Where these types of interagency relationships exist, a role in ensuring single-agency appropriateness therefore takes on increasing significance for the professional involved. For example, within one initiative focused on the assessment of children with disabilities, an Education manager commented that:

Well, my role is obviously to support what the team are doing from an educational position, but it's also to ensure, as far as I can, pupils that are coming in ... are being placed here for sound educational reasons and that the education issues are fully considered because, at the end of the day, we are acting as an LEA, working on the joint agency basis with other agencies. Nevertheless, we have our own responsibilities and where there are suggestions that we might be statementing children, we need to be clear that those recommendations are based on the criteria for formal assessment and not for other reasons (Education manager).

When involved in multi-agency work, being able to take a stance on what was and what was not appropriate to be involved in, however, was not always considered an easy task. A social worker within the same initiative as the interviewee above, for example, felt that, in order to fulfil this role successfully, it was important that s/he had experience and security in his/her own role, and for this reason did not consider it a job for a newly qualified worker:

I think they could have got submerged and it would have been quite hard to have actually stood your ground about things. So I think you have just got to be really clear on what your legal remit is, what your role is, and for me you have got to be quite strong professionally (social worker).

Implementation and planning

Eleven interviewees referred to having a key role in ensuring that the project was planned and implemented, and equally represented within this group were those at strategic and operational level. In essence they saw their role as '*making it happen.*' Some talked about ensuring that the initiative was involved in the authority's strategic plan, whilst others talked about ensuring that there was an action plan and that it was actually implemented. One interviewee, for example, described their role as '*to keep a watching brief on the plans and ideas, and make sure that they are actually happening*'. Another went further and described it as '*essentially a change management role*' and the need to have the ability to '*identify blockages and go to the right people to make sure that they are unblocked*'. Another interviewee was clear that this role involved linking between strategic and operational level as without this they might never get off the ground:

Because I think the decisions that are made at strategic level and the links that are made there, that's essential and it's really, really useful. But, unless people on the ground are actually using them and putting things into practice, it's going to fall by the wayside, isn't it? (behaviour support teacher).

Sometimes this role entailed ensuring that action plans were implemented in other agencies, as well as their own. However, where this involved trying to get the commitment and involvement of a range of agencies, it was reported by one Social Services representative to be time consuming and extremely difficult: *'trying to get GPs, health visitors and teachers to look at looked-after children and trying to get social workers to look at their education and health needs specifically is extremely difficult.'*

Budget or funding management

Where budget responsibility specifically was discussed, in two cases (one focused on children in public care and one on children with disabilities), Social Services was described as having responsibility for the funding or the budget, in a further two cases (focused on information and counselling and children with speech and language difficulties), Health reportedly provided the bulk of the funding, whilst in one case (focused on prostitution), Education reportedly had this responsibility. This would therefore appear to be linked to the target group.

When interviewees were asked about their own role, in addition to project or staff management, the issue of budget management was also raised. Budget or funding responsibility was referred to most often in connection with coordinated and operational-team delivery, suggesting that, in the types of multi-agency activity where professionals work in close proximity, the issue of budget responsibility takes on increasing significance, perhaps because it is more difficult to distinguish budget demarcations. Whilst eight out of the 11 interviewees who mentioned budget management were Education personnel, six out of the 11 also indicated that this was a joint responsibility between the agencies involved:

> *Myself and the Children's Services manager have just agreed that one of the things that's been holding us back is having two separate budgets being poured into the same bucket, but nobody's really holding the bucket's handle. So we've just decided between ourselves that I should carry the bucket, but it could equally have been Social Services* (Education access manager).

Issues concerning budget and funding are addressed more fully in Chapter 6 on challenges.

Initiating multi-agency projects

When asked about roles and responsibilities generally, Education was described as having a role in initiating projects in four cases (albeit only by Education workers), and this role was not mentioned in relation to Health or Social Services. However, when individuals were asked about their own role, nine interviewees from seven different projects indicated that they had a role in initiating joint working, and five of these nine were Health professionals. Which agency took on this role appeared to be related to the focus of the work or the target group. Thus Health professionals had been particularly influential in setting up projects focused in areas such as mental health and speech and language difficulties, which are generally considered to be their remit.

> *Giving it the links it needs within the Mental Health Trust, to try and open what doors I can, to try and connect it to whatever people … If they needed some family therapy, that's a job I would go*

*away and try and find. I would put it through the mental health system to see if we could find somebody to do it ... it is about having that connection to the mental health agency really (*Health manager).

A coordinating role

In the majority of cases, it was evident that the coordinator role was taken on by someone from a single agency, although in one early years initiative, this was a joint funded post. In five of the remaining eight coordinator-led initiatives, as noted by professionals from each of the agencies, this was a role taken on by Education staff. In one (focused on children's health), it was taken on by Health; in another (focused on early years), it was taken on by Social Services and in the remaining initiative (focused on disaffection), by a professional classified as belonging to another agency. Coordinator roles were also mentioned in connection with initiatives of other types. Thus, in one centre-based initiative focused on children in need, this role was taken on by Social Services and in another focused on assessing children with disabilities, a voluntary agency fulfilled this role. Where the coordinator role was taken on by the voluntary agency, this was reported by the Social Services manager to be beneficial because of its independence from a single statutory agency: '*I think the voluntary sector has quite a useful role to play by not bringing a particular agency perspective as opposed to Education's view on* [the service] *which might be the case if one of the agencies chaired it.*' Similarly, in an operational team based within a centre, a voluntary agency had taken on this key role and they were perceived as being in an especially good position, being neutral, to get agencies talking and working together. This voluntary worker described him/herself as '*holding it all together*'.

When asked about their own role, interviewees at both strategic and operational level referred to the coordinating role they undertook in ensuring multi-agency partnerships or bringing agencies together. This role, perhaps not surprisingly as this was the essence of this type of delivery, was a particular feature of coordinator-led projects. Those engaged in a coordination role included representatives from all three agencies, and it may have been that the base agency of the coordinator was more often linked to the target group on which the initiative was focused. For example, within the projects under study, Health took on this role in some mental health and health education projects, whilst Education or Social Services took on this role in early years projects. The coordinator role was key to coordinator-led delivery, perhaps over and above any significant management role.

Providing an agency perspective

When interviewees talked about agency roles generally, it was felt that individual agencies had an important role in being able to offer their own perspective and to offer specific areas of expertise and thus to make a unique contribution to joint working. Health professionals were described as offering a medical perspective and staff and expertise in areas such as speech and language therapy and occupational therapy. Similarly, Education professionals were described as being able to offer an educational perspective and a focus on learning or the school environment. Social Services, on the other hand, whilst also offering a different perspective, was seen as focused on the family or children who were vulnerable or 'in need', as well as being able to offer expertise in the area of child protection.

For some individual interviewees, particularly those involved in decision-making groups, being able to offer an agency 'view' on the issues being discussed was considered part of their role. Those involved in such groups were expected to be able to speak on behalf of their agency, and considerable responsibility was therefore attached to such a role. A Social Services manager involved in a multi-agency decision-making group, for example, stated that part of his role was:

> To facilitate this department forming its own view about what it wants from the strategy and what it can build into the strategy. So it's not just about passing on messages because the department has to make decisions ... it needs a position it can negotiate from or can negotiate around (service manager for children's services planning, Social Services).

Key points

- ◆ With regard to the determination of roles and responsibilities, some interviewees indicated that nothing definite had been established from the outset or that they simply evolved over time, whilst others stated that they were discussed jointly between the agencies, determined according to expertise and experience or decided at strategic level.

- ◆ Conflicting views, however, arose about whether roles were determined primarily by the skills and expertise of the professionals involved or whether this was secondary to the personal qualities of individuals. Exploring the skills involved in multi-agency working (Chapter 7) may therefore shed more light on this.

- ◆ Key features of the roles and responsibilities generally undertaken in multi-agency work were, according to interviewees, the multi-agency steering or management group, which was a key phenomenon in all types of multi-agency activity, the shared responsibility between the agencies involved and an overlap or merging of roles.

- ◆ An overlap or a merging of roles indicated that boundaries between the agencies had become blurred, and in the main this was felt to have been beneficial. However, others felt that maintaining distinct roles was crucial in allowing individual agencies to make a valuable and unique contribution to multi-agency working.

♦   A wide range of roles and responsibilities was felt to be involved in multi-agency working, and those identified suggested that a complex hierarchy of roles and responsibilities may exist, for example, at the level of the initiative itself, at an interagency level and at the level of individual agencies. Professional working in collaboration with other agencies therefore has to balance roles and responsibilities at all these different levels.

♦   Whilst some roles were described as being taken on by any or all of the agencies involved, or were a joint responsibility, others were described as being the remit of a single agency.

♦   Some roles appeared to take on more significance within certain models of multi-agency working or were more significant for certain agencies.

5. IMPACT

5.1 Introduction

This section of the report focuses on the impact of multi-agency activity. Interviewees were asked a number of questions about the impact of the initiative in which they were involved. This included the impact on the target group, impact on their agency, on them as individual professionals and on multi-agency working generally within their authority. They were also asked about the less successful aspects of the initiative. These impacts are therefore discussed in turn.

5.2 Impact on the target group

Interviewees were asked about the impact they felt the initiative had on the target group, which included, in some cases, parents as well as children. Eighteen interviewees from within 11 different initiatives felt that it was too early to say what the benefits to the target group might be as yet, although they anticipated more long-term impact. All but one of these initiatives were classified as decision-making groups or multi-agency coordinated delivery, suggesting that these types of multi-agency activity were more focused on long-term, indirect impact. Eight interviewees felt that, whilst impact on individual children had been noted or they were aware of anecdotal evidence of a positive effect, they were unable to comment on the overall impact.

The most commonly identified impacts on the target group are shown in Table 5.1, and these are ranked according to the number of initiatives within which they were highlighted, although the number of interviewees identifying them is also presented.

Examples of the most commonly raised impacts are shown in the illustrations on pages 94–95. Interviewees expressed their views on impact in a variety of ways, as indicated in the table, but, in the main, the impacts identified centred on three broad areas, which were also areas highlighted, perhaps not surprisingly, when interviewees were asked about aims, and these were:

♦ *improved services*, e.g. easier/quicker access to services and a coordinated approach

♦ *direct outcomes for children and families*, e.g. improved educational attainment, support for parents

♦ *prevention*, e.g. early identification and intervention, and prevention of the need for more specialist services.

The most commonly identified impacts (in terms of both the number of interviewees identifying them and the number of initiatives within which

Table 5.1   Impact on the target group

Impact	Initiatives (N=30)		Interviewees (N=139)	
	No.	%	No.	%
Access to services not available previously	15	50	19	14
Easier/quicker access to services or expertise	13	43	28	20
Improved educational attainment	13	43	16	12
Early identification and intervention	12	40	12	9
More children engaged/maintained in education	11	37	16	12
Coordinated approach	11	37	16	12
Support for children/young people	10	33	16	12
Support for parents	10	33	21	15
Children's needs addressed more appropriately	10	33	17	12
Raised awareness/profile of the target group	9	30	15	11
Better-quality services	8	27	10	7
Prevention of the need for more specialist services	7	23	10	7
Increased or wider range of services	6	20	7	5

A multiple-response question; therefore, percentages may not sum to 100
Source: *Interviews in Phase Two of the NFER study, 2001*

they were highlighted) centred around improved access to services for clients. Multi-agency working in many cases resulted in the target group being able to access services that were previously unavailable to them, and this was identified as an impact within half of all the initiatives. Within a mental health initiative, for example, a Health manager described how Social Services and schools were now able to access mental health services for children and young people, for which there was a recognised need, whereas these had been previously unavailable to them.

As well as greater availability, easier or quicker access to services or expertise was also highlighted in 13 of the initiatives, and raised by a fifth of all interviewees. All types of multi-agency activity reportedly led to improved access to services for the target group. Easier and speedier access to services was reported for a variety of reasons. These included professionals having a better understanding of the systems of other agencies, individuals knowing who to contact within other agencies, raised awareness of what other agencies could offer and improved relationships between agencies, or, as with centre-based provision, the siting of a range of agencies within one central location. Also in relation to access, a key feature of multi-agency consultation and training (though also mentioned in other initiatives) appeared to be that it enabled a greater number of children to access services and had a wider impact than just the target group (noted by seven interviewees in total). In one initiative, for example, by working alongside teachers, speech and language therapists (presently in short supply nationally as well as locally) were able to pass on their skills to teachers, who were then able to apply them in their work with all children.

Illustrative examples of the impacts on the target group

Access to services not available previously	*So Social Services would argue that a lot more of their clients are getting services that they knew needed services but couldn't access for them and that they are having more say in that and are able to direct the families towards those services. And Education would say that schools, local schools, are getting services that previously weren't there for children that they have long recognised to have a need, but won't get that need met until they reach a certain criteria [sic] on the SEN* (Health manager).
Easier/quicker access to services or expertise	*Oh, because I think they don't have to get to 101 different places, first and foremost, and get 101 different people involved. I think they can come to one place. I mean, that's a massive advantage for a parent who has got a child that has very challenging needs, which is tough enough on its own. Then they have to go down to the hospital, down to the LEA office, down to the Social Services office, and then wait for the social worker to come, and you know how it goes and so on and so forth. Lots of different people in lots of different places all carrying out lots of different assessments. I think the parents gained considerably from having everything in one place and just coming here and hopefully getting things sorted* (SEN manager).
Early identification and intervention	*If you work with an autistic child early when they are much more amenable to change, you can modify their behaviours. The pressures on families become less, so you don't work the reverse, which is to leave the child and let those behaviours become more entrenched, which then destroys the family and leaves everybody picking up the pieces – Education putting the child in residential special school, Social Services coping with family breakdown, etc. So the logic is everybody benefits – the agencies, the parents, the families* (Education development manager).
More children engaged/ maintained in education	*I think residential workers and social workers have come round to the notion that it is their responsibility to ensure that schools are found and school places are maintained. And they also know the legalities about exclusions now, whereas at one time a kid might get sent home and they'd say 'All right, fair enough'. Now if the kid's going to be sent home, they're going to say 'I'm sorry, but you can't do this. I need it in writing'* (teacher for looked-after children).
Coordinated approach	*I think certainly that there's not one group of people who are feeling responsible – it's not just an educational problem, not just a Social Services problem. I think there is a genuine feeling that people are working together to try to coordinate efforts. So I think the young people themselves are benefiting in that way* (behaviour support teacher).
Support for children/young people	*They come here and feel listened to, empowered, and have been given information. They are not forced to do anything – something they were a bit worried about. Even if they have not used the service, we have spoken in school assemblies, and they have said they are glad to know about it. It is security for them that they know we exist even if they do not need it right now* (senior project worker, voluntary agency).

Support for parents	*They will come here and won't feel uncomfortable about it. There is still that stigma for some people about contacting Social Services. We are based in the Education Development Centre and they see it as a bit more respectable* (social worker).
Children's needs addressed more appropriately	*I think there's a lot more* [children] *that are being looked at and getting individual education plans and packages that are tailored to their needs really, rather than just trying to slot them into gaps* (behaviour support teacher).

In addition to impacts focused on improved services, many direct outcomes for children and their families were noted. Improved educational attainment (and the maintenance of children within education) both featured highly and were both identified as an impact of multi-agency working in over a third of all the initiatives. Since the initial approach for the research was through LEAs, perhaps it is not surprising that access to, and attainment in, education was such a major focus. However, this also suggests that by addressing the holistic needs of children, educational gains can be made and emphasises the importance of educational professionals recognising the contribution that other agencies can make to educational attainment and the inclusion agenda. This was illustrated, for example, by a teacher who described the contribution that social workers made to the education of children in public care when they took on the responsibility of ensuring that these children received education. Other more direct effects on children that were noted by interviewees included improved behaviour, increased self-esteem or confidence and improved motivation.

Early identification and intervention were also raised as an impact of joint working in 12 initiatives and were overall the fourth most common effect highlighted. This appeared to be a key feature of decision-making groups and initiatives in which a coordinated approach to delivery was adopted. By pooling expertise and focusing agencies on the target group in this way, it would appear that needs can be flagged up earlier, as well as being addressed more appropriately. This was reported to lead to benefits for agencies (discussed next), as well as the children and their families, since problems were tackled before they became entrenched and more difficult to address, as described by an education development manager in an initiative focused on autistic children. Linked to this, in both these types of initiatives, multi-agency intervention was reported to prevent the need for access to more specialist services, or out-of-county services, an impact noted within over a fifth of all the initiatives, together with, as some interviewees noted, attendant cost savings. Multi-agency working, it was reported, sometimes led to a pressure on local services to respond to meet the needs of children who might otherwise require specialist out-of-county services and a building up of the skill level locally to meet increasingly more specialist needs. The multi-agency work being undertaken in a children's centre focused on pre-school children with complex needs, for example, was felt, by the consultant paediatrician involved to have developed the skills of mainstream nurseries such that they could accommodate children with more specialist health care needs. Similarly, a multi-agency initiative focused on the assessment of children with disabilities had reportedly led to the development of range of local provision for these children during the holidays and for those who were out of school.

Multi-agency working was also reported to have led to a more coordinated approach between agencies, and this was raised in over a third of all the initiatives. Alongside this, there was often a view that no one single agency was responsible for addressing the needs of the target group, especially where their needs were complex, since they intersect all agencies. In this way, multi-agency initiatives also allowed children's needs to be addressed more appropriately (also raised within a third of the initiatives), and many professionals believed that this had led to better-quality services and provision (raised by ten interviewees). The raised awareness, or higher profile, of the target group in the eyes of other agencies was also an issue mentioned by a number of interviewees.

Support for parents, as well as children, was highlighted as an impact in a third of all the multi-agency initiatives. A multi-agency service was sometimes felt to be able to offer support to parents who might otherwise not seek help because of the stigma involved in contacting a single agency. A social worker involved in a therapeutic service attached to Education, for example, felt that parents might seek advice from such a service as opposed to Social Services *'because they see it as respectable'* and *'because they don't see themselves as the type of family that would go to Social Services'*. Where family work was concerned, the way in which the work of one agency could support the work of another was also mentioned. Thus, an education social worker reported that having *'an open dialogue'* with families about the work of the Child and Adolescent Mental Health Services was felt to help them develop trust in these services and thereby encouraged them to continue to engage with them even when treatment became challenging. In addition, importantly, parents' increased satisfaction with services provided on a multi-agency basis was also highlighted, as was improved home–school relations.

5.3 Impact on agencies

Interviewees were asked what they felt the impact on their agency had been as a result of being involved in the different multi-agency initiatives. Overall, the most often cited impacts identified are shown in Table 5.2, and they are ranked according to the number of initiatives they were identified in, although the number of interviewees they were highlighted by is also presented.

Illustrative examples of the most commonly cited agency impacts are presented on pages 97 – 98.

Table 5.2   Impact on agencies

Impact	Initiatives (N=30)		Interviewees (N=139)	
	No.	%	No.	%
Broader perspective or focus	16	53	23	17
Improved understanding or raised awareness of issues	14	47	20	14
Improved understanding and knowledge of other agencies	12	40	22	16
Increased demands or pressures	10	33	11	8
Raised profile/status	10	33	11	8
Improved access to other services or expertise	9	30	18	13
Addressing an unmet need	9	30	10	7
Improved planning	8	27	11	8
Improved information sharing	8	27	11	8
Highlighted the value of multi-agency working	7	23	11	8
Successful example/model of working	7	23	9	7
Improved relationships	7	23	8	6

A multiple-response question; therefore, percentages may not sum to 100
Source: *Interviews in Phase Two of the NFER study, 2001*

Illustrative examples of the impacts on agencies

Broader perspective or focus	*It's very stimulating and I think contributes to job satisfaction when you feel you are part of a picture rather than just one person out there banging your head against a brick wall to get certain services. You feel much more part of a framework which is doing something* (team manager, Social Services).
Improved understanding or raised awareness of issues	*Certainly in terms of making mainstream schools more aware of complex and multiple difficulties, yes, on a small scale so far ... I would hope as well that the IEP work we do with individual teachers, that's going to impact on them professionally and individually* (Education manager).
Improved understanding and knowledge of other agencies	*I think the impact has been to have an understanding of who's going to do that role, you know, it doesn't really matter ... what we are saying to people is 'Look, we ourselves can't do this role any more, going into schools and working with the teachers, that's what the behaviour support teacher does'. That has had an impact on us in letting go. Letting go and letting the behaviour support teachers do that job that they are being paid to do* (social worker).

Illustrative examples of the impacts on agencies (continued)

Increased demands or pressures	*A major impact on the Mental Health Trust – increased referrals into the service which have been sustained ... A benefit in that more young people with mental health problems are being identified earlier and requiring a mental health input, but this has increased the workload of the Mental Health Trust* (Health manager).
Raised profile/ status	*Well it raises the status of the school, its reputation, the fact that we are a school that certainly attends to difficulties and parents pick up on this. We are certainly not one who pass them off on to other people, or refuse to recognise problems. We are a school that are very up front about difficulties and do what we can and, if we are actually implementing something for them, the parents are very appreciative and that makes for a better relationship between the school and the community and it enhances everything we do* (headteacher).
Improved access to other services or expertise	*Certainly in terms of improving practice, in terms of a range of strategies, ways of looking at things, but also enabling our clients, whether that be school or individual pupils or families, given them easier access to the CAMHS, I think, and, in terms of support for our workers and our team, and also in some ways, in terms of gelling our team, our support workers, as I say, it's sometimes an opportunity for people to meet together in a safe protected, reliable, predictable environment and actually gives us access to each other* (multi-disciplinary behaviour support team coordinator).
Addressing an unmet need	*Fewer exclusions from school. Schools know they should not be excluding children looked after particularly, although we do have young people out of school. A lot of energy goes into trying to resolve that situation so there is far less danger of them being left or adrift in the system. They might be out of school but they are not going to be ignored. There will be a lot of work going on between Education and Social Services trying to piece something together. It is far less likely that they will just drop out altogether. When that does happen, it is disastrous ... I think on the whole it has been quite energising because it feels like a real response to real unmet need. People rally round that* (principal educational psychologist).
Improved planning	*We have a care coordinator now, who's employed by Social Services, so that if children are complex, they'll have a care coordination plan for them ... so there's a real cohesive plan for that child and that family, and the Children's Centre is just a part of that ... it's an integral part of that ... it doesn't stand alone in any way* (Health manager).

Whilst a large number of different impacts were noted by interviewees, as indicated in the table, these clustered into five main areas:

♦ *understanding within agencies*, e.g. a broad perspective or focus and improved understanding and knowledge of other agencies

♦ *interactions between agencies*, e.g. improved relationships and shared responsibility

♦ *agency practices*, e.g. access to other services or expertise and early identification and intervention

♦ *extension to other areas of work*, e.g. highlighted the value of joint working and increased joint working in other areas

♦ *single-agency gains or losses*, e.g. raised profile/status, achieved targets and increased workload or pressure.

In over half of all the multi-agency initiatives and within all five of the different types, joint working was reported to have broadened the perspective of professionals from all three agencies, although this was highlighted mainly by Education staff. Within Education, multi-agency decision making, for example, was reported to have '*widened people's thinking*' and '*broadened the scope of the work*' and therefore to have strengthened Education's role. It was also reported to have helped educational professionals recognise that a focus solely on education with disengaged children was unlikely to be effective. Similarly, it was felt to have led to a broader, whole-systems approach within Social Services and to highlight to social workers the need to constantly think about education when considering the placement of children. One Social Services manager, for example, stated that it had '*radically broadened their view on the world*'. Multi-agency work was also reported by one Social Services team manager to be more stimulating and more interesting work for professionals because it enabled them to see the broader picture.

Raised awareness and improved understanding of the issues concerning the focus or target group were also highlighted as a significant impact by interviewees from within almost half of all the initiatives. For example, a Social Services planning officer reported that involvement in a mental heath strategic planning group had improved social workers' understanding of mental health issues. Similarly, involvement in a multi-agency initiative focused on disaffected young people was felt to have raised awareness within Social Services of the experiences of these young people.

As well as improved understanding of the issues, improved understanding and knowledge of other agencies were also one of the most common impacts cited, identified in 12 out of the 30 multi-agency initiatives. However, perhaps because of the more indirect contact between professionals, it appeared not to be a feature in coordinated or centre-based delivery. The benefits of improved understanding and knowledge of other agencies were highlighted. Increased knowledge of educational processes by social workers, for example, was felt to have enabled them to secure more educational provision for children and to save time in trying to find out who was responsible for providing education for them. Understanding the roles of different professionals and the constraints and difficulties of other agencies meant that expectations were more realistic. The deputy head of a high school involved in an initiative focused on children in public care, for example, referred to the knock-on effect that the lack of foster carers had for Social Services. Similarly, a Social Services planning officer reported a better understanding of the way Health colleagues operated such that he now understood why they were reluctant to get involved in cases when there were already a large number of other professionals involved. In addition, improved understanding of the roles of other agencies had sometimes led to the professionals in one agency having to stand back and '*let go*' in order to allow other professionals to do their job.

Interestingly, whilst ten interviewees from just under a third of all the initiatives highlighted one of the only negative aspects raised – increased demands and pressures on agencies – five interviewees also highlighted reduced pressure or a reduced workload as a result of multi-agency work. Increased demands featured particularly highly within decision-making groups and coordinated delivery, although, especially within coordinated delivery, reduced pressure was also noted. A service manager within Social Services, for example, reported that knowledge of the education system meant that social workers were now able to challenge school practice, placing increasing demands on schools. Similarly, in another initiative, the fact that children with mental health problems were identified earlier meant an increase in referrals to mental health services was perhaps inevitable.

Other professionals reported that involvement in the initiative had raised the profile of their agency in the eyes of others, an impact also identified in a third of the initiatives. This appeared to feature highly, particularly as a result of involvement in multi-agency decision-making groups and especially for Education staff. Eight out of the 11 interviewees citing this were from Education, suggesting this as an added benefit of joint decision making for them in particular. According to one headteacher, interagency input into the school through a project helping to address pupils' difficulties was felt to have raised its status in the eyes of parents (see illustrative quote on page 98).

Involvement in multi-agency work was also reported to have improved access to other services or expertise for single agencies, and this was identified in just under a third of the initiatives. Whilst raised by professionals from all three agencies, this impact featured particularly highly within multi-agency consultation and training and in two out of the three initiatives classified as operational-team delivery. As well as leading to improved access for children and parents, agencies themselves therefore sometimes gained access to a wider range of skills and expertise. This was the case, for example, in one initiative where mental health workers offered consultation and training to members of an educational behavioural support team.

Ten interviewees, also from just under a third of the initiatives, reported that involvement in joint working had enabled their agency to address a previously unmet need that had been identified. Proportionally, this was again raised more within consultation and training and within operational-team delivery than other types of joint work. A principal officer within Social Services, for example, reported that it was reassuring to know that someone was dealing with the issue of prostitution and that before there had been '*a sense of frustration that nothing could be done and that services could not meet their needs*'. Similarly, where an initiative focused on addressing the educational needs of children in public care, providing multi-agency input for those not in school was also reported to '*feel like a real response to real unmet need*'.

Improved planning, both in terms of strategy and for individual children, and information sharing were also highlighted. Information sharing was thought to provide a broader view of cases and therefore more effective intervention. A number of interviewees also felt that the multi-agency initiative had reinforced the value of multi-agency working generally within their agency and had provided a good model for others to follow.

Other impacts, each mentioned within a fifth of the initiatives, included: being able to engage in open and honest discussion with other agencies; shared responsibility between agencies; early identification and intervention (a particular feature of coordinated delivery); increased joint working in other areas; improved services; achievement of agency targets and changed policies or practice. Clarity about responsibilities, as well as shared responsibilities, was also noted, specifically as an impact within decision-making groups and identified by Social Services and Educational professionals only. A Social Services planning manager, for example, stated: '*The fact that partnership working does not mean passing the buck to another agency, but does mean each agency being clear about its area of responsibility and expertise.*'

Other specific impacts were raised within certain types of multi-agency activity. The development of trust between agencies, for example, was noted only by interviewees within four initiatives, three of which were decision-making groups, and being able to talk and have open discussion with other agencies was also raised by a number of interviewees within this type of multi-agency working. Consultation and training multi-agency initiatives were felt to facilitate collaboration with other agencies, an issue raised by Health professionals only, and to improve working relationships. Interestingly, a move towards the integration of services as a result of involvement in joint working was highlighted as an impact in two of the three centre-based delivery initiatives. An interesting feature of the initiatives focused on centre-based delivery was that joint working was helping individual agencies to achieve statutory targets. A director of Social Services stated, for example, that: '*I think, gradually, it's having a great impact, because we're seeing that none of us can achieve the objectives and targets that either were set nationally, or we want to achieve, alone.*' Also in three centre-based delivery initiatives, interviewees (two out of three being Health professionals) highlighted that professionals within their agency felt threatened by this type of multi-agency work as it encroached on their own agency work, although two also highlighted the enthusiasm generated by such activity. The development of policies and procedures within their own agency featured more highly in operational-team delivery than others and was raised by one Social Services and one Health professional.

5.4 Impact on individual professionals

Interviewees were asked what they felt had been the impact of involvement in the multi-agency initiative on them as individuals. The most frequent responses to this question are shown in Table 5.3, and they are ranked according to the number of interviewees referring to them, although the number of initiatives is also presented.

Table 5.3 Impact on individual professionals

Impact	Initiatives (N=30)		Interviewees (N=139)	
	No.	%	No.	%
Rewarding, satisfying or enjoyable	21	70	42	30
Increased work or pressure	15	50	23	17
A broader or more holistic perspective	10	33	14	10
Raised awareness of how other agencies work	10	33	13	9
Meeting different professionals	9	30	10	7
Experience of, or learning how to engage in, multi-agency working	9	30	10	7
Enhanced or new working relationships	8	27	9	7
Increased knowledge/learning	8	27	9	7
Raised awareness of issues	6	20	8	6

A multiple-response question; therefore, percentages may not sum to 100

Source: *Interviews in Phase Two of the NFER study, 2001*

Illustrations of the most common impacts on individuals cited by interviewees are provided on pages 103–104. Although a large number of different types of impact were noted by interviewees, as can be seen from the table, those raised were similar to interviewee responses given when asked about impact on their agency and, in a similar manner, these could be grouped into the following areas:

♦ ***understanding***, e.g. raised awareness of how other agencies worked and raised awareness of the issues

♦ ***interactions with other professionals***, e.g. meeting different professionals and enhanced or new working relationships

♦ ***individual gains or losses***, e.g. rewarding, satisfying or enjoyable, and increased work or pressure

♦ ***professional practice***, e.g. experience or learning how to engage in multi-agency working.

Illustrations of the most common impacts on individuals

Rewarding, satisfying or enjoyable	*I have thoroughly enjoyed working with a different agency, working with people outside Education. It has been fantastic and very, very good ... It is all about actually promoting good practice, whatever your field of expertise, and to have the opportunity to work with people from a different background has been fantastic – in terms of professional development, in terms of breadth of knowledge and understanding and this whole notion about joined-up thinking, which is very much the flavour of the month in the authority* (education adviser).
Increased work or pressure	*I have aged considerably. Working across two agencies is extremely time consuming. I think people need to understand that they have to put in the effort to keep contact with both agencies and it is very easy to lose contact with one or the other. Just, we shouldn't diminish the importance of showing your face. So I make a lot of effort to get into both the Education Department down at the Civic Centre and also into the Health Authority and keep getting known; otherwise they say 'Who are you, again?' ... So I think there is a danger that people lose their sense of identity and other people lose their sense of who you are as well, so we have to work hard at keeping that* (head of health promotion).
A broader or more holistic perspective	*There is a small group, but they are a very significant group, I think, of children that we were looking at who actually had statements of special educational needs and yet appeared on these panels, which said to me, well, what was the statement doing? If they were statemented, then they should be in school and they should be being supported if the statement got it right and if the resources were there, so that I got anxious and worried about the wider implications for us having, seeing statemented pupils who were out of school and things like that* (consultant paediatrician).
Raised awareness of how other agencies work	*I know if I have got a difficulty about a child now, I am much clearer about who to go and talk to about it and how I can give them the information that they need to know, so I can be more precise in my referrals and conversations with other people, so I know who to go to, I know how to say it and I am much clearer about what they can and can't do* (social worker).
Meeting different professionals	[The conference] *gave us a lot of opportunity to meet with a large number of teachers and special needs coordinators, and that was really good ... and that has had a spin-off because we have been using some of the discussion and the lessons from that, some of the ideas that came from the teachers, and actually incorporating them into other multi-agency thinking* (consultant paediatrician).

Illustrations of the most common impacts on individuals (*continued*)

Experience of, or learning how to engage in, multi-agency working	*I think one of the mistakes I made early on was assuming that everybody was at the same stage of partnership and tried to perhaps rush things through sometimes and we've had to go back and bring people on board ... on a personal level I've learnt a lot about working across boundaries and I've learnt a lot about chairing meetings with people sometimes who don't want to be there and how hard it is to actually turn the rhetoric into action and get some outcomes* (director of Social Services).
Enhanced or new working relationships	*The fact that* [the principal officer for the education of looked-after children] *and I have such a strong relationship is to do with* [the project], *you know. If not, without* [the project] *I think we would still be in different camps and keeping our distance, but the fact that we have had to work quite close together on this project has affected working together on all sorts of other projects* (clinical coordinator for the mental health team).
Increased knowledge/ learning and raised awareness of the issues	*It's made me much more aware of the range of work that CAMHS are able to offer and also about how families actually sometimes find that work very, very difficult and therefore need some encouragement quite often to sustain it, and I wasn't aware of that previously. I assumed that families went along just as they did, see the doctor and went along with the service provided and took the tablets, so to speak* (education social worker).

Whilst overwhelmingly, the most often cited impact on individuals was that they found participation in multi-agency working rewarding or enjoyable, ten of these 38 interviewees also highlighted the increased pressure or workload that had resulted, the second most commonly cited impact. The rewarding nature and the increased pressure involved were evident, regardless of the type of initiative. Whilst interviewees who stated that they had found the work satisfying came from all three agencies at strategic and operational levels, those who reported that they experienced increased pressure or workload were representatives mainly from Education and Health. This might suggest that there was sometimes more to be gained from multi-agency working for Social Services staff. Interviewees talked, on the one hand, about enjoying having the opportunity to work with professionals from a range of different backgrounds because they found this stimulating and thought provoking. They described the work as '*motivating*' and, in one case, '*a morale boost*'. On the other hand, multi-agency work was felt to be time consuming and to require a lot of effort. An education adviser in a coordinator-led initiative, for example, referred to '*a trade off*' between the increased pressure and the professional gains. One interviewee stressed that there was a danger that those engaged in multi-agency activity lost their identity, and s/he intimated that it required considerable stamina to maintain this.

A tenth of all interviewees, from all three agencies and involved in all types of initiatives, felt that their participation in joint working had resulted in them having a broader perspective or more holistic view of the issues. This, however, appeared not to be a feature in centre-based and operational-team delivery. A number of individuals stated that involvement in multi-agency work had enabled them to see the '*bigger picture*', that it '*makes you think about different things*', or that it had changed their thinking. Health workers and social workers, for example, reported that they thought more about educational issues, and vice versa. Having a broad perspective, according to interviewees, enabled them to address a range of children's needs, allowed them to look at joint solutions and, above all, allowed them to see the wider implications of their own work and where the work of other agencies might contribute.

Almost a tenth of all interviewees referred to their increased awareness of how other agencies operate. This appeared to be more a result of involvement in multi-agency operational teams and centre-based delivery, where the day-to-day close proximity of professionals was more likely, as well as in consultation and training. It was also something that those working at operational level were more likely to gain from working together rather than those at strategic level. Thus, a number of interviewees, from different agencies working at operational level stated that they had greater awareness of the policies, practices and systems of other agencies. Knowledge of referral procedures, for example, meant that they were able to access help from other agencies for children and families more easily, or that they knew who to go to for help. Some interviewees also reported that they were now more aware of what other agencies could, or could not, offer.

The opportunity to meet with professionals from other agencies was cited by ten interviewees as a positive gain for individuals, especially within decision-making groups and coordinated multi-agency delivery. Many interviewees talked about the benefits of simply having the opportunity of meeting with professionals from different agencies. Face-to-face contact, getting to know individuals and being able '*to put a face to a name*' were all felt to be beneficial. According to some interviewees, contact with those from other agencies helped develop '*mutual understanding*' and '*break down barriers*'. In some cases, it was reported to have led to other '*spin-offs*', such as incorporating new ideas into practice. The importance of meeting with other professionals is reinforced by interviewee comments about the key factors for the success of multi-agency working, since having the opportunity to discuss issues in this way was high on their list of requirements (see Chapter 7).

A further ten interviewees from all the different types of initiative and from each of the three agencies felt that they had gained significant experience of, or had learnt how to do, multi-agency working through their involvement. A strategic-level Social Services representative, for example, stated that they now felt experienced at '*establishing and promoting partnership working*'. Some interviewees elaborated on their experiences and indicated ways in which they would do things differently another time since they felt they had made mistakes, particularly in the early stages of setting up initiatives (see illustration). The challenges associated with developing multi-agency projects are discussed in Chapter 6, and ways of overcoming them in Chapter 7. Other interviewees indicated that they had gone on to use their experiences in other areas of their work, in this way taking with them both the positive and negative things they had gained.

Nine interviewees reported that they had developed new or had enhanced working relationships with colleagues from other agencies. This was more frequently cited as an impact where individuals were engaged in consultation and training and operational teams than other types of multi-agency activity, perhaps because of the close contact between agencies that might be expected in these types of work. These interviewees stated that they had developed close personal relationships with counterparts in other agencies, and, as well as the professional gains which this brought, such as improved communication, some interviewees indicated that they had enjoyed such experiences. For one principal educational psychologist involved in a project focused on children in public care, this aspect was felt to be '*a big plus*'.

The fact that individuals had undergone '*a steep learning curve*' and had increased their knowledge enormously was also raised by almost a tenth of interviewees. More specifically, an increased awareness of the issues related to the target group or focus of the work was felt to be an additional benefit of joint working, a factor also highlighted by eight interviewees. These interviewees reported having gained greater insight into relevant issues for children and young people. An educational professional involved in a mental health project, for example, reported that s/he was more aware of the mental health issues relating to children and young people. In a project focused on young people involved in prostitution, a number of those involved acknowledged greater awareness of the plight of these young people and the family issues involved. Similarly, an advisory teacher for SEN linked to a project bringing speech and language therapists into schools commented that s/he was far more aware of speech and language therapy issues.

Other factors mentioned, each raised by six interviewees, included: a feeling of empowerment or liberation; increased confidence (mainly for Education staff); development of skills; a reinforced belief in multi-agency working; exposure to different ways of working and extension to other areas of work. Some interviewees felt that involvement in multi-agency work had liberated or freed them up from the constraints sometimes felt when working solely within their own agency, thus leading to a feeling of empowerment. However, multi-agency working was also reported to be challenging and to have raised concerns for some professionals about the working practices of other agencies. In the majority of cases, such concerns were expressed by Health and Social Services staff and centred on the practices of Education.

5.5 Impact on general multi-agency activity

Interviewees were also asked what they considered had been the impact of the initiative on general multi-agency working within the authority that they worked in. Seven interviewees noted that a lot of multi-agency working was already taking place within their authority and three that good relationships were already established (see Chapter 3). Five felt that their initiative was not widely known about and therefore was less likely to have had an impact on general multi-agency working, whilst another seven indicated that any impact might be limited to a small area of work or a small location. Four also suggested that this one initiative was one of a number that contributed to wider development and that it was therefore difficult to isolate whether it alone had an effect in this respect.

However, interviewees referred to a variety of impacts on general multi-agency activity. Table 5.4 shows these responses, and they are ranked according to the number of initiatives within which they were identified, although the number of interviewees is also presented. Illustrations of the common impacts cited at this level are provided on pages 109–110.

Table 5.4   **Impact on general multi-agency activity**

Impact	Initiatives (N=30)		Interviewees (N=139)	
	No.	%	No.	%
Applied to other areas of work	16	53	22	16
An example of effective practice	12	40	28	20
Improved relationships between agencies	12	40	15	11
Increased multi-agency activity	10	33	12	9
Raised profile of multi-agency work	10	33	10	7
More willingness to be involved	9	30	11	8
Provided a model for use in other work	7	23	8	6
Widening networking/increased links	7	23	8	6
Strengthened or enhanced	7	23	7	5
Improved quality of joint working	6	20	7	5
Identifying ways to overcome difficulties	6	20	6	4
Joined-up thinking	6	20	6	4

A multiple-response question; therefore, percentages may not sum to 100
Source: *Interviews in Phase Two of the NFER study, 2001*

In over half of the 30 initiatives, multi-agency working was felt to have had a knock-on effect for multi-agency practice in other areas of work. Twenty-two interviewees, half of whom were from Education, stated that they had applied what they had learnt to other areas of work, thereby extending its usefulness. This was the case in all the different types of multi-agency activity. Interviewees reported that the multi-agency initiatives they were involved in had '*set the tone*' or '*set the precedent*' or had been '*a vehicle*' for other initiatives being conducted in a multi-agency way. In some cases, for example, other joint posts were developed, or the work was extended to other agencies or individuals had, as a knock-on effect, been invited to other interagency meetings that then led to further joint work. In one case, a multi-agency project focused on children with disabilities had, reportedly, led to joint work in other areas, for example, where mental health services offered support to EBD schools.

In over a third of the initiatives, interviewees indicated that the work they had been involved in had been held as a good example, thereby demonstrating the benefits of joint working. This was the most frequently cited impact on general multi-agency activity, being identified by 28 interviewees, the majority of whom were strategic-level personnel, and it was the case in all types of activity. Interviewees reported that initiatives had demonstrated what could be achieved through working together and, perhaps more importantly, that many of the obstacles to joint working could be overcome. Where projects were perceived as successful, this was considered to be motivating to others and the fact that those involved perceived it as a positive experience was felt to encourage others to become involved. In one case, a multi-agency operational team focused on children in public care had been held up as a good example nationally by the Audit Commission.

Also in over a third of all the initiatives, but only cited by 15 interviewees, mainly from Education and Health, was a general improvement in interagency relationships. This was highlighted in all models of multi-agency working except centre-based delivery. These interviewees indicated that initiatives they had been involved in had influenced relationships between agencies. They reported that relationships had changed for the better and that by getting to know people in different agencies they were now more confident with each other and trusted one another and were able to be more open and honest. One interviewee stated, for example, that agencies were '*not as frightened of each other as they were*'. The building up of trust and confidence between agencies in this way was also raised as a separate issue by seven interviewees. Improved relationships had often then led to other issues between agencies being discussed and addressed.

Multi-agency activity was reported to have increased or grown as a result of a third of all the initiatives, but all but one of the interviewees who felt this was the case were from decision-making groups or initiatives classified as coordinated delivery. This might suggest that these types of activity, rather than others, are more likely to lead to more joint work. Some of those working at strategic level indicated that there was now '*an assumption*' that joint working would take place. One director of Social Services reported, for example, that multi-agency working had increased at all levels and that '*there is now an assumption that we work in partnership*', and the manager of the Primary Care Group involved in the same initiative agreed and stated that '*more and more it seems to be multi-agency*'. One interviewee, from Education, indicated that it was more common because there were now '*more routine structures in place*' to support and facilitate multi-agency work.

In a third of the projects ten interviewees, all from Education or Health, reported the raised profile of multi-agency working. They described an increasing interest in developing multi-agency activity. Concomitant with this, a greater willingness to be involved in joint working was highlighted as an impact in almost a third of all projects, and the majority of those who raised this were Educational personnel. However, this was not an outcome cited of decision-making groups. One headteacher involved in a speech and language therapy initiative, for example, stated that he would now be willing to '*give other health initiatives a try*' because school staff had found the experience '*non-threatening and valued the experience*'. Interviewees suggested that, having been involved in one multi-agency project, agencies were more able to see the benefits of being involved in such ventures and stressed this as an important factor. An Education representative stated that Health had not been willing to engage with them before, but they were now able to see some advantages in working together. One voluntary agency representative pointed to the increasing willingness of statutory agencies to be involved with them, as opposed to other statutory agencies. S/he felt, for example, that Health was less willing to be involved with Education because they were uncertain how they might use information about clients that was passed to them and therefore what the consequences of their involvement might be.

Illustrations of the common impacts on general multi-agency working

Applied to other areas of work	*So now we have looked-after social workers inside the CAMHS teams, employed by local authorities and, as I say, we have education posts being employed inside Health, we have that being explored here. We have other connections. Health workers are going out there and connecting up to voluntary ... So for me, as a CAMHS manager, it's opened up all sorts of doors about creativity of the workers, because I think that we had quite a closed shop position, and I feel that it's allowed me to open that up and I have really enjoyed working with these groups of people* (clinical coordinator for the mental health team).
An example of effective practice	*The success of it is the important thing and that's hugely motivating and means that there is going to be more multi-agency working in the future, because it has been so successful* (headteacher).
Improved relationships between agencies	*Yes, I think so. I don't think we are so frightened of each other as we were, so this whole issue about sharing things openly happens a lot more now* (team manager, Social Services).
Increased multi-agency activity	*I think it must do, yes, because it's making links, it's forging links. And the idea of joined-up working is definitely what a lot of the managers are actually talking about now, and what we're doing is actually doing it, really ... there is a lot more going on in the borough that is sort of multi-agency work and so I think it is obviously, it seems to be what's wanted and what works, really* (health worker).

Illustrations of the common impacts on general multi-agency working (*continued*)

Raised profile of multi-agency work	*Well maybe the best indicator I can give you is that ... well I think a couple of months ago, I was invited to talk ... with a paediatrician from Health to a group of Health professionals ... to talk about multi-agency work and what we did and that was across the country. So clearly there is an interest in developing multi-agency work and it was a well-received thing. It's a dry subject, multi-agency work; you can't make it terribly sexy, but it was well received, they enjoyed it and they had a lot of questions to ask afterwards. So I think there's a level of interest in developing this. You would have to say the Government is pushing it through, through social inclusion and you are looking at things like the Connexions service establishment* (head of Behaviour Support Service).
More willingness to be involved	*I don't think, as I said, in the previous climate that there was much of a willingness to be partners in this sense but I think the whole context has changed now and I think they needed to experience such success in order to experience what benefits there are in this style of working* (headteacher).
Provided a model for use in other work	*It gives a very clear message to everyone within the organisations, that we are working together. That this is just how we do business now. I hope we now have a culture where there's an assumption that we work in partnership and I think at the strategic level we are modelling to the organisations that this is how we work together. I think on the ground, people are working very close together* (director of Social Services).
Widening networking / increased links	*I'd like to think it has made it easier for Education to have simpler routes of referral, and they know where their team members are, how to contact, how to access key workers* (school health manager).

Other effects on general multi-agency working noted included: widening networks or increased links between agencies; strengthened or enhanced joint working; identifying ways to overcome interagency difficulties and joined-up thinking. Networking appeared to be a key feature of initiatives focused on coordinated delivery, whilst the building of trust and confidence between agencies was most commonly cited in relation to consultation and training.

Interviewees were also asked whether they felt there had been any less successful aspects to the type of multi-agency work they were engaged in. The responses to this question were similar to some of the issues raised when interviewees were asked about challenges associated with multi-agency working, discussed in Chapter 6. For this reason, the least successful aspects are presented here in Research Vignette 3, although illustrative examples of interviewee responses are also provided on pages 112–113.

Research Vignette 3   Less successful aspects

Issues to do with **funding and budgets** were the most commonly identified aspects reported to have been unsuccessful, cited as an issue within over a third of all the 30 multi-agency initiatives. Despite being the most common aspect raised, funding was an issue raised mainly by interviewees within certain types of multi-agency activity – decision-making groups, coordinated delivery and operational teams, although it was an issue raised equally by personnel from all three agencies. Issues raised concerned short-term funding, which led to uncertainty as to whether the project would continue and an inability to retain qualified staff, as well as inadequate funding and separate agency rather than pooled budgets. All these issues are discussed in depth in Chapter 6 on challenges.

Pressure of work and competing demands, which led to professionals being unable to devote adequate time to multi-agency work, was highlighted as the next most common less successful aspect, raised by 14 interviewees. This was noted particularly in relation to coordinated multi-agency delivery, perhaps reflecting the particular demands placed on personnel taking on a coordinator role. Where such a person was absent, the need for a key person who could devote a substantial part of their time to pulling things together and who could form the focal point of coordinated delivery was also considered a less successful aspect. Half of the interviewees identifying this as an issue were Health personnel, perhaps suggesting particular demands being placed on them at this time.

Engaging others or the lack of commitment of others was the third least successful aspect of initiatives cited and this was noted within a third of all the initiatives and by 14 interviewees. This was highlighted mainly as an issue by personnel from Education with regard to Health staff or vice versa, and it was most evident in initiatives classified as coordinated delivery and decision-making groups. It may be that those involved in these types of multi-agency activity found it more difficult to see the direct benefits for their agency.

An **inability to meet the needs of all children** was highlighted as an issue in almost a third of the initiatives and by 13 interviewees from all three agencies. This was the only issue raised as a less successful aspect that was not also raised as a challenge. There was often a small group of children for whom the provision or intervention in question remained inadequate, despite multi-agency involvement. This was an issue raised within all types of joint working. Though highlighted mainly within decision-making groups and coordinated delivery, it was also one of only two issues raised within more than one of the four initiatives focused on centre-based delivery.

Staffing difficulties, such as recruitment and staff changes, were also commonly referred to, although these tended to be more of an issue where services were being delivered, particularly in operational teams. Lack of staff with the relevant expertise, such as speech and language therapists within Health, and personnel changes within Social Services and Health were highlighted by Education staff as being a particular obstacle to joint working. This was often reported to lead to a waste of time and the need to repeat a lot of work since effective working relationships had to be built all over again.

Finding **accommodation**, often for a large number of staff from different agencies, was another issue that particularly related to centre-based delivery, although it was also an issue in decision-making groups, where often large numbers of professionals needed to meet together.

Other less successful aspects included: time; agency constraints; evaluation; planning; implementation and the different priorities of agencies. Agencies were sometimes felt by Education and Social Services personnel to be constrained by their own legal and statutory requirements (although only highlighted in decision-making groups and operational-team delivery), making it very difficult for them to engage effectively in multi-agency working. Evaluation was a particular issue within coordinated delivery, because of the different agency priorities and the long-term nature of the work. In addition, within decision-making groups, the difficulties of sometimes actually putting into practice the decisions made was also considered by a few interviewees to be a less successful aspect. Different agency priorities, specifically agency targets, were reported to be an obstacle where agencies were brought together in operational teams. It may be that the blurring of boundaries within operational teams made it difficult to distinguish more clearly how the work contributed towards agency targets, thus making it difficult to justify engaging in this type of multi-agency work. Many of the issues raised here are discussed in more detail in Chapter 6 on challenges.

Illustrations of the most common less successful aspects

Funding and budgets	*The only thing from a Health perspective is that Health is expected to contribute to all these things, but Education has been given money from the Government, Social Services have been given money from the Government, but we've been given nothing. So it makes life very difficult for us because our health targets are all adult focused – waiting lists and it means that anything we do for children ... it's not because the will isn't there, it's the fact that the resources aren't there. I do think that if the Government want partnership working to be successful, and they fund one agency to do an interagency piece of work, then other agencies should have the same, and then we're all working to the same song sheet really* (children's strategy manager, Health).
Pressure of work/ competing demands	*I think that one of the difficulties has been in the sort of timescales we work to in trying to share information with colleagues for them then to feed back and because of the pressures of work that I mentioned previously, colleagues have commented to me that they find it difficult to work to those timescales and feel sometimes that, while they would like to be able to contribute more fully, that they feel frustrated that they are not able to* (consultant community paediatrician).
Engaging/getting the commitment of others	*Other people are not as enthusiastic because they have got other pressures. They have to make sure that the OFSTED is good and focus on exam results etc. This is what they are measured on so the Healthy Schools Initiative is not top of their list* (director of public health).

Illustrations of the most common less successful aspects (continued)

Inability to meet all children's needs	*I don't think we have sufficiently well succeeded in interacting with the kind of client for whom the project has been set up for ... we still need to be reaching pupils and families at a very, very much earlier level of difficulty. I think we are seeing pupils and families that are finding the problems that are presenting to us, as being for them out of control rather than just a difficulty that they see if we don't get a handle on this it's going to become out of control, and they are the sorts of families and children that I think we were set up to deal with* (education welfare officer).
Recruitment/lack of staff	*Yes. I must admit I think that is a huge pressure when you are short of staff. There's one side of me that says 'God, that is a luxury' and at the moment can we afford luxuries? I think it's the fact that I have been in* [the service] *and so am committed to ... I have threatened at times when I have been so short staffed and said 'If you don't give me more staff, this is something that I might have to do is pull this worker out', never actually thinking I would do it, but that's the pressure* (social worker).
Accommodation	*We haven't been able to get everyone under the same roof, so that has had an impact, because one of the things that the staff in the team will tell you is that that is a very important aspect of things – that they are actually based in the room, so that they can have conversations over desks, and that communication is eased by that very fact. It has been a real pain that we haven't been able to get everyone under the same roof* (Social Services manager).
Personnel changes	*I mean there are frustrations when you see things like the moves that the children have to take and the changes in the personnel side of things, such as the number of social workers that come and go, and you think I've got to start again and raise their awareness of what's going on in* [the authority]. *And there's a lot of repetition going on in things like that and it becomes a bit frustrating* (secondee to a Quality Protects initiative, Social Services).

Key points

- A wide range of direct benefits of working in a multi-agency way was identified for children and their families. These centred on three main areas: improved services, direct outcomes and prevention. Improved access to services was commonly highlighted, as well as an improvement in children's educational attainment and their access to education. This points to the contribution that other agencies can make to children's education. Multi-agency support for parents was also noted, and sometimes felt to be preferable to single agency intervention where there may be some stigma attached. Collaborative work was also considered to reduce the need for specialist provision, thereby reducing costs.

- For the agencies involved, the advantages of multi-agency work centred on offering them a broader perspective, a better understanding of the issues, and increased understanding of, and improved interactions with, other agencies. However, whilst it was sometimes felt to have raised their profile, it was also commonly reported to create increased demands and pressures on individual agencies.

- For the individual professionals involved, on the one hand, working with professionals from other backgrounds was rewarding and stimulating, but, on the other, it often led to increased work or pressure. They commonly reported that their work alongside other professionals gave them a broad perspective and raised their awareness of the operation of other agencies. Simply meeting with other professionals was reported to provide an opportunity to discuss issues and gain understanding.

- Some initiatives were also reported to have had an impact on general multi-agency activity within the authorities in which they were taking place. The multi-agency lessons learnt within a project had often been usefully applied to other areas of work and successful initiatives held as examples of good practice thereby motivating others to become involved. A general improvement in interagency relationships was also often noted.

- A number of less successful aspects of multi-agency work were also mentioned. These included issues about funding, the pressure of work and competing demands made on an individual's time and about engaging the commitment of other agencies. With many of these issues also raised as challenges, we now move on to examine them in more depth.

114

6. KEY CHALLENGES TO MULTI-AGENCY WORKING

6.1 Introduction

From existing research, it is possible to discern a range of challenges facing those working within a multi-agency context, specifically those factors that might help or hinder effective practice. However, what remains unclear is the extent to which these factors, or challenges, are prevalent across initiatives, the extent to which they are agency specific, felt by those working at a strategic or operational level, or contingent on different models or 'types' of multi-agency partnerships. The NFER research examined examples of successful multi-agency practice so that the factors facilitating successful practice may be examined alongside challenges to that success, across a range of agencies and models of working. It is therefore possible to move beyond specific examples of success, to look at the key features challenging successful practice across a range of contexts. This chapter sets out the key challenges to multi-agency working.

The overall challenges are discussed, but interviewee responses to questions about conflicting agency and project aims and the difficulties in the early stages of development of initiatives are also incorporated into this chapter. Areas of overlap are highlighted where relevant, but the problems encountered in the early stages are also presented separately for clarity (see Research Vignette 4).

Those participating in multi-agency initiatives were asked to identify the main challenges they faced, and responses were clustered into seven main categories. Table 6.1 shows these main categories, which are ranked according to the frequency with which they were cited. Each of these is now discussed in turn.

Table 6.1   Key challenges to multi-agency working

	Interviewees	
Main challenge	**No.**	**% (N=139)**
Fiscal resources	46	33
Roles and responsibilities	44	32
Competing priorities	36	26
Non-fiscal resources (time, staff, space)	27	19
Communication	19	14
Professional and agency cultures	14	10
Management	14	10

A multiple-response question; therefore, percentages may not sum to 100

Source: *Interviews in Phase Two of NFER study, 2001*

6.2 Fiscal resources

During Phase One of the research, funding and resources emerged as the major challenge to multi-agency working. In Phase Two, funding was identified as the greatest challenge by a third of all interviewees, above all other issues. It was also identified as the most common problem in the early stages of development of initiatives (see Research Vignette 4). Within this broader challenge of funding, interviewees identified three main concerns and these, in rank order, were:

♦ conflicts within or between agencies

♦ a general lack of funding

♦ concerns about sustainability.

6.2.1 Fiscal resources: conflicts within or between agencies

Overall, of the 46 interviewees who referred to fiscal resources as a key challenge, over half identified such conflicts within or between agencies. Conflicts over fiscal resources were not felt as strongly at the operational level, with only a minority of interviewees at this level reporting a concern, compared with around a quarter of those at both the strategic level and the strategic–operational interface. However, impact at operational level on clients was reported, for example, '*bickering*' over funding was reported to delay provision of appropriate services to children. Conflicts over funding were reported more commonly within initiatives classified as operational-team delivery and coordinated delivery, less so for all other types. Bearing in mind that the challenge of funding was not perceived as strongly overall at operational level, this suggests that these specific types of delivery may exacerbate existing conflicts, perhaps because of working proximity at that level.

At strategic level, the experience of budget management within a multi-agency context was not wholly positive. Numerous interviewees cited the impact of elected members on budgetary considerations, with multi-agency working removing the power elected members had over services:

Our elected members don't always understand. They see their role as the keepers of the public purse and providers of public services, and with some members there perhaps still is a culture of: 'Why are we giving money to Health?'. And I've had to work hard with our elected members to say: 'Well no. This is all of our business and it's not about giving, it's about giving and taking, and reciprocal arrangements, and we're all bigger for it'. It's not an easy message (director of Social Services).

It actually becomes quite hard, because you are no longer giving the elected members the same sort of platform for championing their own corner, which is the bedrock they've been founded on. You're actually trying to move away from that to say: 'Here are some issues that we need to address jointly', and so on. And the table thumping – 'My ward, my people' – is actually, that sort of role is diminishing. We are encouraging people to look beyond that. And I think that is one of the challenges (Health Service planning manager).

Whereas some interviewees reported that multi-agency working required the sort of budgetary flexibility that destabilised elected members, others were concerned that political influences on service providers impacted on the effectiveness of provision, particularly where there was pressure to use private provision:

Research Vignette 4   Difficulties in the early stages of development

Not only was **funding** considered to be the main challenge generally, but it was also the difficulty most frequently encountered in the early stages of setting up the initiatives. This was the case in all types of initiative, but particularly so in coordinated and operational-team delivery, and it was an issue highlighted predominantly by interviewees at strategic level. Interviewees spoke, in the main, of the problems created by projects having different funding streams. In some cases, this led to administration difficulties, such as those which occurred when one agency was responsible for an individual's salary, but responsibility for the accountancy process rested with another. Disagreements between agencies over who paid for what and concerns over the general lack of funding for multi-agency initiatives and ensuring sustainability once the pump-primed money ceased were also highlighted.

Finding the time to set the initiative up and actually do the work was highlighted as the second most common problem. As indicated in the main challenges, interviewees felt that prioritising time for multi-agency work was often difficult when there were other, conflicting priorities within their own agencies: '*It seemed like running all the time, trying to keep ahead of everything*'.

Thirdly, in ten initiatives, **different agency policies and procedures** were noted. This was believed to affect the day-to-day running of initiatives, especially where complexities arose around the expectations placed on agencies under different forms of legislation. Also in ten initiatives, **accommodation** issues were raised. Interviewees referred to logistical problems in finding a suitable venue in which to locate staff, especially where different agencies were involved. In one initiative offering an operational-team delivery, it had not been possible to place every member of the team in the same location and this was felt to have an adverse effect on communication and information sharing.

The next most frequently mentioned difficulty was **the appointment process**, especially when different agencies had different procedures *re* recruitment and selection. Recruitment was thought to be particularly difficult when projects were short-term. As one manager of an operational team noted: '*Advertising a post for three years – who is going to move for a limited time? Good staff would then need to be looking for another job after two years.*' At the same time, within this initiative, the illness and subsequent long-term absence of the original project leader had impacted significantly on the team in the early stages. It had caused difficulties with team management, the employment of further team members and had resulted in a loss of morale. Also mentioned by interviewees in five of the initiatives was the problem of sustaining initiatives in the face of **changes in personnel**.

In nine initiatives, interviewees referred to the difficulty of **ensuring people's commitment**. This was linked to the lack of time for multi-agency work, often in the face of conflicting priorities. In five cases, the difficulty of **involving Health** as a partner agency was particularly highlighted. There was a recognition that, in some cases, the goodwill existed; it was more to do with the pressures of the agency's own agenda.

In seven initiatives, **old attitudes or prejudices** were believed to impede progress. Ingrained ideas could result in people being initially resistant to change. **Relationships between agencies**, highlighted in six initiatives, were felt to be something that took time and effort to develop. In the formative stages, professionals could be quite '*prickly*' with each other, not wanting to share or cooperate fully. Interestingly, the majority of those referring to the above difficulties were Health professionals, while no interviewees from Social Services referred to either. Also in six initiatives, interviewees referred to difficulties in **getting the right people together** in the right place and at the right time, especially those capable of making the necessary decisions. This was a difficulty highlighted predominantly within decision-making groups and only where all three agencies were involved. This perhaps reflects the problems inherent in coordinating meetings involving personnel, often with conflicting commitments, from a number of different agencies.

Other difficulties highlighted included: agencies having unequal roles, and therefore power differentials (mentioned predominantly by strategic-level professionals from Health); identifying the remit of the initiative; different ways of working or different terminology; blame throwing and/or negativity; lack of clarity about roles and responsibilities; decision making when so many people from different agencies were involved – '*you think "Oh no, another delay"*'; and incompatible IT systems.

> *There's this thing: 'We'll give you some money but we want you to go away and not worry us about it'. Very much a local perspective on that, and there's also an attitude about: 'Well, if you have to pay for it, it must be better than if it's provided directly'. And a lot of our members have that view as well. So that's why we get put under intense pressure to use the independent, non-maintained sector, when I could put my hand on my heart and say the quality of what we can offer in our own schools, especially our mainstream, surpasses anything you can get in the private sector* (head of Children's Service).

Those at the strategic level, therefore, had to balance a range of pressures when deciding which services should be asked to provide services, and the degree to which funding could be used across services; in addition to which, interviewees reported a degree of reticence on the part of the agencies themselves to share resources. There was evidence that, at the strategic level, individuals were to some degree constrained by their agency identity. That is, their responsibility to 'the agency' took precedence over both the needs of the client and their professional judgement:

> *People guard their own pots and can become very defensive, and it's hard to actually move people out of the corner from that point, and if you are also thinking: 'Well what I might want to say as a professional might not be what I'm allowed to say from my agency'. So you have to be, sometimes you have a double dialogue going on about what you want to say and what you can say* (social worker).

The conflicts over fiscal resources were also linked to agencies in other ways, with personnel from Health, for example, reporting a widespread perception among personnel from other agencies that Health was very well funded. Where there was a lack of resources, the impact on multi-agency working was perceived to be negative, particularly when cuts had to be made. One interviewee stated that '*When budgets become tight, agencies retreat back to their core business*'; and another referred to similar experiences:

> *My experience is that when the money gets tight, they look at who is doing some work that is not anything to do with them, crossing the boundaries, and that is tremendously damaging, because usually that's the very work that is crucial, in my mind, in terms of providing services for families. In the past, when there have been multi-agency posts, or posts where one agency has funded somebody who works across agencies, whenever money gets tight, the temptation, often the reality, is to pull that post first* (consultant psychiatrist).

The evidence suggests that a fiscal 'precariousness' was often associated with multi-agency working. At one level, there was an acceptance that, under budgetary pressure, service providers often retrenched into a more minimalist role; at another level, there was the perception that multi-agency working was a more effective use of resources, reducing repetition, or overlap. At strategic level, where these pressures were felt the most, conflicts over fiscal resources were part of the process of working in new ways, for different purposes. That is, conflicts were an inevitable feature of doing things differently.

6.2.2 Fiscal resources: a general lack of funding

Over a third of the interviewees who referred to fiscal resources as a key challenge cited a general lack of funding for multi-agency work. This fiscal precariousness is therefore linked to the perception among some interviewees that it was difficult to fund multi-agency working. These concerns were twofold: firstly, that there were insufficient funds to implement what was required; and secondly, that those funds that were provided often had strings attached:

> *First of all, I think there is always an issue about resourcing and how you organise that, especially when most agencies are having real problems of resourcing – we are here in this area – or if there are other problems with resources, it comes with very specific funding labels attached to it; that means it's quite difficult to move it around, because the Government has said that you can only spend it on 'X'* (strategic director, voluntary organisation).

Within a concern with the challenges posed by a lack of resources were issues such as start-up costs, where these were not included in those funds made available. There was concern over the constant 'hassle' of having to bid for funds, often against criteria that were not ideal in encouraging joint working. Moreover, once funds were provided, there were concerns that a single agency could be seen as 'cash rich' by others, and expected to fund things beyond the resources provided.

6.2.3 Fiscal resources: the challenge of sustainability

Over a fifth of interviewees specifically identified sustainability as the major resource challenge: '*You can do all this good work and get the schools so far down the line, and then, all of a sudden, somebody just pulls the plug and you have to, just literally, walk away*' (school nurse and team leader).

There was concern that the multi-agency teams that had come together around specific client needs or service delivery, and that were developing successful multi-agency practice, could be fragmented by a lack of consideration of if, or how, their work should, or could, be sustained.

The association with initiatives identified as offering some form of delivery (as opposed to consultation and training or decision-making groups) continued to emerge in the evidence, with a greater perception of the lack of resources and the sustainability of resources, moving from operational-team delivery to coordinated delivery and centre-based delivery respectively. However, there was a comparatively high degree of concern with sustainability within initiatives classified as offering centre-based delivery, compared with an absence of concern within the four other types. This may suggest that the level of 'precariousness' identified above was felt strongest within these sites. That is, within those initiatives classified as non-delivery, interviewees expressed concerns across the broad range of fiscal challenges.

6.3 Roles and responsibilities

The second main challenge, mentioned by a third of those interviewed, concerned the roles and responsibilities adopted by those individuals working within multi-agency initiatives. Issues around roles and responsibilities fell into three main areas:

- ◆ understanding the roles of others
- ◆ conflicts over areas of responsibility
- ◆ the need to move beyond existing roles.

6.3.1 Roles and responsibilities: understanding the roles of others

Two-thirds of those who reported roles and responsibilities as a challenge specified a need to understand the role of others and to recognise the limitations that an individual's role placed on their actions. However, greater understanding of the roles of different personnel was also cited as an outcome of multi-agency working, something that followed on from practice. When the data was examined in relation to the different types of multi-agency initiative, there was evidence that this challenge was not perceived to be significant across all types. For example, understanding the role of others was not cited as a challenge by any of the 38 interviewees working within those initiatives classified as coordinated delivery, whereas it was cited by seven of the 17 interviewees working within those classified as operational-team delivery. There was evidence that understanding each other's role was a challenge primarily associated with those working at the strategic–operational interface. That is, whereas less than one in ten of the interviewees at either strategic or operational level thought that this was an issue, over two-thirds of those 'straddling' strategic and operational roles did. It is possible to suggest that understanding the roles of others is both more important and more difficult for those working at the strategic–operational interface.

Linked to the challenge of understanding individuals' roles was understanding that of the various agencies and voluntary organisations. Almost a third of interviewees made a distinction between understanding the individual and the agency role, and drew attention to some of the conflicts that could emerge between those who adopted a similar role within a different agency. For example, in an initiative classified as coordinated delivery, the distinct 'identity' afforded by association with one agency was perceived to be diluted by involvement with another:

> *I think the big challenge is actually taking the agency you come from with you, because they see you as joining a different department and no longer being part of their department, and it's very easy for them to think that you've moved on, to a completely different area, and it's not relevant to them anymore. They don't see you still in your old role; people say: 'Well, now you're working for the local authority...'. They find it difficult to see that this is the way things are going to be in the future, that we've got to work with other agencies and bring the skills together. I think it's quite difficult for people to understand that: 'You're not a proper health visitor anymore,' they'll say* (health visitor).

This task of '*taking your agency with you*' presents itself as a major challenge to those working across agencies, where the roles of the agencies are perceived to be different.

When asked about conflicting agency and project aims, other areas of tension identified centred on individuals having different roles within the project and within their agency, or, as one interviewee put it '*having to wear two caps*'. The difficulties that a headteacher might have in adopting an advocacy role for young people when they were also expected to be the disciplinarian within that system, for example, was raised by an educational psychologist in an initiative focused on children in public care. Similarly, an education welfare officer who was also a project worker felt that there may be issues for him/her if a child s/he saw in connection with the multi-agency project was not attending school.

6.3.2 Roles and responsibilities: conflicts over areas of responsibility

When asked about conflicting agency and project aims, tensions over areas of responsibility were highlighted, particularly in relation to initiatives focused on consultation and training, and they were raised mainly by Health representatives. Where Health provided consultation for Education professionals around speech and language difficulties, for example, this was sometimes seen by Education as a way of offloading their responsibilities on to them when Education staff did not feel that they were qualified to take them on. Consequently, Health personnel felt that Educational professionals sometimes still regarded speech and language difficulties as the sole responsibility of Health professionals and expected them to come into school to solve children's problems, and there was reluctance among Education to take the issue on board:

> *There was a little bit of reluctance on the part of some members of staff because maybe they had in their own minds the idea that they are not speech therapists, somebody else who was qualified at this should be taking the children and doing something for them ... in a way some people felt that it was a bit of a cop out in the sense that, oh, OK, right then, in school the teachers can deal with it* (SENCO).

Tensions were also evident, particularly for Education, where decisions, normally considered the remit of Education, were taken out of their hands, as in the educational placement of children with complex needs, since this had attendant resource and funding implications:

> *Well I wouldn't say conflicts but there can be difficulties in that, say from a Social Services perspective that they may find it advantageous for a child to attend a particular school, but from an Education perspective it might not fit in with our policies if a child is from a different area of* [the authority]. *How feasible it is to provide transport, for example, from one area of* [the authority] *to another, and that sort of thing* (SEN officer).

Similarly, Education found it difficult to be part of a joint assessment process where this meant passing the decision for formal educational assessment to other agencies. The attendant resource implications and the trust between the agencies that this would require were made explicit:

> *Well I think it's a leap of faith because, as I said, the historic model is Education managers, having gathered the appendices for the formal assessment, they then make the decision unilaterally, and to allow potentially the appendix writers to sit down and say 'Yes, there should be a statement and it will require this amount of money to be spent; now go away and write it', that's treading on some historic toes. That isn't the way we do things, or the way things have been done, so who wears the trousers round here, you? It will need a little bit of flexible thinking* (head of children's services development team, Education).

In addition, the lack of clarity of roles and responsibilities was also mentioned, albeit by only a few interviewees, as one of the difficulties in the early stages of multi-agency projects (see Research Vignette 4), especially where one agency had more of a role than another.

6.3.3 Roles and responsibilities: moving beyond existing roles

Interestingly, the research also found that there was a perceived need not only to understand and respect roles and for there to be clear roles and responsibilities, but to move beyond existing roles to work in new ways. For example, in an initiative classified as operational-team delivery, involving Social Services, Health and Education, individuals were required to move beyond the limits they set themselves, or that were set by usual practice:

> It's no good saying 'I have respect for and I understand your professional boundary and we will keep those boundaries exactly where they were when you entered this job, or when you worked somewhere else'. You've got to build some way of changing them. I call it 'blurring the edges'. I don't know what else to call it (head of special educational needs support team,).

This 'blurring the edges' is not without difficulty. For example, participants reported that it required a degree of reflection, or even a capacity for self-criticism on the part of individuals and, at the same time, questioned their sense of identity, gained through following existing practice or procedure:

> It's bloody hard. It's much easier to work on your own, to what you are used to. So it can be more draining, more time consuming, and you have to work through [that], challenge your own beliefs...it's complex enough in child mental health anyway! (child psychiatrist).

Another issue concerned the statutory responsibilities or obligations on an individual or agency. For example, in one initiative between Health and Social Services, some of those involved wanted to 'stretch others more than they could go'. In this case, a nurse was asked to prescribe specific drugs in order to meet the immediate needs of a client, but was professionally unable to do so. In this example, different personnel were not fully aware of where the boundaries were.

6.4 Competing priorities

The third most frequently cited challenge to multi-agency working, mentioned by over a quarter of the interviewees, were the competing individual and agency priorities within the initiative. When this data was examined alongside the classification of the different multi-agency initiatives, there was a tendency for those working within initiatives classified as operational-team delivery to cite this challenge most. Over half of those working at the strategic–operational interface cited that competing agency and professional priorities posed a challenge to their work, compared to under a fifth of those working at the purely operational level. In addition, less than a fifth of those working within Social Services were likely to perceive these difficulties, compared to a third of those working within voluntary organisations.

When asked about the existence of any conflict between the aims of their agency and the aims of the project, in the vast majority of cases, interviewees felt that agency and project aims were closely aligned (in only four projects were significant areas of conflict reported). However, even so, most went on to describe '*different priorities*' or '*tensions*' and they elaborated on some of the conflicting areas of priority that existed, which included, for example, differences in the target group, different Government targets and a focus on preventative work versus crisis intervention.

Differences concerning the target group were highlighted as one of the most common reasons for tension, as well as commonality of target group being referred to as one of the most common rationales for lack of it. It was an issue raised by professionals from all three agencies. For example, the fact that Social Services worked with individual children with problems, whilst Education worked with all children, was raised a number of times:

> *There is some tension about the project in terms of where it fits in at a broader level for all children, and where it's specifically targeted at children looked after, because if you can improve the baseline for all children, then children looked after are children in schools, so if you can do work that's going to improve it across the board ... but the project has got to deliver some specifics for children looked after in my view to be able to justify its funding* (assistant director, Social Services).

Similarly, tension arose where the target group for the initiative did not fit fully the criteria for one of the agencies, as in one project where some children accessing the service offered did not fit into the criteria for 'learning disabled' children as identified by Social Services:

> *I think issues have arisen in terms of the staff involved and the children that come in, because not all the children meet the registration criteria for the disability register, yet the input from Social Services is from the disability team, so that creates, not necessarily a clash, but a tension around how we resolve those issues* (commissioning manager, Social Services).

The focus on different target groups clearly had potential implications for the involvement of professionals in multi-agency working, as illustrated by this example:

> *A good example of this is the meningitis vaccination programme where school nurses ... they have a universal role as well, they don't just work with children in need, and suddenly the school*

nurses were involved in this massive programme which basically meant that they were absent from the team (children's services manager, Social Services).

Further, in relation to differing agency priorities, different Government targets were also reported to be a potential area of tension and, where multi-agency work was in alignment with individual agency targets, conflict was felt to be reduced. The focus on reducing waiting lists in Health, for example, meant that areas of work, such as interagency working, that were unlikely to address waiting lists directly would be the first to be abandoned when resources were tight:

> *What are we being measured on? We know the links are there, that a healthy child does better in school, but that is not what people are getting measured on. They are looking for immediate measures and in the short term and this is not helpful. In Health, for example, heads will roll if you do not meet your waiting list targets. So people are measured on other things. The timescales are different. A holistic measure of a healthy child needs a raft of indicators, but Education is measured on theirs and Health on a different set* (director of public health).

Similarly, the focus on literacy within schools was reported by an Educational professional to mean that focusing on the health and social needs of children was difficult, and this created a tension for those involved in this type of work:

> *It might be difficult to get across to schools who are being driven by governments, as we are, how making sure children have very good dental checks is going to impact on their ability to get level 4 at key stage 2 ... and because of the prescriptiveness of the curriculum, although it is getting better now in terms of that, how you get a school to spend time on talking about health issues, social issues, when they could do that superbly, but if they can't get the kids reading they'll be judged to be failing ... that is a tension* (assistant director of Education).

Engagement in preventative work versus crisis intervention was also raised as an issue, mainly by Health and Education professionals. Health professionals, for example, felt that a lack of resources meant that it was difficult for them to focus their attention on prevention, creating tension when this was expected. Whilst this was the same for some Educational professionals, such as educational psychologists, others felt that earlier intervention was more appropriate.

As well as needing to be able to manage competing priorities, another of the challenges reported by those working within multi-agency initiatives (of all types), was to ascertain, maintain, or increase the level of priority granted to the initiative by those agencies (or voluntary bodies) involved. For some participants, this process involved a 'mapping' exercise, an attempt to judge the degree of commitment on the part of those involved. A range of 'clues' to commitment was identified by participants, such as a strategic presence at initiative meetings, the provision of fiscal resources, levels of staffing or the provision of physical space. The priority of an initiative within an agency could be judged from such clues, but there was evidence that this mapping could also lead to misunderstandings. For example, in a speech and language therapy multi-agency initiative, clinical obligations prevented strategic-level involvement in some meetings, leading to an assumption that the initiative had a low priority within the Speech and Language Service.

6.5 Non-fiscal resources

Fiscal resources, the lack of them, or conflicts concerning them, were not the only resource issues faced by those working in multi-agency initiatives. What emerged from the analysis of interviews with participants at different levels within the initiatives was that non-fiscal resources were implicated in both developing *and* sustaining successful multi-agency initiatives. The 'right' staff had to be available and come together in order to work out any different perspectives on the same issue. By working in a multi-agency context, such issues were overcome, but fragmentation could result in the same individuals having to tread the same ground time and time again. Issues about the allocation of time, the provision of staff and the physical space in which to work together effectively were identified as challenges by a fifth of those working across agencies.

6.5.1 Non-fiscal resources: the challenge of time

Across agencies and voluntary organisations, there was evidence that personnel were under a great deal of pressure, with the time available to move beyond core roles at a premium. In some areas, such pressure was exacerbated by the small size of the authority, with individuals having overlapping responsibilities and limited time in which to meet them. The interviewees who specifically drew attention to the lack of time were equally represented within the different types of multi-agency initiatives, although slightly less so in those offering consultation and training. However, when the data was compared to an individual's role, there was a tendency away from operational level. Under a fifth of those working at an operational level reported that a lack of time posed a challenge to their work, compared to half of those at a strategic level.

The evidence suggests that multi-agency working was time demanding, that is, it took individuals *more* time to work with other agencies than it did for them to work in a single agency capacity. In part, this was linked to familiarity, where single agency work could proceed on the basis of common understandings of purpose, acknowledgements and acceptance of the role of others, a shared professional language, or shared assumptions. Working with others, in a voluntary or statutory capacity, meant that these could no longer be taken for granted and new relationships were required:

> *Building up cultures of confidence and trust and that does take*
> *time and it does depend on individual commitments of the people*
> *to make the group. Some agencies find it a more comfortable fit*
> *than others* (director of Social Services).

Moreover, where some agencies were used to working in time-limited, or time-restricted ways with clients, others were not. For example, in an advice and information service for young people, the Social Services personnel were used to working with young people in a more open-ended manner, with an ability to extend the service where required, whereas the Health workers were not:

> *The way we work is different to the way the Health Service work.*
> *The way we relate to young people is possibly different and the*
> *way we follow things up is different as well. We're not just stuck*
> *with the two-hour period; again, it's not a criticism of the way*
> *health workers work. They're paid for a session, but we tend to*
> *follow things up, we have the staff and the ability to follow things*
> *up during the night, or the next day, or at the weekend. We have*
> *that follow-up support* (assistant principal youth worker).

Time was therefore differently available to those working in multi-agency contexts. Where many participants reported being under similar pressures of time (there never being enough of it), existing practices and time use varied considerably. When agencies came together, these practices influenced perception, with misconceptions about the time use models within different agencies leading to assumptions of differential commitment or capacity.

6.5.2 Non-fiscal resources: the challenge of staffing

Another issue of resources was staff, with staff shortage (or compatibility) reported as affecting successful multi-agency working in, particularly, but not solely, those authorities in the south and south-east. Moreover, these challenges were not felt equally at all levels within an agency; there was an operational dimension to staff shortages:

> *Lack of staffing is a problem here, in that people can't be recruited*
> *to do the operational work. We all have recruitment difficulties*
> *because of the low pay in comparison with the high cost of housing*
> *that inevitably affects partnership working.* [And] *because we're*
> *all working understaffed, you end up doing the work that hits the*
> *desk, like I said, and you don't necessarily realise that taking some*
> *time to do some work together might help* (children's strategy
> manager, Health).

The staffing pressures that were reported by strategic-level staff linked to this lack of capacity to work together, a 'retreat' into essential, single-agency activities. Related to the shortage of staff was their turnover, with three participants specifically citing the disruption caused within multi-agency working when teams fragment:

I think sometimes it can be difficult. You have a key person that you have from an agency that you build a relationship with, who you know you can ring up. Sometimes, what happens is that person moves on, and then you get somebody new. In a sense, you take a couple of backward steps before you have to establish a new relationship and start again, and that causes difficulties (childcare development officer, Education).

6.5.3 Non-fiscal resources: the challenge of accommodation

In some cases, finding suitable accommodation was also an issue. For example, in one authority, a successful team experienced difficulties over space, with counselling services having to share office space with Health. While this was central to the objectives of the initiative, there remained different interpretations of that space and its suitability for different purposes:

For instance, next door, and particularly in this room, I, personally, through my experience of working with people, would really not want to see anybody in here, because there's all stuff about family planning, about sex everywhere. In that room [next door], *there's a bed, with a huge whacking great big lamp, and if like somebody is coming in who is confused about their sexuality, or has been, like, sexually abused in some way, they go in that room and there's that huge bed and all that symbolises. And I have said this and all my manager said was: 'Well, why don't you cover the posters up and draw the curtains over?'. But I think that's worse, because then it's hidden, and so the emotional impact of that is ...* (senior counsellor).

6.6 Communication

An issue that emerged during both Phase One and Phase Two was that of communication, specifically a lack of communication within and *between* agencies. A tenth of all interviewees reported poor communication between agencies as a major challenge to successful multi-agency working. This could be the communication of the general objectives of the initiative within it, or, more frequently, a concern with the day-to-day communication between those involved. The issue of difficulties in day-to-day communication appeared to be broadly perceived across the different agencies and voluntary organisations, with a slight tendency to identify it specifically within Education. The data also suggested that there was an operational/educational dimension to the perception of poor communication between agencies, although, on the basis of the evidence, it is impossible to suggest that this was solely an educational issue. The tendency may be explained by the contexts in which different individuals worked, where operational personnel working in educational settings had different degrees of access to methods of communication and had different availability during which they could be communicated *with*. That is, whereas Health professionals and those working in Social Services or voluntary organisations had access to the telephone during office hours, or had internet access at work, and were available to be contacted during office hours, teachers did not, and were not. Moreover, teachers were not available in ways that other professionals were, leading to missed opportunities. Where the time they had available to communicate with others was limited, and the resources were not available for others to communicate with them, this could lead to frustration:

It's actually the problem of getting to talk to someone; time is the issue. Being able to talk to the right person, missing each other, problems with messages. People also choosing not to reply, not to be involved in the work (teacher).

The issue was not, however, solely related to teachers. Those in other agencies were concerned that communication could be hindered by availability, that people were too busy to respond to messages. Additionally, there were difficulties of communication within an agency, that is, there were communication problems between those working at strategic and operational level.

A comparison of responses to the type of initiative pointed to an absence of reports of such difficulties within those classified as operational-team delivery, with the majority of the concerns (over a third) emerging from those initiatives classified as coordinated delivery, perhaps due to the large numbers and relatively dispersed nature of the people with whom they had to communicate. This in itself was quite interesting. Given that there was a tendency towards operational roles, the absence of concern within operational-team delivery suggests that communication, and problems with it, may be ironed out in practice.

There was also some evidence of a strategic–operational distinction as to the location of any difficulties, with the operational-level personnel locating the source of any difficulties at strategic level, and strategic-level personnel locating the source of any difficulties at operational level. This was partly due to general difficulties in communication within agencies:

There are lots of instances where communication from top to bottom in organisations is a major difficulty. There have been lots of instances where our directors and assistant directors and senior managers can be saying: 'We work together very well'. But the people operating at the bottom level say: 'Well we don't know each other' (family worker, Social Services).

Interviews with strategic-level personnel pointed to a difficulty of communication that was formulated around issues and interpretation, whereas at operational level the difficulty was formulated around poor communication. This suggests that communication difficulties were of a different dimension, depending on location. Different interpretations were therefore indicative of different perceptions of the source of the 'problem'. The general challenge of communication masked a range of inter and intra-agency issues.

A difficulty that *was* specific to those at strategic level was that of 'balancing' multiple multi-agency initiatives. Here, the challenge of communication was at the policy level, and there was a perception that successful multi-agency working was being undermined by poor communication at Government departmental level:

I do believe, and I have said many times, publicly, privately, in writing and to the House of Commons Health Committee and everybody else who'll listen, that the DTR and the DoH and the DfEE, and the Cabinet Office and the Social Exclusion Unit, you know ... how dare they keep issuing all these free-standing initiatives – Sure Start, neighbourhood regeneration – and just keep throwing these little bombs out into the system and not making them joined up? It is ridiculous and creates a huge amount of work for people, and also, I mean, it stops us from working together locally (deputy director of health strategy).

Communication was therefore an issue that extended throughout and beyond the multi-agency practices examined. Where difficulties were reported, they were at every level within and across agencies. Although not the major challenge facing those working in multi-agency contexts, difficulties of communication could remain unresolved.

6.7 Professional and agency cultures

One of the purposes of the Phase Two research was to examine the impact of joint working on the practice of professionals and their service. An issue that was identified by a tenth of interviewees as having the potential to affect practice was the 'agency culture' within which practice took place. In this sense, the culture of an agency should be seen as those things held in common – not its *modus operandi*, but those values, customs and accomplishments that underpin and inform its practices. None the less, conflicting policies and procedures were also sometimes reported to lead to tensions, and these are therefore discussed briefly at the end of this section.

6.7.1 The challenge to agency cultures

There was a perception that multi-agency working disrupted, or intruded on, existing agency cultures, and that some people found this unsettling:

Some organisations are very structured and their workforce look for a culture of routine, focus, agreed aims. The early years team is like a butterfly, jumping about all over the place, to create things and bring things together. And sometimes that generates difficulties for people who are not used to working in that frame. So it is very much about training, support, enabling, and also about building the confidence of those organisations who have never embarked on things like that before (early years and children's manager, Social Services).

This perception was associated primarily with those at a strategic level (over two-thirds of the respondents), but none of the interviewees at operational level reported finding the agency culture (their own or other's) challenging. Moreover, it was only associated with individuals within those initiatives classified as coordinated delivery (two-thirds of respondents) and decision-making groups (a third of respondents). Across the different agencies, it was associated with those working in Education and Social Services, rather than in Health or the voluntary sector. Overall, the challenge posed to successful multi-agency working was felt by some, but not others, and this required further examination.

The research found that when demands were made on those who sought security in existing practices, or where (inadvertently or purposefully) the agency culture was challenged, participants reported resistance to multi-agency working. This was greater when the aims of the initiative were not clearly articulated, received, shared, valued, or understood by all parties – in short, where there was lack of common purpose:

> *I think the difficulties are historical, and historical national, not just historical local. I think Education and Social Services have traditionally seen themselves as rivals, and, in a sense, genuinely don't have a shared philosophy of what the problem is that they're dealing with, or what the outcomes are that they ought to be looking towards. I think, when you then add Health into that equation, it's even more problematic. So we don't have, almost a shared starting point, in terms of philosophy* (care planning and review officer, Social Services).

The response to the challenges brought about by multi-agency working was, in some cases a retreat into the security of single-agency culture. Engaging with other agencies brought the participants into contact with different systems of values, and these could be different to those experienced within their own agency:

> *Social Services is, to me, fairly flexible. Moving into Education was like a whole new culture. They are very status conscious, and where I would anticipate that the person at the bottom of my team, in terms of payment and grade, should be able to talk to somebody in Education, to ask the same questions that I could phone up and ask, and receive the same answers. But that's not always the case and, I must say, that's very frustrating* (early years and children's manager, Social Services).

Another feature of experience was that multi-agency working was instrumental in exposing each agency (and individual personnel within it) to external scrutiny, a form of interagency peer review. The sensitivity of participants in multi-agency teams to criticism (perceived or actual) was therefore heightened by the presence of professionals from other agencies, or personnel from the voluntary sector, often with different ways of working with the same client group. The culture of the agency, often underpinning practices, but not evident in them, was therefore exposed. The resistance to change that participants reported was indicative of a response to this exposure.

Adding to any sensitivity individuals may feel in multi-agency contexts were the related issues of divergent priorities, budgets, roles and responsibilities discussed above. At the strategic level, there was a perception that such considerations mitigated against the needs of the clients, and that strategic-level personnel had, in some cases, an agency-led agenda:

> *People at this* [senior management] *level, and I include myself, tend to spend a lot of time developing and protecting their own little empire. It's all politicking. It's not just about self-aggrandisement, although there's a bit of that. It's a genuine desire, I think, for most people in the public services, most senior managers want to protect services* (education access manager).

Moreover, there was also a perception that addressing the needs of the clients, and the development of successful practice at the operational level, could fall victim to this tendency to resist change:

> *I mean, the purpose of the organisation is to deliver good services to people, whether it's Health, whether it's Social Services, whether it's Education. So if you go at base level, you can start to identify a lot of common ground. If you then start to examine how, and against what value base, people think that change can be achieved, you very quickly start to get divergent views. I mean, the culture within Education, within Health, within Social Services, to use just three organisations within the social and health care arena, are really quite different. I mean, democratic accountability is different, decision making is different, professional disciplines and professional cultures are different. So you have a major issue about that. There has to be a preparedness at senior level to embrace* [it] *and look at your value base and work together. And it's only by doing that that I think that better outcomes, better use of resources, would actually be achieved* (assistant director, Children's Services, Social Services).

On the basis of the data, it was therefore possible to suggest that strategic-level personnel had to confront the culture of their own agency within multi-agency initiatives, specifically any detrimental impact it may have had on the client group. Their concern that their own, or other agency cultures, challenged successful multi-agency working was therefore based on this reflection on it, or its exposure to critical scrutiny.

6.7.2 Policies and procedures

As well as cultural differences, specific policy and procedural differences were also reported to create challenges for those working in a multi-agency environment. These sometimes, however, also reflected fundamental differences in principles and philosophies and hence were closely linked to cultural issues. Thus, when asked about conflicting agency and project aims, professionals highlighted issues such as the compulsory nature of Education compared to the voluntary nature of Health or Social Services intervention. Where Educational professionals were able to refer to Health services for treatment, for example, they were often felt by Health professionals to insist on children and parents attending for treatment or sometimes even to make it a condition of access to education, which goes against their own philosophy:

> *Sometimes they are placed on the waiting list and when you get to the parents they don't want the service, they are not committed and that's it ... I was at two stage three reviews last week where we have had parents on the waiting list and parents don't want our involvement* (children and family service manager, Education).

Basic differences in principles of operation were reported sometimes to lead to the unrealistic expectations of other agencies. One interviewee from a voluntary organisation involved in providing counselling for young people, for example, indicated that teachers found it difficult to understand the concept of 'voluntary' treatment:

> *Then Education are saying 'What did you do? You saw them once. What use is that? We want them to have ongoing counselling. We want them to have this and we want them to have that', and it's really frustrating for the people in Education, that we're saying 'But that's not what the young people wanted'. We don't force anyone to do anything. We will tell them what the options are but in the end what choices they make are up to them. Some people in Education find that terribly difficult and I would have as a teacher as well* (senior project worker, voluntary agency).

Similarly, different policies were also sometimes reported to create problems. Different policies on confidentiality, for example, were raised as an issue, mainly by operational personnel, and this was sometimes reported to inhibit effective multi-agency working:

> *We did think about pooling referrals or having joint allocation meetings, but that was going to be difficult ... what can happen with politics and guidelines that are supposed to protect can actually hinder things ... That couldn't happen because children referred to our services couldn't be discussed within a Social Services setting without the parents' permission and we couldn't obtain that until we had seen the family and there was also the issue of the GP, who said they were referring to a mental a health team; I am not referring to Social Services* (clinical psychologist).

Procedural differences were also felt to create problems. Differences in personnel procedures, for example, were at times felt to have created barriers to multi-agency working. This was also raised as an issue in the early stages of development of projects (see Research Vignette 1 in Chapter 2). This issue is illustrated by the following comment:

The biggest thing at the moment is beyond the day-to-day running of the team, such as personnel issues. There was a redeployment issue within Health which was not identified by the other agencies as in the best interests of the team, but it was in the best interests of the Health agency. Because there are separate personnel procedures and disciplinary procedures, those areas are possible areas of difficulty. This will need a lot of working through. (children's services manager, Social Services).

6.8 Management

One of the challenges raised by multi-agency working is how any single initiative (or series of multi-agency initiatives) is managed at the strategic level. Working across agencies raised a number of difficulties, often linked to conflicts of interest within interagency management teams. There was evidence that the 'people upstairs' needed to be on board, and perceived to be both equally committed to making the specific initiative work and to working well together at an agency level, for an initiative to have credibility across agencies and for it to enjoy both strategic and operational level support. This was certainly reported by interviewees to be one of the key factors for success, as discussed in depth in Chapter 7. The research found that management challenges were disproportionately reported (and perhaps felt most keenly) within those initiatives classified as offering coordinated delivery, suggesting management difficulties were exposed in interagency coordination, rather than, for example, centre-based delivery. There were also differences linked to agency and role, for example, half of those reporting these challenges worked at the strategic level and half were in Health. However, this does not suggest any lack of clear management within any agency or at a specific level; rather that where certain agencies came together at the strategic level, it was perceived to pose management challenges.

The absence of the challenge of management within certain types of multi-agency practice also points to possible sources of conflict. For example, in those initiatives offering centre-based delivery, there may have been greater opportunity for strategic coordination linked to the proximity of individuals or their coming together around provision (such as in sharing a site). Furthermore, with less than a quarter of respondents citing management challenges working at an operational level, it may be the case that any difficulties or conflicts are not felt outside the strategic group. However, while strategic conflicts may be contained, the perception of coherence remained important, with participants looking for evidence of commitment:

All parties need to be equally committed, and need to be seen to be equally committed. And maybe, if the managers aren't going to the strategic meetings, that's sending out a message that it's not a priority (community outreach facilitator, Health).

Where managers did face difficulty was in marrying the need for direction with an avoidance of 'top down' implementation, perceived as heavy-handed management at the operational level. There was evidence that multi-agency initiatives had to be seen as strongly supported and promoted at the strategic level in order to remain credible at the operational level, yet that this strategic drive had in itself to be very carefully managed in order to carry along all the various participants. This was considered a difficult task within a single agency, and the multi-agency dimension simply made it more so. One of the challenges was therefore engaging the 'right' people at strategic level, like-minded individuals, often with experience of practice in more than one agency. These individuals could be conceived of as the 'creative entrepreneurs' of the public sector, individuals who sought new ways of working in order to meet shared goals and who worked within, beneath and across existing management structures in order to achieve change. Over a third of those interviewed had experience of working in more than one agency. In the words of one participant: '*These people know who should be engaged and know why, they know who is doing what and what the agendas are (within and between agencies), they should be able to move things, to get the right people around the table, and, perhaps importantly, they should also know who not to invite.*'

6.9   Other challenges

Other challenges to successful multi-agency working identified by participants included:

- ♦ data collection and data sharing
- ♦ staff training
- ♦ geographical factors (rurality)
- ♦ issues specific to the client group.

While the frequency with which these issues were cited means that they were not ranked among the seven most highly rated challenges, they remain potential sources of difficulty.

Challenges around data collection had two main components: client assessment and data sharing. In terms of assessment, there was evidence of different tools and/or procedures in operation, with different agencies requiring the same and sometimes additional information for different purposes. Data sharing was considered difficult on two fronts: the actual mechanics and the underlying ethical principles. Mechanical issues were the incompatible (often outdated) computer systems or software, but more concern was expressed at the underlying ethical principles: who would have access to the data and the purposes to which it would be put. Within a single agency, there were often clear procedures for data gathering, storage, retrieval and use; when this data was requested by another agency, these procedures were exposed to outside scrutiny.

Staff training also had two components: that required and that missed. Because multi-agency working could involve new ways of working, it posed challenges to those involved. There was therefore a perception among some participants that they required additional or enhanced training in order to meet the demands of any role. Linked to this was a concern that those working within a multi-agency team could miss out on professional development delivered at 'base', within a single agency context. For example, a nurse may gain training in child protection, but miss training on a new form of inoculation for children.

Challenges linked to the geographical location of the initiative, or to the site of intervention were only raised by two participants, but both of these drew attention to the difficulty of working in multi-agency initiatives in rural areas. This was linked to the distance between teams and the difficulty of coordinating or attending meetings when many hours' travel was required. Related to this was the lack of coterminous boundaries in rural areas between different agencies, with some having very large areas to cover with few members of staff. While this also affected urban initiatives, the perception in rural areas was that resources (particularly human resources) were spread too thinly.

Issues related to the client group were raised in the context of whether the initiatives which focus on their needs, and on more effective ways of meeting their needs, are able to overcome any interagency tensions, avoid replication and enhance what already exists. While this was not significantly reported across the research, the desire to improve on what already existed remained implicit in many of the accounts of those professionals working in multi-agency contexts.

It was often reported that, whilst multi-agency working went smoothly at strategic level, conflicts arose in trying to put things into practice at operational level. The majority of those citing this worked at strategic rather than operational level, although they were from all three agencies. As one Social Services manager stated:

> *It's ever so easy to get everybody to agree that what we should all be doing is improving the life chances of children. Nobody is going to sit at a table and say 'No, we shouldn't; we should be making their life chances worse'. The conflict becomes then, or can arise – it doesn't always arise – that there is quite regular areas of dispute if you like about how we are going to go about doing that, very strategically, but more specifically and more regularly, operationally* (service manager, Social Services).

Key points

- The challenges identified in association with multi-agency working were numerous and reflected the complexities involved when professionals engage in collaborative ventures. The issues involved, however, centred broadly around the areas of funding and resources, roles and responsibilities, competing priorities, communication, professional and agency cultures and management.

- Perhaps not surprisingly, issues around funding were the most often cited challenges, not only generally, but also in the early stages of development of projects, and the challenges involved conflicts over funding within and between agencies, a general lack of funding for multi-agency work and concerns about sustainability. This was the case regardless of the type of multi-agency activity. Other types of resources were also an issue: multi-agency work being cited in some cases, particularly demanding of staff, time and accommodation, compared to a single agency approach.

- Communication was identified as a challenge at all levels of working, although different interpretations of the problem were evident at strategic and operational level. Communication was most commonly reported as a difficulty within coordinator-led initiatives, where those involved were more disparate, and least in operational teams, where close working may have ironed out such problems.

- Conflicting professional and agency cultures surfaced as a challenge and particularly by those at strategic level.

- Many of the same issues were highlighted as difficulties in the early stages of development of multi-agency initiatives. However, particular common challenges at this stage included funding, time, different policies and procedures, finding accommodation, the appointment of staff, changes in personnel, ensuring agency commitment and in particular involving Health.

7. KEY FACTORS AND SKILLS FOR MULTI-AGENCY WORKING

7.1 Introduction

This chapter focuses on the key factors for the success of multi-agency activity and, linked to these, the skills that interviewees felt professionals needed or were beneficial to engage in it effectively. In both cases, a wide range of factors was identified. The overall key factors are presented and then these are each discussed in depth, whilst the skills required are presented in Research Vignette 5 and referred to in the text where relevant. Linked with the factors required for success, interviewee responses to the question of overcoming challenges are also referred to where they add to the discussion. The reasons interviewees gave for lack of conflicting priorities between the project and their agency, and specific responses relating to overcoming difficulties in the early stages of development, are presented in Research Vignettes 6 and 7 respectively and also discussed where relevant.

Interviewees were asked, in general terms, to describe what they felt were the key factors in determining the success of a multi-agency initiative. As with other such open-ended questions, interviewees provided a large number of different responses. The most frequently mentioned factors are summarised in Table 7.1, in rank order according to the number of interviewees citing them, although the number of initiatives in which they were highlighted is also presented.

Table 7.1   The key factors in the success of multi-agency working

Key factor	Initiatives (N=30)		Interviewees (N=139)	
	No.	%	No.	%
Commitment or willingness	28	93	81	58
Understanding roles/responsibilities	25	83	45	32
Common aims and objectives	23	77	35	25
Communication/info sharing	21	70	35	25
Leadership or drive	21	70	32	23
Involving relevant personnel	22	73	25	18
Funding/resources	20	67	24	17
Good working relationships	17	57	24	17
Having adequate time	14	47	21	15

A multiple-response question; therefore, percentages may not sum to 100

Source: *Interviews in Phase Two of NFER study, 2001*

A wide range of factors was considered important for effective multi-agency working, thus pointing to the enormity of the task. Whilst some interviewees suggested that personal qualities of the professionals involved, such as commitment, were important (see also the skills required in Research Vignette 5), others indicated the need for effective processes between individuals, such as communication, whilst yet others referred to external factors, such as funding. Those highlighted will now each be discussed in turn.

7.2   Commitment or willingness to be involved

As in Phase One of this study, the most commonly identified factor felt to be key to effective multi-agency working was overwhelmingly the commitment of those involved, identified by over half of all interviewees and highlighted by interviewees in all but two of the 30 initiatives. Although more a quality than a skill, this was also the third most commonly mentioned factor when interviewees were asked to describe the skills required (see Research Vignette 5). Examining the data by different variables showed that this was considered an important requirement regardless of the agency to which professionals were aligned, whether interviewees were strategic or operational, or the type of multi-agency activity. In each model, commitment was identified as a key factor by a third or more of all interviewees and in coordinator-led initiatives, by over three-quarters, although it was found to be secondary to understanding roles and responsibilities by those involved in decision-making groups and centre-based initiatives.

The most commonly reported issue relating to commitment (noted by 34 interviewees) was that commitment at strategic level was crucial. This was so much so that interviewees stated that, without this, 'you're knocking your head against a brick wall' and 'it would be hard to go anywhere'. From a management point of view, for some interviewees, this meant putting the structures and conditions in place to allow staff to be involved in multi-agency work. As one manager put it: 'you maintain that commitment by seeing it as a priority so that you enable people to have the time devoted to it and not it being eroded over time because the priorities change'. Many thought that strong management commitment was required to sustain joint working, for example:

> You need all those people to commit one hundred per cent. If they commit 50 per cent, it's not worth it; they have to be in it all the way or not at all because otherwise you just kind of put in and pull out again and it makes it not a very stable project at all. You really need strong commitment from everybody (project worker, Social Services).

Five interviewees stressed the commitment required at operational level, with one stating that there had got to be 'champions lower down' and another that to make it work you had to have 'good strong commitment at grass roots level'. Operational level commitment reportedly involved seeing the work as a priority and sometimes sacrificing your needs over those of others.

Others (14 interviewees), however, considered that commitment was needed at all levels and that multi-agency working could not be sustained by commitment at strategic or operational level alone and that a '*bottom up*' as well as a '*top down*' approach was essential, for example:

> *If it just exists in senior and policy makers' minds and they are expected to happen at the grass roots, that won't work, and if people try to get something ... at the grass roots but hasn't got the backing of senior managers and planners and policy makers, then that runs the risk of failing as well* (group manager, Social Services).

When asked in more detail about what commitment meant, the need for participants to have a belief in multi-agency working (noted by 12 interviewees) and to actively want to engage with other agencies (noted by eight interviewees) were identified. Interviewees reiterated, for example, that '*people have got to want to do it*' and '*you have to have people who believe in it*'. Ultimately, for one interviewee, a belief in the fact that workers were doing their best for children lay at the heart of their commitment: '*I think if you don't have those levels of real kind of human and emotional kind of commitment to what you are trying to do, then you are just going to give up.*' Thus those involved had to want to participate and to feel that it was worthwhile. Whilst one interviewee stated that it would be easy to direct people to do multi-agency work, s/he felt that individuals should be asked if they wanted to be involved. Alongside this was a need for individuals to take ownership of the process. Tangible commitment was felt to involve giving time, seeing multi-agency working as a priority, and being prepared to resolve issues that arose and '*not to say it can't be done*'.

7.3   Understanding roles and responsibilities

The second most common factor identified as important for effective multi-agency working was an understanding of the roles and responsibilities of different professionals and different agencies, highlighted by almost a third of all interviewees from over three-quarters of all the initiatives. This was also highlighted as the most important 'skill' involved in multi-agency work (see Research Vignette 5). Again, when examining a range of variables, this was found to be key to multi-agency working regardless of agency alignment, level of working or the type of multi-agency activity, although for those involved in decision-making groups and centre-based delivery it was raised by more interviewees than those who raised commitment as a key factor.

When asked in more detail about understanding others' roles and responsibilities, for many interviewees (19), this was about all those involved having a clear understanding of what was expected of them. Linked to this, interviewees raised the importance of understanding the constraints under which other agencies operated so that expectations were realistic. Without clear roles and responsibilities, it was considered easy for agencies to work on different agendas, to assume that a piece of work was somebody else's responsibility, for misunderstandings to develop, or for clients to receive conflicting information:

> *I think being very clear really about boundaries and limitations and roles and who's responsible for what and to make sure that there's kind of mutual understanding about that, and so at the planning stages to be very, very clear about who's going to do what and to make sure that it's realistic and it's actually going to happen, because I think in the past there has been a tendency to assume that it's someone else's responsibility or to think an agency is capable of passing it over to them, to think they deal with that* (behaviour support teacher).

> *I think that's where most of the conflict occurs and that's where we are in danger of raising parental expectations and one agency is suggesting that 'Oh yes, this can be done' and another one is saying 'Well actually, not really' and the parent is being caught in the middle* (special needs manager, Education).

In addition to understanding, when probed in more depth, interviewees referred to having mutual respect for the professional roles of other agencies and to valuing each other's contribution. Without professional respect, one interviewee described multi-agency working as '*almost a non-starter*'. One interviewee stressed the need for an understanding that everyone, regardless of their agency or their professional role, was equal:

> *An understanding that everybody is equal and that there are no status symbols in this and that one knows more than the other... even looking in the mental health arena, you have got hierarchical positions, and yes we know that if you are a psychiatrist you have had this training and that training and you have trained for ten years as opposed to five, but it's about they themselves understanding that maybe, just something that someone says is just as important* (LAC support teacher, Social Services).

Being able to put yourself in the shoes of others, to see their point of view and their priorities, was considered one of the keys to success, as was also, according to one interviewee, the willingness to work together on the priorities of other agencies '*on a quid pro quo basis*'. For one interviewee, being able to empathise with others also involved a level of self-awareness, without which, reportedly, difficulties could arise:

> *Where I have had difficulties in the past, it's not necessarily been to do with the agency; it's been the person perhaps representing that agency who cannot see the viewpoint of anybody else ... a school nurse who can think of nothing but the priorities of the school nurse and cannot understand the school, who are concerned about OFSTED inspections, meeting another target, exam results, league tables. You've got to take that on board, and if you can't, that's where multi-agency working doesn't work* (school nurse).

Research Vignette 5   Skills required for multi-agency working

In many cases, linked with key factors, interviewees described a wide range of different skills as being required or beneficial for multi-agency work. The most common will now be discussed.

Understanding other agencies, although not really a skill, was clearly a major requirement identified as important – being mentioned by half of all interviewees from over three-quarters of all initiatives. In addition, over a quarter of all interviewees referred to the importance of **understanding individuals' roles** (also the second most common key factor cited) – both their own and those of others. One of the interviewees explained: '… *you have to understand from the other agencies' perspective why they may not be able to do something in a particular way rather than it becoming an issue that you fight over*' (head of children's services, Social Services).

Communication skills were identified by interviewees as particularly important in multi-agency working, as well as communication itself being raised as the fourth most cited key factor. Effective communication clearly provided an opportunity to establish the understanding of agencies and roles that has already been deemed so important. One interviewee said: '*Communication is the key, isn't it?*', and this was a sentiment frequently repeated: '*If you can't clearly communicate with each other, whether it's at strategic or operational level, then it's not going to work.*' One facet of communication particularly – **listening skills** – was seen as valuable for multi-agency working, and cited by a quarter of interviewees. One interviewee made the point: '… *when you are on this team and we are all coming from very different angles and the language is different, you have got to hear behind the language where somebody is coming from*' (education welfare officer). Interestingly, operational-level interviewees made more comments relating to the importance of listening skills than those from higher in the management hierarchy.

Negotiating and compromising skills (another aspect of communication – a specific form of communication relating to conflict resolution) were also mentioned by a high percentage of the interviewees. These comments were made more commonly by strategic-level interviewees and those from Social Services than those with operational roles or from Health or Education. However, almost a third of interviewees from Education cited **flexibility** of attitudes and working patterns as an important issue, compared with only around a tenth of those from Social Services and from Health.

The third most commonly mentioned issue, although more an attitude than a skill perhaps, was a genuine **willingness to work together**. One interviewee explained how this had been an important factor in the success of their initiative: '*There's got to be some willingness to see the other person's point and view and try and move forward.*' Another interviewee, from Education, also highlighted where a lack of determination to work together could result in a '*retreat into one's own zone of comfort*' when '*the going gets tough*'.

Other 'skills' raised as important included: not defending agency boundaries, openness to new ideas, social and interpersonal skills, understanding strategy, having vision, relationship building and networking.

Subtle differences were seen in the skills described as useful by interviewees from initiatives involving different types of multi-agency working. Understanding other agencies, for example, was a skill mentioned by over half of the interviewees involved in decision-making groups, whilst other skills commonly referred to by these interviewees included negotiation and compromise, communication skills, and a genuine willingness to work together. On the other hand, the need for flexibility was mentioned by fewer interviewees from decision-making groups than from any other type of multi-agency initiative. This perhaps suggests that the decision-making process requires less flexibility, but more active communication skills. Interviewees from consultation and training initiatives mentioned a willingness to work together less frequently than interviewees from all other types of multi-agency working, suggesting that this can take place without the genuine desire to work together. However, those interviewees from centre-based initiatives or operational teams cited a willingness to work together as an important skill more frequently than any other group. They also placed similar emphasis on not being defensive or precious about agency boundaries. It would seem that these initiatives, where active multi-agency working happens at an operational level (as opposed to those with a coordinator, or consultation) require much more commitment from individuals in terms of their willingness to work together and overlap their agency boundaries.

The ability to understand the position of other agencies and their different priorities was mentioned specifically in alleviating issues over budgets:

> *I mean Education obviously have limited resources, Social Services, I think, even more so and Health perhaps even more than that. I don't know, but again, with the Health Authorities we are very conscious that they have a whole range of priorities and they are not all about children with special needs, and sometimes their resources are directed towards other things and we would quite like them to come in the direction of SEN children, but again it's about understanding the different pressures and priorities that everybody has to work to, and to some extent actually being realistic, I think* (SEN manager).

Clear roles and responsibilities for different agencies within multi-agency initiatives were also reported to prevent conflict over dual roles for individuals, although the assertiveness to say no when asked to do something beyond your agency remit was also noted.

7.4 Common aims and objectives

One of the third most important factors cited by interviewees was having common aims and objectives between agencies, cited by a quarter of all interviewees from over three-quarters of the 30 initiatives. Having common aims, however, appeared to be higher on the agenda for Education personnel, for whom it was ranked the third most important factor, than for those from Health and Social Services, for whom it was ranked eighth and sixth respectively. The establishment of common aims was also found to be less important for those at operational than at strategic level, but it did appear to be important within all types of multi-agency activity.

When probed in more depth about the need for common aims, some interviewees stated that there needed to be 'a unifying factor' or 'some common ground'. Others went further and described the need for 'like-minded' people to get together or for there to be 'a coming together of *minds'.* Yet others stressed the need for shared goals to be ones which all those involved believed in. The importance of there being *'a real purpose'* to joint working and that it was not something that was better achieved by a single agency was also noted because *'people don't want things to be token'.*

Others, when probed for more detail, stressed the need to be clear about what a multi-agency project was trying to achieve, that the aims needed to be clearly defined and that there needed to be agreed outcomes. Similarly, when asked about overcoming some of the challenges posed by multi-agency working, one in ten participants cited setting clear priorities within an initiative. However, when the responses were compared to agency, there was greater evidence that Educational personnel (half of respondents) found this strategy important, with fewer (less than a third) of personnel at the strategic level citing the success of such an approach. In part, the concern with priority setting was linked to the issue of operational credibility, where those working at an operational level needed to feel confident that those with strategic responsibility were aware of their workload and the context of practice:

> [We need to] *work with people's existing priorities, recognising the pressures. This is where operational credibility is essential. To sell it at the operational level requires a degree of honesty and an awareness of the terrain, the conflicts and the strategic–operational relationship* (school nurse).

Where priorities reflected this contextual awareness, and displayed role and responsibility recognition, operational personnel were engaged more effectively. For example, teachers required others to recognise the pressures of assessment procedures at specific times in the year, or that their availability over lunchtime was often impacted by school duties. Where priorities reflected, or were sensitive to pressures, the credibility of the initiative was enhanced. However, there was also a perception that the process of multi-agency service delivery in itself necessarily 'disrupted' existing priorities, and this was not always a bad thing:

> *What other people see as limits can be seen as quite positive and what is limiting in one sense is liberating in another.* [We should] *allow the professional to really define what they are able to provide, with the emphasis on who can do it best in their own role* (health coordinator).

Setting priorities was not, therefore, a simple case of clarity or prescription, but a complex negotiation of role and the creation of a context where 'what works' replaced any individual or agency-specific agenda. This required those individuals involved in multi-agency initiatives to assess the basis of their priorities, for example: was patrolling the school field a reasonable use of an Educational professional's time compared to addressing the needs of children in public care? As a consequence, the process could reveal the extent to which agencies served client needs, or existed in a state of 'crisis management' that prevented a clear focus on need:

I think it goes back to being focused on what you are trying to achieve. And again, if you get that from real [client] *need, I think that becomes quite clear. And that to me is incredibly simple, but I don't think many agencies are able to. That's not their natural way of doing things. It's mostly just reacting to crises and coping with very difficult situations* (children's project coordinator).

The common theme across initiatives, regardless of type, was the focus on client need and the shaping of priorities to best serve or meet that need: '*Everyone has to be sure that what they're doing makes a difference, because if it doesn't, they shouldn't be doing it*' (headteacher). Where there was a common target group or at least an overlap and where there was a focus on children and their families, for example, interviewees also reported that conflicting priorities were reduced (see Research Vignette 6). Thus, ensuring or promoting a clearer client focus within and between agencies was considered important. When meeting the needs of the client group became a priority within or between agencies, this meant putting to one side any issues of professional territoriality, or pursuing an agency-specific aim. Those working within an agency had to recognise that others outside it had something to offer, and did not necessarily seek to usurp their professional role by becoming involved. For example, in an initiative that focused on children in public care, the needs of the clients became the priority, not the differing priorities within Education and Social Services. The catalysts for this were both internal and external. Externally, there were growing political concerns about educational provision for children in public care and research evidence of 'gaps' in the system. Internally, there was a desire to change some of the practices that led to misunderstandings between professionals, based on their different priorities concerning the client group:

My interest in the education of looked-after children really started with the realisation that, when I came in to working within Education, that the complaints that education social workers had about Social Services not being interested in education were actually true. Because I'd been a social worker for 13 years and although I paid lip-service to them, visiting school and doing some work with the education welfare officer, or the class teacher, it wasn't really what I was interested in. I was always of the view then that some of these kids have got so much to deal with, we shouldn't really worry too much about their education. I quickly realised when I came into Education, and learnt from my colleagues here, that really you can't underestimate the value of education: for everybody, but particularly for disadvantaged groups and especially the poorest performing groups, which were children in care (education manager).

The coming together of a small team of individuals, most of whom had experience of *both* Education and Social Services, led to pressure to change practice. According to interviewees, this coincided with external pressure, based on growing evidence of problems in this area. But in order to change practice, the priorities of the respective agencies had to be reorientated towards the priorities proposed by the team: focused on the needs of children. That is not to suggest that the needs of children were previously ignored, but that the basis of the low priority given to educational outcomes within Social Services was challenged internally and externally by this multi-agency team. As a consequence, the authority put in place strategies that in some respects preceded the policy debate at the national level.

Such client-focused priorities had the potential of disrupting existing practice or procedure and risked running into resistance (or entrenched interests). Where clarity was required, therefore, was in the *process* of setting out the basis for action, a collaborative engagement with participants, rather than the imposition of a single vision or way forward. In those multi-agency initiatives examined, there was evidence that the priorities of statutory and voluntary agencies congealed around specific priorities (such as unmet need), but represented a more general pattern of the willingness and/or capacity to address the efficiency of current professional roles, responsibilities and practices. While further research would be required to fully map the extent and impact of such a shift, the research points to potential changes in professional practice across a range of services.

Raising the priority of multi-agency working may be less problematic when there is the existence of external pressure for change to services. None the less, the research found evidence of numerous 'goal-orientated' teams working within authorities to achieve change:

> *The commitment to the end goal, the shared goal, to make it work, irrespective of what barriers you might find, I think, we had that right from the beginning. And that does kind of enable you to sail through things and overcome more traditional barriers. When you have worked in these situations for some time, almost get blasé about some of the barriers. Yes, it is accepted as a barrier to multi-agency working, but it can't carry on any longer. Once you get to that point, where you've made that decision, the rest becomes easy. You have to work around them, or nothing would change for some of these children* (chief educational psychologist).

The shared priority of the team acted as a means of maintaining or enhancing the priority of the initiative across agencies, but once more the focus remained the client group. Maintaining the priority of an initiative was linked to starting with, or developing, shared objectives or goals. Successful multi-agency working accepted that priorities would differ between agencies, but within agencies individuals were brought together around a common goal:

> [The challenge is] *the understanding of people with common agendas and try to line them up. Trying to make, trying to demonstrate, how each of our agendas has relevance to everybody else. Because I think people will get engaged if they see it is*

going to be relevant, and if they see it is going to be beneficial, and multi-agency working needs to demonstrate that relevance and benefit. Otherwise, why get involved? (head of health promotion).

However, the data also suggests that multi-agency teams were more likely to shape agency priorities by demonstrating success, rather than seeking confrontation over perceived shortcomings in existing provision.

Research Vignette 6   Rationales for the absence of conflicting priorities

Interviewees offered a variety of rationales for the absence of conflicting priorities between projects and their agencies. Conflict was reportedly reduced where:

- **there was an overlap of, or a common, target group**

The most common rationale offered for the alignment of aims and lack of conflict was that the target group for the project was the same, or overlapped with, the target group of the agency. Although cited by interviewees involved in all types of multi-agency activity, this appeared to be particularly relevant in centre-based and operational-team delivery.

- **aims were linked to agency plans, policies or statutory responsibilities**

The second most commonly cited factor was that the multi-agency work being undertaken was linked to agency plans or policies or to agency statutory responsibilities or targets, thus making it a key part of the agency's core business. Perhaps not surprisingly, in both cases, all except one of the professionals citing these as rationales were strategic-level personnel from each of the three agencies.

- **links between different areas were recognised or a broad approach adopted**

Others noted that, by taking a broad perspective (or holistic approach) or by recognising the links, or the knock-on effects, of the work of different agencies, alignment of aims was more likely and conflict reduced. Health professionals were overrepresented in those who cited both these rationales, perhaps suggesting a greater willingness on the part of Health professionals to take a broad view and in this way extend work beyond their normal agency boundaries. In addition, initiatives focused on coordinated delivery featured highly within both groups. The priority many placed on the need to recognise the areas of overlap was often expressed, for example: '*I believe that for raising achievement the ethos of the school and health of individual children and their families is important and that it is interlinked and as important as literacy and numeracy and ICT*' (director of education).

- **there were common aims**

Conflicting priorities were reduced where all agencies were reported to be '*working to the same ends*' and '*all pulling together*' towards a common goal. The need for common aims was also raised as the third most common key factor overall, and this is discussed in more depth within the text.

- **there was a focus on social inclusion**

A focus on social inclusion was felt to legitimise multi-agency working and to ensure that aims were consistent within all agencies. One interviewee, for example, felt that such a focus made multi-agency working almost imperative: '*With inclusion ... I think we're finding more we have to work in a multi-disciplinary way, because the children are needing so much more.*'

- **there was a focus on children or young people and their families**

The need to focus on the needs of children was also raised. Where this was the case, a single-agency focus was reportedly avoided. Linked to the need for common aims, the issues involved are discussed in more depth within the text.

- **multi-agency work was made a priority and there was support from the very top**

Insisting that multi-agency working was a priority and having support from the top within all the agencies involved was also reported to be influential in the absence or resolution of conflict, for example: '*We decided that it had to be a core priority for the overall aims in both agencies. We raised the profile. Directors were also heavily involved*' (chief educational psychologist) and '*I think one of the crucial things is getting those chief officers to send out that* [the] *message, if you like, is we have an organisational perspective that's absolutely legitimate*' (service manager, Social Services).

7.5 Communication and information sharing

Communication and information sharing was also raised as a key factor by a quarter of all interviewees and considered equally important by professionals from each of the agencies, although rated as more important by those involved at operational level, over a third of whom cited it as a key factor compared to just under a fifth at strategic level. Communication and information sharing appeared to be a particularly important factor for those involved in consultation and training, for whom it was the second most important factor identified compared to fourth or fifth in other types of multi-agency activity. For one interviewee, the focus on communication was crucial because often '*this can be where it falls apart*'. When interviewees were asked to elaborate on the issue of communication, they raised a number of key factors centred around:

- providing opportunities for dialogue

- communication skills

- information dissemination.

7.5.1 Providing opportunities for dialogue

Some interviewees indicated the importance of keeping lines of communication open and providing the opportunity for dialogue between different agencies. Alongside this, the need for people to be willing to discuss issues with others and for them to be open and honest was also raised. One of the most important factors cited in the resolution of conflicting agency and project aims, regardless of the focus of joint working, was felt by interviewees to be to provide the opportunity for agencies to discuss the issues: '*The best way to resolve these things is, in my view, getting the people who are responsible for the provision of these services talking to each other.*' This was also raised by others when they were asked about overcoming challenges generally, and it was felt particularly important in the early stages of development to continually highlight the issues (see Research Vignette 7). Thus, delivering training opportunities in multi-agency contexts that included professionals from a range of agencies and engaged the expertise of the voluntary sector, as well as setting up structured meetings between participants and clients prior to interventions to map out agendas and priorities, were highlighted. Such dialogue was thought to facilitate a better understanding of how other agencies functioned and thereby resolve many of the day-to-day issues:

> *I think I need to plan to get into school staff meetings and say this is what we are about and this is how we work so people referring to us understand what might happen ... So it's about information and education really of teachers about the way that we work ... I think they need to hear that. Also so they can challenge that and say that we don't think that is any use so we can have some dialogue. So we each go away with an understanding of each other's perspective* (senior project worker, voluntary agency).

> *Some of the day-to-day issues, I feel, weren't fully addressed at the outset, and they may not have reared their heads at the beginning of the pilot, but suddenly they can surface ... and if we'd had some initial joint training about each other's policies – simple things like that ... I'm sure some of that would have given a greater insight and a clearer understanding* (school health manager).

In one initiative, for example, the location of a Health Promotion Service within Education was felt to have facilitated communication and helped overcome conflicts between the agencies:

> *It is almost an educative process as well in that there is a danger sometimes that, when somebody says no or disagrees with your point of view, that you feel they are just being bloody-minded or whatever, whereas being with Education and being able to talk informally to people, sort of on a day-to-day basis, it helps to demonstrate that people may be saying no because of very good reasons because of organisational or professional constraints and there are real barriers that we need to sort of negotiate together and the same thing so often the real barrier to progress is misperception between two people, and being in the same one organisation can actually help to overcome that* (head of health promotion).

Conflict resolution was also felt to be facilitated by some of the professionals involved in multi-agency initiatives having worked within other agencies, since having first-hand experience enabled them to empathise with professionals from other agencies.

7.5.2 Communication skills

Communication skills, perhaps not surprisingly, featured highly in the list of skills that professionals considered important for multi-agency working, as did also listening skills, negotiation and compromise, and building personal relationships (see Research Vignette 5). When probed about the issue of communication, and linked to the need for dialogue just discussed, interviewees again spoke about the need for professionals to be prepared to listen to the point of view of other agencies. Concomitant with this was a recognised need for negotiation and the ability to reach a compromise between the agencies, as was also forging personal links with professionals from other agencies. The importance of negotiation and compromise was emphasised by this interviewee:

Being able to accept and being able to acknowledge other people's point of view and work together. Sometimes people will have one perspective and sometimes people will have another. Sometimes you have got to meet in the middle and sometimes it's OK to agree to disagree. It is being able to recognise people's individual points and different perspectives they may be coming from and planning from there. For example, sometimes you may have a very disruptive child and Social Services don't want him to be at home all day and the teacher does not want him to be at school all day. It is trying to work out some kind of plan that is going to work and be acceptable to everybody because you can see all sides in that situation. It is not fair to the other 30 children in the class to have this child, but equally it is not good just to have that child languishing out of school and excluded. It's trying to negotiate to try to find a practical solution (social worker, Education).

7.5.3 Dissemination of information

The dissemination of information and the need to give everyone feedback on a regular basis and to keep everyone '*up to speed*' were also raised. Having a named person to contact within an agency and being able to put a face to a name were mentioned as factors that facilitated such communication, as was having protocols that were put in writing. In addition, it was felt that there was a need to share data more effectively to avoid the replication of services or repeat requests for data from key individuals. Communication was also raised as the second most important factor in overcoming the challenges to multi-agency working generally. Participants reported that a range of strategies could be adopted through which communication could be improved, and these strategies (mainly focused on information dissemination) operated at three broad levels:

♦ Enhancing the *procedures* of communication, for example, by establishing clear protocols and principles underpinning communication between individuals or agencies, so that some individuals or parties were aware of their responsibilities to others.

♦ Improving *systems* of communication, for example, by setting up an intranet or email groups, so that communication was not hindered by over-reliance on agency-specific systems (such as internal memos).

♦ Communicating more frequently with other professionals at the *human* level, for example, by physically sharing workspace and enhancing opportunities for face-to-face contact with partners in frequent interagency meetings at both strategic and operational level.

At each level of communication, strategies to overcome difficulties were reported, and a sample of these is presented below.

Illustrative examples of overcoming challenges to poor communication

Level	Strategy
Procedures	• Developing protocols that establish responsibilities and setting out clear communication frameworks that purposefully cut across agency boundaries. • Scheduling certain aspects of interagency communication (such as establishing a newsletter) so that participants are regularly updated. • Establishing contingency procedures, such as naming a second person to deal with enquiries during illness, holidays, or when an individual is in the field.
Systems	• Establishing an intranet system within an agency, so that all parties can access and input information, exchange ideas and be alerted to initiative developments and timescales. • Establishing a mailing list (electronic or otherwise) so that key players are not left out of developments. • Setting out a communication matrix, setting up systems of communication, establishing reviews of effectiveness and revision strategies.
Human-level	• Talking to others, regularly, face-to-face, if possible. • Working together, sharing space and resources. • Taking time to listen to the perspectives of others, especially those individuals working in other agencies, who may bring a new perspective on an old problem. • Establishing a forum to encourage self-reflection and to air interagency assumptions (even stereotypical assumptions) of other professionals. • Identifying key individuals (or key players) in each agency who are able to communicate well across agencies and communicate effectively at both strategic and operational level.

Source: *Interviews in Phase Two of NFER study, 2001*

Where the nature of service delivery was a factor in the reports of poor communication posing a challenge to multi-agency working (with specific types of initiative reporting greater difficulties), the ways of overcoming this challenge were not as clearly type specific. None the less, some of the strategies at each of the three levels lent themselves to certain contexts. For example, improving communication at the human level may have been easier within those initiatives typified as operational teams, where individuals worked in closer physical proximity to each other in service delivery. However, that does not suggest that such initiatives were free of difficulties, or had found the answers to challenges of communication. Communication within initiatives could remain problematical, despite successful strategies in its operational dimension.

7.6   Leadership or drive

Leadership or drive, the next most important key factor identified, was considered equally important by staff from all three agencies, but whilst it was considered important at strategic level and across the strategic–operational divide, those working only at ground level did not raise it at all. For those involved in operational teams and coordinator-led delivery the need for leadership and drive ranked more highly and was raised by over a third and over quarter respectively, compared to about a tenth of interviewees in other types of joint working.

One interviewee, amongst others, described leadership as '*critically important*', and many interviewees stressed the importance of clear direction at strategic level. When asked about what leadership in relation to multi-agency work involved, interviewees talked about having people who were '*dynamic*', '*on the ball*' and who were able to motivate and encourage others: '*when you speak to her, you feel motivated yourself*'. They talked about having someone with '*authority*' who was able to empower others to '*make it happen*', without which, reportedly, it would not happen.

In general, the participants identified two broad aspects of leadership: leadership as a strategic drive and tenacity that could surmount any obstacles to progress; and leadership as a strategic vision that could bring together the team required in order to effect change. Effective leadership was a combination of the two. Leaders or 'drivers' were thought to require tenacity and not to be fazed by obstacles. For one interviewee, this meant going beyond the realms of his/her normal job:

> *In that simple sense we have all got a day job, the fact that I am sure that's beyond his/her day job, you need that one person who is prepared to keep it going and not let it slip, keep badgering people and pushing and poking and prodding and manipulating* (head of Children's Services, Education).

In addition, leaders were also felt to need a '*breadth of vision*' because this type of work involved '*opening out to other ideas and to other people*'. 'Vision' was also mentioned as a skill required for multi-agency work by over a tenth of interviewees (see Research Vignette 5). Getting multi-agency work off the ground was thought to require one or two people with a vision who were not prepared to be side-tracked by other issues:

> *Well, sometimes it feels as if everybody talks about how wonderful multi-agency working is, but it takes the vision of one or two particular people who manage to get together and actually then say 'Yes, we are going to make this happen' ... somebody in voluntary and somebody in Social Services, who actually had a vision, they didn't get side-tracked by the nitty gritty of the other staff and they really went ahead for it and then you get the strategic discussion but the vision bit has got to come first* (social worker).

The need for the leader to maintain the focus, whilst also recognising the contribution of each of the agencies involved, was also raised:

It's about having a leader who can manage all those differences, who can create a trusting environment and can encourage the sort of personal growth in all of those different agencies, that are all people who feel involved, and maintain the focus of the client group, or the patient group or whatever the word might be you choose to use, but the multi-agency working doesn't become the purpose in itself, that it continues to be related to what's needed (clinical coordinator, Health).

Leadership was also the third most important factor identified by interviewees in response to the question on overcoming challenges. Strong leadership of a multi-agency initiative was reported as an effective way of overcoming some of the challenges to multi-agency by over ten per cent of the research participants. Perhaps unsurprisingly, two-thirds of those proposing this strategy were located at the strategic level; less than an eighth were working purely at the operational level. Despite this strategic bias within the response, the participants did not necessarily associate strong leadership with a 'top down' drive, but with vision and the ability to implement management strategies that effect change:

The top down leadership issue is important, but you cannot rely on that alone. There are lots of examples where casework collaboration can bring people together and feed up the system. So you have it from both ends (educational psychologist).

When the data was examined in terms of agency, there was a greater emphasis on leadership within Health and Education, less so within Social Services and the voluntary sector. Within Social Services, there was greater emphasis on integrated management systems, where collaboration extended to strategic management level. Perhaps the distinctiveness of leadership within successful multi-agency contexts was the repertoire of management skills required of those individuals with strategic responsibility for an initiative, for example: the ability to accept and, in some respects, be confident in working alongside any tension and ambiguities that were raised when working across agencies; or to calibrate leadership style to purpose, driving an agenda forward when required and letting it go when necessary. Those with strategic-level responsibility for an initiative were, in some respects, perceived as something of a 'different animal', emerging from, and responsible for, new ways of working. In this context, strong and effective leadership was not locked into a specific model of management, but indicative of a responsiveness and capacity for change.

Added to the perception that, at the level of practice, effective leadership could overcome the challenges posed by multi-agency working was a perception that effective local and national-level leadership was also important. The ability of elected members to think and move beyond current demarcations of responsibility and accountability was referred to previously, but participants also cited a desire for more commitment to multi-agency working at the national level, to encourage agencies to move beyond the view of it as an additional burden:

I actually think, to make agencies commit and work together, it needs legislation. In the real world of budget pressures, if an agency has got to do 'this' and they can also do 'that' if they want … [then] I think on some of the things it will take legislation. Not good practice and not guidance. I think agencies will need to be required to (assistant director, Education).

Having clear directives from managers at strategic level from all the agencies involved and from the Government was also felt to be important in overcoming conflicting agency and project aims:

Better directives from the Department of Health and DfEE. Now Health and Social Services have to get together over certain things else they will not get any money, but not the same type of thing coming from the DfEE, separate lines of communication and not the impetus from the top. New SEN document not sure even if it was sent to Health and it is seen as an education document. If you make partnership a cultural thing, it forces those lower down to do it and have to consult each other (chief executive, Health).

Although this was a minority view, there remains evidence of some scepticism of the ability of those working within multi-agency contexts to effect change within a national context that, in their view, fails to fully support multi-agency working, by for example, preventing or discouraging budgetary flexibility and/or linking budgets to very specific targets.

7.7   Involving the relevant personnel

The sixth most frequently identified key factor overall was the need to involve the relevant personnel. This was an issue raised mainly by Education and Health staff and raised slightly more frequently by those working across the strategic–operational divide, which perhaps indicated that the relevant personnel were more difficult to identify at this level. In particular involvement of the people at the right level of responsibility was mentioned, thus having people who could make the required decisions or activate the right services or mechanisms within their own agency:

It's going to be better if you can have a manager or at least someone who is going to be able to give a firm commitment to putting services in, rather than someone who is going to have to take that back to talk to their manager because that's … there's time limitations on that (deputy unit manager, Social Services).

Involvement of the right people, however, was felt to depend on the availability of resources and the priority given to the work by individual agencies. For example, it was recognised that teachers were very busy, but some teachers reportedly *'bend over backwards'* to engage with speech and language therapists whilst others were thought not give it the priority required.

7.8 Sharing and access to funding and resources

Following the need to involve the relevant personnel, funding and resources were the next most common key factor referred to, raised by over a quarter of interviewees. This was raised by almost a third of all Health staff, less so by Education staff and did not feature in the top ten issues for Social Services staff at all. Perhaps not surprisingly, it was also an issue raised in the main by those at strategic level and appeared to be less important for those involved in operational teams and coordinator-led delivery, where it was ranked eighth or ninth, compared to fifth for other types of multi-agency working.

Although only raised as the seventh most important key factor by interviewees, sharing funding and resources was the most common strategy identified for overcoming challenges. Perhaps this is not surprising, since issues over funding were the most commonly reported challenge encountered and issues around other resources were the fourth most common. Over a third of all interviewees identified a lack of, or conflicts over, fiscal resources as the greatest challenge to multi-agency working. A fifth of interviewees also identified how resource issues were (or could be) overcome by adopting three broad strategies:

♦   Pooled budgets – where one or more agency met some or all of the costs associated with personnel from other agencies (or voluntary bodies), or provided 'in kind' resources.

♦   Joint funding – where resources were provided by all those involved in an initiative, often on an equal, or like-for-like basis.

♦   The identification and use of alternative or additional sources of income to pump-prime or enhance multi-agency services.

The distinction between pooled budgets and joint funding related to delegation and control; where joint funding involved a degree of delegation, it allowed an agency to retain control over the uses to which resources were put. Pooled budgets were the distribution of resources to a budget, with less retention of managerial control by the contributing agency:

> *I think you've got to learn to trust people. You've got to lead by example. Go to somebody and say: 'Look. If you'd be prepared to do this, I'll do that'. Or: 'What do you think if we did this together?'. Or: 'I'm prepared to give up something to do this'. That's a good example of what's happening with the budget on this. Social Services are actually saying: 'Well, actually we will relinquish a bit of control'* (Education manager).

The factors underpinning the willingness of agencies to delegate control of resources varied. In one case, it was seen as a recognition that, following cuts to budgets and under conditions of greater scrutiny of resource use, pooled budgets were a way of delivering services and meeting statutory obligations:

One of the things that has helped is actually financial stringency in local authorities, because, actually, no one department can really deliver everything anymore. The realism nowadays is that unless we work with other people, we cannot deliver services. So, I think that's helped. People would see it as a bad thing, but that has actually made people think (principal educational psychologist).

Joint funding, on the other hand, was a way of showing commitment to multi-agency working, even where resources were under pressure. That is, it was a way of highlighting the importance of ways of working, or of the needs of particular groups. Fiscal pressures were associated with retrenchment into core roles, with clear boundaries and a reluctance to take on a role that could be identified as more properly the responsibility of another agency.

Some agencies had more capacity for working in different ways, or were more able to pool budgets. For example, in one initiative, the Health Service and voluntary organisation were reported to have greater flexibility than Education and Social Services:

Health and the voluntary sector are generally in a better position to tie up the resource end of joint projects than Social Services and Education. Now I think that is partly an external problem and relates to the ways in which the standard spending assessments are still worked out for local authorities, and therefore what they do, or rather don't have, to be able to spend on the pace of change. And they have rather less access, Social Services have less access to additional pots of money to make that change, and although Education have access to the money, it's so often that it has to be matched, and their inability to do that, plus, they have major priority drivers, they have got to get their school standards sorted out if they want to hold on to schools. That is an all-consuming requirement. Social Services have the Quality Protects agenda, which, although it may appear to be a good opportunity to use interagency work, or CAMHS, in fact, the way they have read it, and managed it, hasn't left them with the resources to change. So, therefore, they are heavily reliant on what Health, and to some extent the voluntary sector, can contribute. Now, that's not to say that they don't find ways [to contribute], *but it's much harder for them to do that* (children's strategy manager, Health).

Research Vignette 7   Overcoming difficulties in the early stages

When asked about overcoming difficulties in the early stages, interviewees referred overall to the need for goodwill, a commitment to working together and being able to talk to each other. Generally, a number of ways in which difficulties could be overcome were raised. These included: continually highlighting the issues; having a joint perspective; being able to access and/or work with people at strategic level; creating and ensuring time (e.g. by having a dedicated post); being flexible; developing trust; demonstrating good practice; having skilled practitioners. Some interviewees, however, offered responses for specific problems:

- **Funding**

Interviewees in one initiative stated that, as the project had developed, it had been able to 'prove' itself by demonstrating '*value-addedness*' and, as a result, had been able to attract other sources of funding.

- **Finding the time to set up initiatives**

Where finding time was a problem, having joint objectives or a shared ambition was proffered as a way of overcoming the problem. This was felt to give the initiative the momentum it required to enable staff to create time by prioritising accordingly. Recognition of the importance of the work and making it a priority, as well as the need for a shorter time scale with less pressure to achieve results '*overnight*', thus allowing more time for discussion and debate, were also raised.

- **Different policies and procedures**

Having a clear structure at strategic level and a commitment to working together were suggested as ways of overcoming differences in policies, procedures and/or priorities. Two interviewees commented that this should be easier now, as multi-agency working had become the recognised route to follow, because '*it's the political agenda*' and '*it isn't an option to go down any other route*'.

- **Recruitment**

It was suggested that recruitment to projects could be facilitated by strategic-level commitment and keeping the issue concerned high on the agenda, for example, through a multi-agency conference. Covering illness, so that long-term absence did not adversely impact on an initiative, was particularly pertinent to interviewees in an operational-team initiative, which had lost its project leader at an early stage.

- **Ensuring commitment**

Interviewees in two decision-making groups suggested having '*away days*' in order to pool ideas and expertise and to generate a genuine will to work together, as energy could be put into developing a group identity. Also highlighted was having a few '*quick wins*' so people could see an immediate impact. This engendered confidence that the initiative could achieve its aims. In one coordinator-led initiative, much energy, it was stated, had been put into winning over people at a senior level.

- **Old attitudes/beliefs and prejudices**

This was thought to involve changing people's perceptions and, as such, was something that took time. Positive feedback from clients and altering structures to allow for more effective multi-agency working (e.g. changing opening times to allow different professionals to work together) were quoted as ways of influencing a change in attitude.

- **Relationships**
Relationship problems had largely been ironed out through discussion and being prepared to see other people's point of view. Where local government reorganisation had taken place, several interviewees spoke of this being seen as an opportunity to overcome traditional relationship problems between agencies. Joint training and consultation, reportedly, could be used to establish '*the foundation for moving forward*'.

- **Getting the right people in the right place at the right time**
Interviewees felt that this could be facilitated by being flexible in order to accommodate the needs of others and sending out up-to-date information in good time to keep things from being overlooked. One decision-making group reported having appointed a multi-agency coordinator to do just that.

The capacity to embrace new ways of working, or to take risks with resources, therefore varied across agencies and across areas. The budget priorities that were either internally set, or externally imposed, prevented some agencies from certain ways of working. However, such budgetary 'constraints' were also reported to be behind some of the strategies that achieved the successful pooling of resources to meet the needs of the client group(s). Where pressures on agency budgets were more keenly felt, or where budgets were closely tied to outcome measures, the capacity to pool resources was reduced, but budgetary innovation could prevent this from having a negative impact on the client group(s). The evidence from those engaged in such strategies suggests that individuals come together to create capacity when there are shared, or clearly defined, objectives between agencies. For example, meeting the educational needs of children in public care in one area was such an interagency priority, that the budgets had to be pooled to meet a pressing need. Where this capacity creation faltered, however, was beyond the strategic level, where policy directives prevented flexibility at a local level.

The need to commit resources to developing better interagency and intra-agency relationships, with an emphasis on finding the best routes to service delivery, was also raised.

7.9 Other key factors

Other key factors that interviewees highlighted included:

- good working relationships
- time
- flexibility
- trust and honesty
- review and development
- using examples of successful multi-agency working as exemplars

◆   developing interagency protocols for shared working

◆   encouraging risk taking.

Although also intimated when talking about communication, good working relationships were also a key factor raised by almost a quarter of all interviewees. In addition, relationship building and networking were also raised as a 'skill' by over a tenth of interviewees (see Research Vignette 5). Interestingly, however, whilst good working relationships were highlighted by about a fifth or more of Education and Social Services personnel, they did not feature in the top ten key factors for Health staff. In addition, they were ranked less importantly by those involved in operational-team delivery than in other types of joint working, perhaps because professionals worked so closely together anyway.

The need for adequate time for joint working was raised by over a fifth of all interviewees. Although raised by just over a fifth of all Health staff and just under a fifth of all Social Services staff, this was considered less important by Education personnel. It also appeared to be more of an issue for interviewees working at either strategic or operational level, where it was raised by almost a fifth of all interviewees, rather than those working in between. Interestingly, although highlighted by just over a fifth of those involved in consultation and training, coordinator-led and operational-team delivery, no one involved in decision-making groups or centre-based delivery raised it as an issue. Alongside this, establishing procedures of time management, where service delivery takes account of the pressures facing professionals and the potential for adding to levels of 'initiative fatigue', was also raised.

Whilst not frequently cited by participants, other key factors and other strategies for overcoming challenges were also suggested. Flexibility, which was also mentioned as a skill (see Research Vignette 5) and recognising the links between different agency remits were important, reportedly, in overcoming specific tensions over budgets and referral routes. Trust and honesty, for example, were considered important ingredients by almost a fifth of all strategic-level interviewees, whilst an additional key factor that emerged as important at operational level was the need for continual review and development. Using examples of successful multi-agency working as exemplars within and between agencies and voluntary bodies, thereby seeking changes to practice on the basis of evidence of success, was also raised. In addition, encouraging risk-taking in supported contexts, where professionals were encouraged to think and act outside usual practices, and developing interagency protocols for shared working and entering into interagency service-level delivery agreements were also mentioned.

Where these strategies were differentially in evidence across initiatives, the range was suggestive of a good deal of innovation and flexibility of response to the challenges thrown up by multi-agency working.

Key points

- ◆ The key factors essential for successful multi-agency working were wide-ranging and varied. They involved setting up effective systems and procedures, such as for communication and involving the relevant people; ensuring adequate resources in terms of funding, staffing and time; and establishing common aims from the outset. In addition, the key factors often included the more personal qualities of the professionals involved, such as their commitment and drive.

- ◆ Commitment to, and a willingness to be involved in, multi-agency working, whatever the type, were felt to be key to effective collaboration. What emerged was the importance of those involved wanting to be involved and having a belief in multi-agency working, rather than being directed to engage in it.

- ◆ Understanding the roles and responsibilities of other agencies was also thought to be key. One particular facet of this was the need to understand the constraints binding other agencies so that there were realistic expectations of what they could offer, but another was the need for mutual respect between professionals so that all contributions were valued.

- ◆ Underlying the need for common aims, also considered important, was the need to establish common ground and a focus on the target group such that this overcame single agency agendas. Direction towards a common goal was seen as vital, but at the same time it was felt important to recognise that different agency priorities existed.

- ◆ A number of facets of communication and information sharing were felt to be important, including providing opportunities for professionals from different agencies to discuss the issues, communication skills and information dissemination. A variety of strategies were suggested for improving communication, which was particularly important in the early stages of multi-agency project development.

- ◆ Leadership or drive at strategic level was considered important in keeping the momentum of multi-agency working going, despite the obstacles encountered. Two essential ingredients of this leadership role were vision and tenacity.

♦ Sharing and access to funding and resources, whilst not raised significantly as a key factor, were, however, deemed the single most important factor in overcoming challenges, since challenges were often focused in this area. Pooled budgets, joint funding and the identification and the use of alternative resources to enhance multi-agency work were discussed in this respect.

♦ Interviewees also described a range of different 'skills' they felt beneficial for multi-agency working. Communication skills, including listening, negotiating and compromising, stood out as important generally, although some skills were felt to be more important within specific models of multi-agency working.

8. CASE STUDIES

Introduction

The purpose of this chapter is to present detailed portrayals of multi-agency activity and the context in which they occurred. Six of the 30 examples of multi-agency initiatives examined in Phase Two of the research were selected for further, more in-depth study in Phase Three. Initiatives were particularly selected to illustrate the different types of multi-agency activity, but also to reflect a range of target groups, as well as having readily observable discrete sessions of multi-agency activity.

For the case studies, information was obtained from a variety of sources. Detailed summative interviews were conducted with key personnel in each of the initiatives, focusing on a strategic and operational overview, funding issues and evaluation. Available documentation relating to evaluation was also collated, and telephone interviews were conducted with 'professional clients' in receipt of a service through the initiative (usually those from each of the referring agencies). Finally, a discrete session of multi-agency activity was observed and a post-observation questionnaire administered. In addition, relevant information was also taken from the interviews conducted in Phase Two.

Each of the case studies presented follows the same format:

◆ description, i.e. the type of activity and the target group

◆ background to the initiative, i.e. the rationale and process of development

◆ funding and resources, i.e. how it was resourced by the different agencies

◆ the aims, i.e. what it set out to achieve

◆ agency involvement at strategic and operational level, including where interagency relationships were felt to be working particularly well or not so well

◆ analysis of the observation of a discrete session of multi-agency activity (discussed further below)

◆ outcomes and evaluation, including the benefits to children and families, and to the professional clients, as well as issues about cost-effectiveness

◆ a summary of the key points raised.

Observation

As part of the case study, analysis and discussion about a session of multi-agency activity that was observed by one of the researchers is presented. It must be borne in mind, throughout this section, that each of the observed sessions analysed here represents just one individual multi-agency session and that the presence of the observer may be an influential factor. However, all agency representatives involved in the multi-agency activities observed were given the opportunity, following the session, during post-observation interviews, to reflect on the activity and the differences between the observed activity and the activity as it usually took place. No such differences were reported. Attempting to capture and convey the subtleties involved in the processes observed was a challenge. Examples were inevitably both spontaneous and responsive, despite, in some cases, a predetermined agenda. In addition, these activities were influenced and bounded by a specific historical context that included the histories of the main participants, their profession and their agency. They were in themselves bound up in their own culture and procedures. The observations presented all follow a similar format and include: the context of the multi-agency session observed; the format of the session; the time spent on different activities; and key points.

In attempting to depict the processes involved in multi-agency activity, five key types of multi-agency activity were identified:

♦ informalities

♦ chairing

♦ presentation of information

♦ discussion

♦ decision making.

Within each of the case studies, therefore, discussion about the time spent on different activities centres around these areas. Times are only approximations since times were simply noted at regular intervals rather than a formal schedule used. Although each of the initiatives under study was originally classified as one type of multi-agency activity, what became clear, on more detailed examination, was that many of the projects entailed elements of more than one, and in some cases, even all of the five models previously presented. Six case studies are therefore presented as follows:

Case study 1

An operational team, with coordinator-led and centre-based elements, providing an assessment service for children with learning disabilities.

Case study 2

An operational team, with a consultation and training element, providing a therapeutic service for children with emotional and behavioural problems and support for their parents.

Case study 3

A specialist health promotion service located within Education – a coordinator-led initiative, with a range of different types of multi-agency activity throughout the service.

Case study 4

A multi-agency strategic decision-making group focused on children in public care, with a multi-agency operational team established to address their educational needs.

Case study 5

Coordinator-led service delivery involving an early years and childcare development team, with a decision-making and an operational-team element to it.

Case study 6

A mental health decision-making strategy group incorporating a number of operational teams and consultation and training at other levels.

CASE STUDY 1

An operational team, with coordinator-led and centre-based elements, providing an assessment service for children with learning disabilities

Description

A multi-agency child assessment service for children with disabilities (under the age of eight years) and their parents. This initiative involved all three of the main agencies but also entailed significant voluntary agency input. It was originally classified as an operational team, and the Social Services manager interviewed felt that the professionals involved did work as a tight-knit unit. However, s/he felt that coordinated delivery might be a more appropriate description since the team was coordinator led and a number of the professionals involved were not based within the centre, but provided services as and when required. When convening to discuss clients or to conduct assessments, the professionals involved met in a central base provided by a voluntary organisation, where services were also provided for children with disabilities, so it also had some characteristics consistent with centre-based delivery.

Background

This service began when local health consultants and a voluntary agency, which already provided services for disabled children in the area, became concerned that '*parents had to go to three different agencies and relate their stories three times*' and then received an uncoordinated response. The project was jointly commissioned and all three agencies, Health, Education and Social Services, agreed the outline and management. They agreed to pool staff resources and to avoid replication by 'seconding' them into a multi-agency team. However, as indicated in the documentation provided, '*each professional remains accountable to their "parent" organisation but are [sic] sanctioned to work within the joint protocol that was developed and ratified by the Joint Management Board*'. The service had been operating for about three years.

Funding and resources

There was a joint commissioning contract for the service. Health, Social Services and Education provided resources in terms of the contribution of staff time. Whilst this was thought to be common practice in multi-agency initiatives, it was considered unusual to have a tripartite contract with voluntary sector involvement. Social Services and Education, however, were only expected to provide 18 hours of support per year compared to the range of input provided by Health '*because of the type of children*'. All three agencies made a contribution to the overheads and the coordinator's salary. The coordinator, who was from the voluntary sector, was considered by the strategic commissioning manager from Social Services to be key to the effective working of the service since his/her independent role meant that the initiative was not aligned solely to one agency.

The use of existing staff was felt to be advantageous as the workers knew the client group and the range of services available in the area. However, when staff moved or were off sick, the Social Services manager reported that their involvement in the team was difficult to cover. Links between the voluntary sector and the statutory agencies reportedly ensured '*connectedness*' to the health and social care agenda. However, because of the way the initiative was funded, difficulties for the social worker, who was from the children with disabilities team, reportedly arose because some of the children assessed fell outside of his/her criteria and this meant that s/he therefore had to sometimes negotiate the involvement of other aspects of Social Services.

Aims

The aims of the service, as indicated in documentation provided, were:

♦ for professionals to work in conjunction with colleagues from other agencies

♦ to provide a coordinated service for children with complex needs

♦ to assist children in maximising their physical, social and emotional potential

♦ to develop more effective, better coordinated plans to meet individual need.

Thus, aims focused on the process of interagency working, as well as client-focused aims, were documented. When asked about the aims of the service, interviewees reiterated the client-focused objectives. They added that one of the overall aims was to enable the child's whole range of needs to be assessed under one roof, effectively providing '*a one-stop shop*' for parents, who, it was felt, had a difficult job coping with a child with disabilities. So, as a representative from the voluntary organisation stated, a primary aim was: '*to make sure that parents felt that they could go through one door and come out through the other having seen everybody that they needed to see*'.

Agency involvement

A diagram showing the strategic- and operational-level involvement of different agencies is presented in Figure 8.1. All three of the main agencies and the voluntary agency were involved at both strategic and operational level. However, the resources, in terms of staffing, provided at operational level varied between the agencies partly because of the nature of the target group and partly because of the pressures of work placed on different agencies.

Figure 8.1   Strategic and operational agency involvement in an assessment service for children with learning disabilities

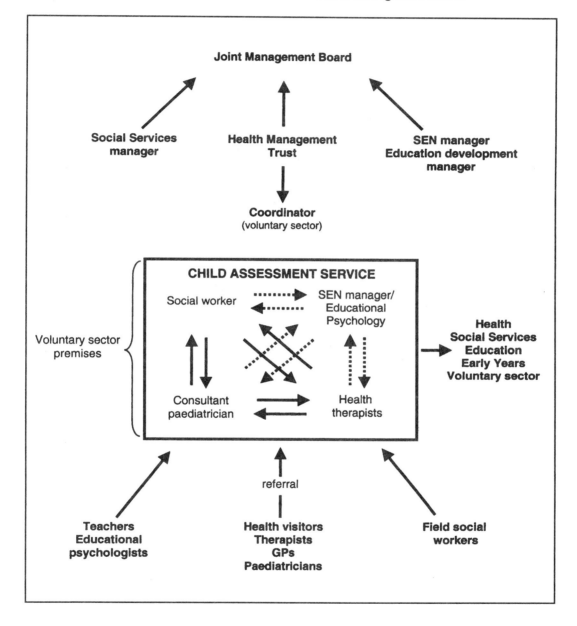

Strategic level

Strategically, overarching the assessment service was a Joint Management Board involving Health, Education and Social Services. This was reported by the commissioning manager from Social Services to be an independent process with no single agency domination, since the director of the voluntary organisation chaired the meeting. As indicated in documentation provided, '*any issues that arise about the need to change working practice or where individual agency policy is an obstacle to making the service function are taken to the Board*'. The relationship between all three of the main agencies at this level was reported by the Social Services manager to be very good.

Operational level

A voluntary organisation provided the premises in which the service operated and employed a coordinator for the service. Whilst employed by the voluntary agency, however, the coordinator role was developed through a joint contract with the three agencies. Professionals from all three agencies (e.g. teachers, educational psychologists, health visitors, GPs, field social workers) were able to refer children to the service for assessment.

The assessment team itself included the coordinator, a range of Health professionals (e.g. speech and language therapists, a consultant paediatrician, occupational therapists and a clinical psychologist), and a social worker, together with Educational professionals, usually an educational psychologist, when relevant. The relationship between the Health professionals and the social worker was reported to be particularly good and to enable '*effective discussions about individual children*' to take place. The relationship with Education in the past was also reportedly good, but since personnel had changed there was felt to be a lack of consistent education input into the service. According to the Social Services manager, a review of education services and of the educational psychology input to the team was reported to be in response to a need to '*rationalise the special educational needs management*'. Ongoing difficulties with psychiatric input to the service were also reported. Input to the team from the psychiatric service highlighted the problems of working across Trust boundaries since the psychiatric consultant was reportedly employed by a different Trust to the one with which the team had a contract. This was felt to '*create some tension*' and provide an obstacle to joint working.

OBSERVATION

Context

Following receipt of a referral, the coordinator conducted a home visit and then a multi-agency planning meeting was set up. The purpose of the meeting was to exchange relevant information about the children to be assessed amongst the team and to set up a date and time for the assessment to take place. Two of these meetings, each of half an hour, were observed in one morning. The meetings generally involved not only members of the assessment team but also relevant professionals from other outside agencies in contact with the child. Present at the meeting were the service coordinator, the consultant paediatrician, an occupational therapist, a nursery nurse, a physiotherapist, two speech and language therapists, the social worker (who joined the meeting after 15 minutes), a secretary (who joined the meeting after five minutes) and a student nurse, as well as the NFER observer.

Format of the planning meeting

The coordinator began by presenting the case and read out a home visit report and relevant reports from others not able to be present at the meeting. The speech and language therapist and the occupational therapist then also read out their reports. Following this, the coordinator and the paediatrician asked a few questions and then a general discussion took place amongst the group. Discussion centred mainly on whether an assessment by the service was relevant and with whom and when this would take place. Finally, once a decision had been agreed, the coordinator told the secretary to fix the dates for the assessment. A similar format was repeated for the second case.

The time spent on different activities

Table 8.1 shows the approximate time spent on different activities.

Table 8.1 Time spent on different activities

Activity	Time (mins)	Time as a percentage of the whole session
Informalities	0	0
Chairing	8	13
Presentation of information	30	50
Discussion/suggestions	7	12
Decision making	15	25

Percentages have been rounded to the nearest whole number, and therefore may not sum to 100

Source: *Observation in Phase Three of the NFER study, 2001*

The overall aim, as indicated in the post-observation questions, was '*to share information amongst our own team*', as well as share concerns. Thus, perhaps not surprisingly, approximately half of the meeting time was devoted to **presentation of information** by different professionals within the group and information from outside agencies.

Another of the key aims of the meeting, as indicated in the post-observation questions, was to decide who was to attend the assessment and when it was to be held. Thus, a quarter of the meeting time was devoted to **decision making**. This was sometimes difficult to separate from discussion as negotiation often took place around decisions. This type of interchange occurred mainly between the coordinator and the paediatrician. The significant role of the consultant perhaps reflects the hierarchy within Health. However, others also provided input based on their unique professional knowledge. At one point, for example, the social worker made a significant contribution in terms of addressing child protection issues and the availability of Social Services support for children and their families. This was reiterated in the post-observation questions as it was stated that the social worker was able to outline when Social Services might be able to offer input that others might not have considered. The involvement of the social worker in working alongside Health workers in this way was also suggested as an example of effective multi-agency working following the observation.

Difficulties sometimes arose in making decisions because key people were absent from the meeting and because the team needed more information about the child under discussion. From responses to the post-observation questions, for example, it was clear that the input of the clinical psychologist, absent at this session, was considered important, as s/he was able to give a '*psychological side*', a perspective that others did not have. Similarly, absence of an educational psychologist created difficulties because other professionals had a very limited understanding of the educational assessment process. The educational psychologist was reported to attend '*infrequently*' as s/he only had 18 hours a year dedicated to the team and, since planning meetings were arranged as soon as possible, pressures of work meant that his/her time was often booked up. The absence of relevant professionals from external agencies was also noted. It was considered helpful, for example, to have a teacher or a health visitor present since they often had day-to-day contact with the child and therefore knew the child well.

Approximately 13 per cent of the meeting time was devoted to **chairing**, which was conducted by the coordinator. However, there were times when the paediatrician undertook a similar role and also moved the meeting on by asking for collective agreement with a decision or by asking a question. The domination of the paediatrician and the coordinator within the meeting was further emphasised by the fact that they both sat at the top of the table. This was evident when asking the post-observation questions as well, as they responded to most of the questions. With the meeting focused mainly on information exchange and decision making, **discussion** between the professionals involved only accounted for a small percentage of the meeting time. Where it did occur, it was limited and appeared to centre on issues around decision making. Overall, the meeting was very business-like with no informalities taking place.

Key points

♦ A formal and business-like meeting that, in the main, focused on information exchange and decision making between the different professionals involved.

♦ The absence of key professionals with expertise in particular areas or different agency perspectives at times impeded the multi-agency decision-making process.

♦ Hierarchical issues were evident. This may be influential in the information exchange and discussion between professionals since it may be that this prevents individuals having equal status in negotiations.

♦ The role that a voluntary agency may adopt in being able to act independently to pull agencies together and coordinate their work was highlighted.

Evaluation and outcomes

A formal internal evaluation, in which both process and outcomes were measured, had been completed by the team. As part of this formal evaluation, information was collected from parents, the teams from which the professionals involved in the service were 'seconded' and the professional users of the service, i.e. the referrers. In addition, for the purposes of this case study, information was obtained through a detailed interview with the strategic commissioning manager from Social Services and from telephone interviews with three 'professional clients' – a headteacher, a Social Services team manager and a health visitor – who had referred children to the service.

The benefits for children and their families:

The formal evaluation that the team themselves had conducted showed that the benefits for children and their families were numerous, and these included:

♦ only having to visit one place for a complete assessment

♦ reduced waiting time for an assessment

♦ not having to repeat their story a number of times

- increased involvement in the assessment process
- increased understanding of the issues
- clarity of their role and professional roles
- holistic understanding of their child's needs
- provision of a comprehensive written report.

However, the formal evaluation also showed that a significant number of parents were unhappy about the lack of provision following the assessment, and some families stated that their involvement with Education suggested that some Educational professionals had not read the report that had been produced. This points to the limited involvement of Education at this time being felt by those in receipt of the service as well as those providing it.

Interviews with the three referrers supported the positive findings of the evaluation. The main benefit to children and their parents, cited by all three interviewees from the three different agencies, was that they only had to go to one place for a range of assessments by different agencies. In addition, they noted that families were offered advice and support and were very much involved throughout the process. Whilst the issue of educational involvement did not surface directly in the telephone interviews, the headteacher interviewed, from their perspective, felt that parents were not always fully informed about who would be involved and that Social Services involvement was not always welcomed by parents because of the stigma attached.

The benefits for 'professional clients'

Outcomes from the formal evaluation showed that the service was well known to the professionals who were able to refer and that the referral process was considered to be straightforward. It also showed that the service was considered efficient, friendly and child centred. Formal evaluation, in addition, indicated that referrers thought that the reports provided were comprehensive, well presented and easy to read. The benefits for agencies included the development of shared criteria of need, joint planning and the avoidance of conflicting information for families. For the professionals directly involved in the team, the benefits included a clear definition of roles, flexibility of approach, a broader view of the evidence presented, shared expertise and shared accountability, as well as saving time and paperwork.

The telephone interviews with referrers indicated that the main advantage, for professionals as well as clients, was that it provided a thorough, holistic assessment which was conducted in one place. A multi-agency assessment was felt to take into account a range of needs that a single agency could not. For individual agencies, as well as families, the service provided a single point of contact for advice and support and a quicker assessment process.

For the health visitor interviewed, for example, being able to discuss his/her concerns prior to making a referral was felt to be particularly helpful. Provision of a detailed report, with clear recommendations, was felt to enable other agencies to provide the most appropriate services and having each of the agencies involved at the heart of the service was felt to facilitate interagency discussion. This meant that one, rather than several, conclusions were reached, leading to a clearer outcome and, subsequently, lack of conflicting information for families.

Whilst the Health and Social Services representatives were unable to highlight any disadvantages to the service, the headteacher interviewed outlined a number. S/he stated that it was difficult to get all the agencies together and particularly difficult to release teachers to attend meetings (although they would always send a report). S/he felt that a single agency might therefore be able to act earlier, whilst multi-agency input might lead to a delay. The confidence required by professionals generally to contribute effectively to multi-agency meetings was also highlighted. Despite these disadvantages, the headteacher maintained that an assessment from the service gave a more rounded picture of children and families' difficulties.

Cost-effectiveness

The service was considered by the commissioning manager from Social Services to be well resourced, good value for money and to be used effectively. Formal assessment showed that the service was felt by individual agencies to be cost-effective since it avoided duplication and encouraged the collaborative use of resources. The Social Services team manager interviewed reported that obtaining separate assessments (as had been the case previously) was both costly and time consuming, whilst the current service was felt to be cost-effective and to provide an intensive assessment, one that was unrivalled elsewhere. The health visitor interviewed also felt that the service was cost-effective since it allowed early diagnosis and intervention, thereby preventing later problems.

Key points

- ◆ This case study highlights the difficulty of gaining commitment from agencies for multi-agency working when, as a single agency, there are other pressures and priorities.

- ◆ Single-agency cultures, such as the internal hierarchy within Health, may be an influential factor in interagency interactions, since it may mean that those around the table are unable to negotiate from an equal starting point.

- ◆ The role that a voluntary agency may contribute, as an independent organisation, in providing opportunities to draw agencies together and coordinate their input was highlighted.

- This case study illustrates the unique expertise that different agency professionals may contribute to multi-agency working.

- A more holistic and cohesive, as well as convenient, service was provided for families by agencies working in a collaborative way.

- A multi-agency assessment provided a more holistic picture of children's needs and therefore a more comprehensive assessment than any single agency, so that their needs could be met more appropriately.

- Lack of coterminous boundaries, particularly in relation to Health Trusts, may provide an obstacle to multi-agency working.

- In order to contribute effectively to multi-agency meetings, professionals need to feel secure and confident in their role within their own agency.

CASE STUDY 2

An operational team, with a consultation and training element, providing a therapeutic service for children with emotional and behavioural problems and support for their parents

Description

A multi-agency team providing advice for parents and therapeutic help and support for children and young people who have emotional and behavioural difficulties, particularly those who have been abused. Social workers employed by Education, as well as Social Services, undertook direct work with clients, but a significant part of the initiative was the consultation, support and training received from Health, such that the Health representative involved was considered an equal part of the team.

Background

Following local government reorganisation, this new authority decided to set up their own local therapeutic service for children who had been sexually abused so that it was more accessible for children and families. The authority had inherited three part-time social workers, who had a lot of experience at working with abused children, from the previous Educational Psychology Service, which had been disbanded. Initially, Social Services seconded two part-time social workers to work alongside the 'education' social workers, but it was reportedly difficult for them to give the team their full commitment. This led to Social Services later matching the staff resources provided by Education so that there were two full-time workers and two part-time workers jointly provided by the two departments. The children and families service manager from Education was appointed manager of the team because she had a social work background. The service remit had recently been widened to include all children with emotional and behavioural problems rather than just those who had been sexually abused.

Funding and resources

Social Services and Education jointly funded the team, but the Health Service also provided training, consultation and support in the form of a clinical psychologist's time, and this was recognised as a valuable contribution. Staff salaries were split half-and-half between Education and Social Services, but the team was based in Education premises and the team manager was employed by Education. Whilst the original plan had been for Education to manage the team some of the time and for Social Services to manage it for some of the time, this '*had not materialised*'.

Issues around funding reportedly arose concerning the provision of training for the team. The team manager stated that there was no specific training budget and the team had to rely on the goodwill of Social Services for access to training. S/he felt that it would be better for Social Services to provide the money. In addition, social workers who were paid for by Social Services but seconded to Education were said to feel vulnerable since they could easily be drafted into mainstream social work should resources become tight.

Aims

The overall aim of the team was to provide therapeutic support and intervention for children experiencing behavioural and emotional problems. Since local government reorganisation, it was considered important to establish such expertise locally rather than children having to travel long distances to receive a service. The educational psychologists at that time, according to one interviewee, were not in a position to offer such a service, because of the constraints imposed on them by the formal SEN assessment procedure. The aim was also to support professionals from a range of agencies in their work with these children and to liaise with them so that they could refer and so that the service was accessible to them. Particularly highlighted were children whose emotional difficulties stemmed from family problems, where input from a field social worker was felt to be insufficient.

Agency involvement

A diagram showing the strategic and operational involvement of different agencies is presented in Figure 8.2. Whilst all three of the main agencies were involved at operational level, Social Services and Health had limited strategic-level involvement.

Strategic level

Although originally set up in close collaboration with the children's services manager from Social Services, the team was managed by the children and families services manager from within Education. Whilst there was no multi-agency group specifically convened to oversee this service, all three agencies came together in a Planning and Implementation Group for Children's Services where, according to the Education manager, issues about the service could be addressed. Although Health had little involvement in the development of the service, the manager was able to feed into health planning through this process, so lack of direct Health involvement at strategic level was not felt to be a problem.

Operational level

The team accepted referrals from the Social Services Department (field social workers), the Education Department (e.g. teachers and educational psychologists), Health professionals (e.g. health visitors and school nurses) and police, as well as directly from parents. The team itself consisted of four social workers, two employed by Social Services and two by Education, who conducted direct work with clients, the manager of the team and the clinical psychologist who offered consultation and training to the team.

Relationships with 'professional clients' from various agencies were described as being at different stages. The clinical psychologist, perceived as an integral part of the team, had links with the local Child and Adolescent Mental Health Service (CAMHS), and the development of the relationship with the CAMHS team was reported to be one of the aspects of the service that was working particularly well. Whilst there had been initial suspicion that the therapeutic team might encroach on CAMHS territory, there was now reported to be a good understanding of each other's roles and a recognition that their work complemented each other. Clear communication between the CAMHS and the team was therefore described as a key feature.

Relationships with schools, on the other hand, were reported by the team manager to be '*improving*', with members of the team being asked to attend stage three SEN reviews held by schools if they thought there was anything that the team could offer. The parents' advice service was specified as an aspect that had been particularly valuable in facilitating the team's relationship with schools, since school staff were sometimes not clear about appropriate referral and in such situations they were able to direct parents to the advice line. Traditionally, good links with the educational psychologists were also cited despite the fact that personnel had changed over the years.

In contrast, links with field social workers were reported not to be working as well. Whilst social workers were expected to conduct some work of their own with children prior to referral, this was frequently not the case and many referrals received from social workers were felt to be inappropriate. This was thought to be due to the increasing pressure of work and the increasing demands placed upon them. The therapeutic team manager had hoped that there would be more cases where the team might work with the child whilst the social worker worked with the family.

Figure 8.2   Strategic and operational agency involvement in the therapeutic team

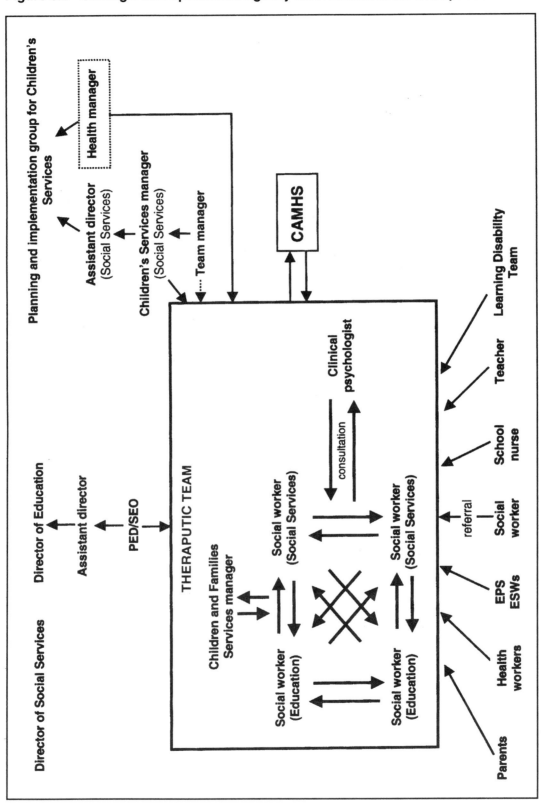

OBSERVATION

Context

The clinical psychologist met fortnightly with the team for two hours to offer supervision on individual cases and general support. One of these meetings was observed as part of the case study. Those present at the session were the four social workers (two from Education and two from Social Services), the Education manager, the clinical psychologist and the NFER observer. The purpose of the meeting was to give the social workers an opportunity to discuss cases, share experiences, gain different perspectives and to move 'stuck' cases forward.

Format of the meeting

One of the social workers presented the case of a child who they were currently seeing. Following this, a general discussion took place about the case and finally a way forward was sought. A second case was then presented by another social worker and this followed the same format. The group sat more or less in a circle in which everyone appeared to have equal status.

The time spent on different activities

Table 8.2 shows the approximate amounts of time spent on different activities within the session observed.

Table 8.2   Time spent on different activities

Activity	Time (mins)	Time as a percentage of the whole session
Informalities	0	0
Chairing	0	0
Presentation of information	36	40
Discussion/suggestions	45	50
Decision making	9	10

Percentages have been rounded to the nearest whole number, and therefore may not sum to 100
Source: *Observation in Phase Three of the NFER study, 2001*

Approximately 50 per cent of the session time was devoted to **discussion**, perhaps not surprising given that the main aim of the session was described as '*problem solving and consultation*', and was felt to provide an opportunity to '*get ideas from others and other perspectives*' by the health consultant. It was also described as '*educational*' since it was reported to support other work conducted by the clinical psychologist in training sessions for the group and to have parallels with other cases that individual workers may be involved with. In fact, one social worker pointed out that s/he had '*four different cases in my head*' when discussing one case, and, in this way, it was thought to be beneficial to all those involved.

The clinical psychologist, perhaps not surprisingly given her consultative role within the group, was especially active in the discussion which took place, although all contributions were welcomed. It was notable that the Education manager appeared to take more of a back seat for most of the time. The clinical psychologist played a key role in asking questions of others to ascertain their views in addition to offering specific expertise in relation to mental health where relevant. This was reiterated in the post-observation questions. The clinical psychologist stressed that s/he was not 'the expert' since s/he stated that '*If things are stuck, it is about highlighting certain things, not that I have the knowledge and you do not*'. At one point in the meeting, s/he stated that s/he felt that regular sessions with the psychiatrist would be helpful for the team, as she was only able to give a psychologist's perspective, and that she would try and organise this. The social workers, however, acknowledged the unique contribution that the clinical psychologist was able to make. One of the social workers, in the post-observation questions, for example, stated that, without the input from the clinical psychologist, s/he would have struggled with such a case. The clinical psychologist's input was also reported to '*make you think more about cases that you might otherwise pass on quicker to other agencies*'. Close working with the psychologist was also thought to avoid clients going to many different services. Links with the local mental health service through the clinical psychologist were cited as an example of effective multi-agency working since these had enabled them to access help quickly and know how each other worked, and there was an understanding that '*it is not about off-loading cases on to other agencies*'.

Others offered their general experience with cases and the fact that '*people chip in from all different aspects and perspectives*' and the importance of having '*a lot of common experience between them but different expertise*', i.e. the difference between a social worker and a psychologist was noted in the post-observation questions.

Approximately 40 per cent of the time was devoted to the **presentation of information** by two of the social workers, although one was employed by Social Services and one by Education. These were presented to the whole group and one stood to use the OHP, whilst the other remained seated.

In contrast, approximately only ten per cent of the session time was devoted to any form of **decision making** and this seemed to merge with, but follow, case discussion. Decisions were made as to how to proceed with cases, and this was identified as one of the main aims of the session in the post-observation questions. Whilst other social workers did contribute minimally to this aspect of the session, the clinical psychologist was particularly instrumental in discussing and negotiating with the social worker whose case it was how to progress. Within the post-observation questions, one of the social workers emphasised the support that the meeting had provided since it had confirmed for her that there were reasons to be concerned about a case and it had enabled her to clarify what they were and where to take them. When asked what would happen now, this was supported by reiteration of the fact that the individual worker would make a referral to the CAMHS.

The session was very informal and relaxed and no time was devoted to chairing. There appeared to be a set format of which all were aware and no chairing role was necessary as this occurred naturally. Two cases were discussed, as had been planned.

There was no real time devoted to informalities in the meeting, although informalities were exchanged between social workers at the beginning of the session. At other points within the session, individuals laughed in response to things others said. The group appeared to feel very relaxed with each other, and this was confirmed in the post-observation questions, in which both the clinical psychologist and a social worker described the sessions as enjoyable, as well as an effective way of working. The 'mutual respect' between the professionals involved in the team was raised as an example of effective multi-agency working, when they were asked about this following the session. The team appeared very close and it may not be insignificant that the listening skills required within their counselling role are also a vital component for multi-agency work.

Key points

◆   The session was conducted in a relaxed, informal atmosphere in which no direction was necessary and where it was evident that the team members got on well together and respected each other as professionals.

◆   It may be that the listening skills which were a key component of their counselling role were also beneficial in helping them work collaboratively together.

◆   All those involved were equally able to offer ideas, share experiences and offer professional expertise where relevant.

◆   As the consultant, the role of the clinical psychologist was one of facilitation more than direction, as s/he herself said s/he did not consider him/herself to be the 'expert'.

◆   A lot of time was devoted to discussion compared to decision making, and this reflected the aims of the session, which were more about sharing ideas and experiences.

Evaluation and outcomes

At the time of this research, a formal evaluation of the work of the team was about to be conducted. In this, the views of parents and children who used the service were being sought with regard to both processes and outcomes, and parent and child questionnaires were the two main tools to be used for this evaluation. Whilst the availability of the service was expected to prevent the need for Social Services intervention in many cases and therefore costly accommodation procedures in the long term, this was reported by the manager to be difficult to evaluate. It was felt, however, that there were some families accessing the service who would be unwilling to contact Social Services directly because of the stigma involved, and the fact that parents returned for further support was cited as an indication of how useful they had found the service. As part of this case study, the 'professional clients' interviewed included a SENCO, a principal practitioner from Social Services and a school nurse.

Benefits for children and parents

Professional clients who were interviewed were asked what they felt the benefits to children and families were, and altogether the three interviewees raised a number of advantages. Overall, the service was felt to be approachable, organised, accessible and responsive. Parents of children with emotional and behavioural difficulties were reported to be able to get help and advice immediately and to have better access to local resources as a result. Whilst a SENCO from a local school felt that children and families were able to get independent advice without having the stigma of having to contact Social Services, the school nurse interviewed felt that this stigma might still exist. The SENCO stressed that the confidentiality aspect was important for children. At the same time, the principal practitioner from Social Services felt that the therapeutic team was closer to Education than field social workers and could therefore offer something over and above what they themselves could offer. This meant being able to take a more holistic approach and being able to take into account educational, as well as social needs.

Benefits for professional clients

Those from referring agencies felt that it was very useful to be able to get advice and support from the team about individual cases, as well as being able to refer children, and, as for parents, the availability of independent advice (i.e. not Social Services or CAMHS) was considered important. For the school nurse, who would normally have to refer such cases to the GP, advice on less severe cases was considered most valuable, whilst, according to the SENCO, the school was able to ask a member of the team to attend internal case reviews if they thought it was relevant. The team was reported to work in partnership with schools where it could (e.g. in the case of school-phobic children) and also to provide training. The SENCO noted the simple referral procedure, which helped, as teachers were often busy. Referrers were said to be kept fully informed, as regular reviews were a feature of the service. The therapeutic effect on children in receipt of support from the service was also considered to reduce the likelihood of problems in school. For the Social Services representative, the fact that the service now covered a wider range of children, i.e. all those with emotional and behavioural difficulties, rather than just abused children, was reported to be advantageous and it was felt to be easier to collaborate with a more local service.

Difficulties raised, however, included the fact that there was often a long waiting list and the stigma attached to contacting social workers, a point raised earlier. All interviewees stated that the service could do with more workers because of the demand for the service.

Cost-effectiveness

Whilst the manager did not consider the service well resourced in terms of training and accommodation, the work was considered good value for money and the resources available were reported to be *'used to the full'*. For the SENCO interviewed, the service was considered good value for money, especially as it was part-funded by the LEA and therefore cost the school nothing. The principal practitioner felt that having a local service saved time and money, although s/he stated that it could also be improved by offering group work. For the school nurse, the early intervention made possible by the service was thought to prevent later crises and was therefore considered cost-effective.

Key points

- ◆ Local government reorganisation can be a significant influential factor in the development of a more collaborative relationship between agencies.

- ◆ Those involved in multi-agency working need to be able to give it their full commitment if it is to work successfully; otherwise there is a tendency to get drawn constantly back into the agency's core business.

- ◆ It is important to give consideration to the way that funding is set up for multi-agency working so that this does not create obstacles to joint working.

- ◆ Where professionals offer consultation and training to other agencies, this can have a knock-on effect of improving understanding across the agencies so that they are less territorial and developing a more effective working relationship between the agencies generally.

- ◆ Where professionals from different agencies are brought together to form a multi-agency team, access to professional development and training needs to be ensured, particularly where they may no longer be line managed by their own agency.

- ◆ For professionals involved in a counselling role, the skills involved may be transferable and equally beneficial for multi-agency work, since listening, respect and empathy would appear to be key components of both.

- ◆ A multi-agency service allows the holistic needs of children to be addressed and in this way offers something over and above single-agency intervention, whilst at the same time may prevent the stigma attached to contacting some agencies.

- ◆ Offering advice and consultation, rather than joint working with other agencies, can facilitate early intervention and prevent inappropriate referrals.

CASE STUDY 3

A specialist Health Promotion Service located within Education – a coordinator-led initiative, with a range of different types of multi-agency activity throughout the service

Description

A specialist health promotion service with a primary and a secondary prevention team. The primary prevention team involved a team that worked specifically with schools, and it is this team that was the main focus for this study. Different parts of the service were reported by the head of service to entail different types of multi-agency activity. The schools team was felt to bring together agencies to deliver INSET or to provide input into the curriculum in schools and therefore to have a significant coordinating role. In addition, they worked as an operational team with schools to develop a health education programme in schools and also worked with LEA advisers and others involved in delivery. The schools team, together with managers from within Education, formed a decision-making forum at managerial level. The team also contributed to the training strategy for the LEA and its delivery. Training officers from the service worked with training officers from the LEA to develop partnership competencies that were delivered through training courses. Only centre-based delivery was therefore felt to be absent.

Background

The Health Promotion Service was reported to be set up in response to new flexibility under the Health Act 1999 (Sections 26–28) and also a local government Bill concerning modernisation and the duty of partnership with the local authority in the development of the Health Improvement Plan. The aim was to develop a service based on the principle of saving lives from 'A Healthier Nation'. A health information partnership was therefore set up to look at how to define and develop shared objectives and performance indicators and to develop basic systems so that managers from different agencies could talk to each other.

Funding and resources

The Health Promotion Service was jointly funded by the Health Authority and the local authority, and was officially commissioned by the Primary Care Trust. They had access to an identified health promotion budget. Two-thirds of the budget came from the Health Authority, a quarter from the LEA base budget and the Standards Fund, which funds the schools team, and one-twelfth from Social Services, which funds work on Quality Protects and children in public care. The health promotion manager stated that health promotion services are usually funded by Health and located within the Health Authority or the NHS Trust. In contrast, in this authority, the service was based in Education, Youth and Leisure and all the staff were local authority staff except for the head of the service, who was an NHS manager. The service was in the process of examining pooling budgets from different agencies so that the funding could be used more flexibly. The head of service felt that the funding was distinctive in that a lot was allocated on trust between the agencies with no '*hard and fast service level agreements to cover it*'. The existence of an NHS manager working within the LEA, accountable to both agencies and having to report back on the appropriate use of the money through both of the agencies, was felt to be influential in establishing such trust. The fact that the funding allocation from different agencies had to be accounted for in this way was reported to make the funding complicated and time consuming to manage, as well as having the added pressure of continually having to ensure that the funding was available from the different agencies. The ability to pool budgets was reported to be helpful as it would mean that the funding would be '*on firmer ground*', there would be less reporting to do (although still accountable) and the manager felt that it would represent a stronger commitment from the agencies.

Aims

The overarching long-term aim of the Health Promotion Service was to improve the health of people within the borough and to improve the '*capability and capacity*' around specialist health promotion locally. Alongside this, the service aimed to coordinate input from the broad range of areas involved in health promotion and to have '*a bigger vision*' rather than one that was '*piecemeal*'. It was felt that by coordinating services in this way it was possible to allocate resources where they were most needed rather than according to '*who shouted the loudest or which department had a bit of turf they were trying to protect*'. At the same time, from an Education perspective, and with respect to the schools team in particular, having embarked on the Government's Healthy Schools Scheme made it imperative that targets were met, i.e. schools were signed up to take part, and that the scheme developed was deemed appropriate for local schools.

Agency involvement

A diagram showing the strategic- and operational-level involvement of different agencies is shown in Figure 8.3. For ease of presentation, only the primary prevention team has been shown, but the secondary prevention team sat alongside the primary team under the umbrella of the Health Promotion Service.

Strategic level

At strategic level, the Health and Social Care Executive (H&SCE) was reported to '*act like a management team*' and made recommendations to the Joint Health Strategy Board to be ratified. Board members then took issues back to their own organisations for agreement. This aspect of the H&SCE was reported to be working particularly well and it was felt to have provided a lot of support, resources and time for the work conducted in schools. Officers from different agencies at the level below the executive developed the programme for the Health Improvement Plan, which also included the Community Plan and the NHS Modernisation Plan. All plans, however, according to the service manager, *'fed into and came from'* the Education Youth and Leisure Plan.

The head of service stated that it was managed from within Education under the Pupil Support Services for ease of management and day-to-day purposes. S/he was therefore managed by, and accountable to, the head of this service. At the same time, however, s/he was also responsible to the Health Authority and the Primary Care Team and had to provide reports to both. This reportedly involved a lot of duplication. Ideally, s/he stated that reports would *'feed right through Education and the Health Authority would then pick up what it needs from that'*. The head of service stated that this also influenced *'people's perceptions of accountability and how others lower down see him/her and the demands they therefore make of him/her'*. S/he reported that those beneath him/her were not always aware of the complexities involved and they often perceived him/her to be part of Health. S/he felt that it was important to have someone in his/her position who was comfortable with the potential conflicts that could arise and s/he cited one of the challenges as *'being able to manage the competing demands and the different perceptions about where your loyalties or priorities lie'*.

Operational level

The Health Promotion Service included a primary and secondary prevention team, the interface of which it was cited *'could be better'*. There was reported to be *'a clash'* between the service wanting to take on a support and advice role for other professionals and other agencies wanting them to respond to the immediate needs of the client group, such as vulnerable pupils. This was also mentioned by one of the participants in the meeting which was observed (see later), who referred to disagreements about practice, particularly relating to the presence of teachers when sexual health workers were working with young people.

The Healthy Schools Partnership, which was reported to include the LEA, the schools team, school representatives from all sectors, Primary Care Trust representatives and other agencies, was responsible for the development of the local Healthy Schools Programme, and oversaw this. The schools team included individuals from different backgrounds, i.e. two teachers and one nurse. This aspect of the service was reported to be working particularly well since it had *'worked through a lot of conflict'* and was still *'producing the goods and working extremely well'*. Both the planning and the delivery of the Healthy Schools Programme were felt to be working particularly effectively.

Figure 8.3   Strategic and operational agency involvement in the joint Health
Promotion Service

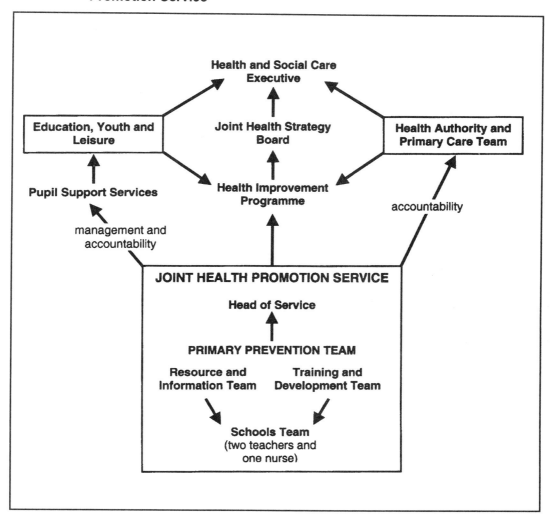

OBSERVATION

Context

The multi-agency activity that was observed was a meeting of the sexual health strategy group. This involved representatives from the schools team, school nursing, the Primary Care Trust, the Children's Service, the Youth Service and various specific sexual health project workers, and was chaired by the sexual health development worker, a member of the joint health promotion service secondary prevention team. Several people arrived during the meeting, and similarly several had to leave before the end. The absence of a Social Services representative at the meeting was commented on in the post-observation questions – they were reported to often not attend. It was felt that their commitment to the meeting was probably influenced by the fact that '*the Social Services' agenda is quite small in comparison to the agenda of the meeting so it probably doesn't have a big impact that they are not there*'. In contrast, another participant commented that it was good that the person involved in child protection had been there since '*he could provide good input that no one else can*', suggesting that particular expertise from different agencies was important for the meeting to progress.

Format of the meeting

The meeting took place in a large room and comfortable chairs were arranged in a circle. Before the meeting began, the sexual health coordinator arranged a buffet lunch on a table in the room for the participants in the meeting. While s/he was doing this, people started arriving and chatting between themselves – some discussing particular areas of joint interest, and some making arrangements for other meetings. It was clear that the beginning of the meeting provided an opportunity for people to communicate with others who were ordinarily difficult to contact.

The sexual health coordinator brought the meeting to order, and then explained the researcher's presence in the room, and the purpose of the research. Following this, s/he moved on to the first agenda item. The meeting followed the planned agenda relatively closely, although the order of items was sometimes altered to take account of the interests of people who arrived late or had to leave early. The meeting took the general form of short presentations or updates of information from relevant individuals, followed by general discussion, brainstorming and information sharing between the group, and a move to resolution or decision making, often on the part of the coordinator. The coordinator generally summed up what had been said by the rest of the group and turned this into a practical decision or action point, and this was often his/her mechanism for moving the meeting on to the next item on the agenda.

Four key agenda items were discussed, taking between ten and 20 minutes each, before the coordinator suggested that the group break for lunch. Thirteen minutes were allocated to everyone getting food from the buffet and informal conversations in small groups before the coordinator moved everyone back to the circle of chairs. Participants continued to eat while the next agenda items were discussed.

After lunch, six further agenda items were discussed, although it was noticeable that each of these lasted between three and ten minutes, and there was more of a sense of urgency from the coordinator about making sure that the group considered all of the items on the agenda. As one group member stated after the meeting: '*There is never enough time*'. For this reason the coordinator chaired the meeting more closely, and encouraged the group to make decisions and move on swiftly.

At the end of the meeting, there was a short time for members of the group to raise further issues, and a date for the next meeting was agreed.

The time spent on different activities

Table 8.3 shows rough approximations of the time spent on different activities.

Table 8.3   Time spent on different activities

Activity	Time (mins)	Time as a percentage of the whole session
Informalities (including lunch)	18	15
Chairing	16	13
Presentation of information	12	10
Discussion/suggestions	63	53
Decision making	7	6

Percentages have been rounded to the nearest whole number, and therefore may not sum to 100
Source: *Observation in Phase Three of the NFER study, 2001*

As may be expected of a meeting of this kind, drawing together professionals from a wide range of agencies and backgrounds to discuss the implementation of the Health Promotion Strategy, the largest percentage of the meeting was spent in **discussion and suggestion**. This also included considerable sharing of information relating to the specific agenda items, although the group were often actively brainstorming and working towards decision making and solutions. From the post-observation questions, it appeared that participants generally felt that the meeting was good since it gave everyone an opportunity to comment on the issues.

Prior to the group discussing each agenda item, one lead individual gave a short **presentation of relevant information** or an update on the progress of the particular issue. In most cases, the coordinator took on this role, although at some points s/he invited others to give their reports. However, this was not a major element of the meeting, and only accounted for ten per cent of activities. The coordinator noted, at the end of the meeting, that pressures of time allowed some people to deliberately avoid giving their reports back to the group, but s/he felt that this was not a major problem.

Surprisingly, only six per cent of the meeting was actually spent in any type of formal **decision making** process, and this often comprised the coordinator summarising what the group had said during discussion, and formulating it into an action point. S/he would then feed this decision back to the group, who would invariably give their assent. Only one other member of the group took on this decision-making role at any point during the meeting, when the decision to be made was in his/her particular area of expertise.

Informalities accounted for a total of 15 per cent of the whole meeting, although much of this time was devoted to lunch. Interviewees clearly valued the lunch provided (and this was commented on in the post-observation questions), but it also provided a timetabled opportunity for informal discussion. During lunch, individuals spoke in small groups and there was evidence of them making practical arrangements and discussing specific issues. One interviewee remarked, after the meeting, that '*because the meeting has put us all in touch, we now meet outside the meeting … it* [the meeting] *has become more focused than it used to be'*. The coordinator explained that s/he tried to chair the meeting in a very '*informal and chatty'* way, which meant that the group were able to laugh at appropriate moments, although this did not disrupt the general flow of conversation, or take time away from the key activities.

The **chairing** role of the sexual health coordinator was clearly apparent during the observation. Although this activity only accounted for 13 per cent of the time, the coordinator clearly steered the group between the agenda items. However, interestingly, s/he often used summaries and decision making as a method of moving the group on to the next item. Chairing became a more important role in the second half of the meeting (after lunch) when it became apparent that time was short, and that there were still many agenda items to cover. The coordinator took a considerably more active role in moving the group forward during this phase of the meeting. Despite this clear steering role throughout the meeting, the coordinator did not appear to have greater status than other members of the group, nor did others appear threatened by his/her management of the agenda.

Key points

♦ The observation illustrates how shortage of time demands very focused chairing, with one individual or agency taking a lead role, although this does not need to lead to that individual monopolising the group.

♦ The meeting was moved between agenda items by the chairperson summarising the group's discussions and decision making and feeding an action point back to them for their assent.

♦ Breaking for lunch provided built-in time for informal discussion, minimising other instances, thus making the meeting more focused on the agenda items.

♦ Having a multi-agency meeting centred on a strategy in this way allowed all those involved to have an opportunity to discuss the issues, as well as meeting with other professional face-to-face.

Evaluation and outcomes

Whilst the head of service felt that the initiative was good value and cost-effective, s/he reported that it was difficult to know how to measure outcomes. S/he saw the continuing commitment to funding of the Primary Care Team as an indication that the service was doing a good job. Individual pieces of work were evaluated against objectives, but no formal evaluation of the whole service had been undertaken. The programme was monitored in relation to individual team action plans, which linked back to the Education Development Plan and, within a performance framework, set out priorities, performance indicators and outcomes. Process issues rather than outcomes tended to be measured, and the head of service acknowledged that measurement of impact might be a very long-term consideration.

As part of this case study, however, two school nurse team leaders and one PSHE coordinator in a secondary school were interviewed about the benefits to children and to their agencies. They reported that the aims of the service were to support schools in terms of health promotion, in the main through training and support to staff, but that they also often engaged in direct work with pupils as well. The PSHE coordinator reported having frequent contact with the schools team. The school nurses reported that they 'worked in partnership' with the team to provide health education/promotion to schools, although the possibilities of also targeting children with certain health problems, such as those with poor hygiene, through a broader whole-school approach was also mentioned. The team provided training for school nurses and worked alongside them in schools doing health education and joint baseline assessments, as well access to a library of resources.

Benefits for children

The PSHE coordinator stated that, whilst the work of the schools team mainly centred on school staff and that it encouraged them to focus their priorities, this then had a knock-on effect for children. S/he also indicated that children were now more actively involved themselves in health promotion and had more say in what they did. In addition, input from the schools team had facilitated links with outside agencies such that, when pupils needed specialist help they were able to access this more easily. One school nurse reported that students now received a broader curriculum as before they would only have received input from Education staff. Similarly the other nurse stated that children were able to access different people's skills and interests and, where individual input was needed, this could be offered in a non-stigmatising way. The only disadvantage for pupils raised was that confidentiality could be a problem if pupils wanted to talk to those from outside of the school.

Benefits for professional clients

With regard to the benefits to the agencies involved, the PSHE coordinator referred to having a more coordinated approach to the involvement of outside agencies. Working with other agencies in this way was reported by one school nurse to '*broaden your horizons*' and develop wider links with other agencies. Input from the team was felt to enable school nurses to become more involved in health promotion in schools as well as with individual children, and provided them with '*more strategies for approaching schools and children*', thereby developing their role considerably.

On the other hand, teachers' workload was reported to make it difficult to prioritise and difficult to contact outside agencies. This meant that teachers had to work on a needs basis if a child had a problem. Similarly, one of the school nurse team leaders mentioned the difficulty of logistically getting everyone together, whilst the other mentioned the difficulty in doing joint work when there were other core agency-focused priorities, such as immunisation programmes. Difficulties arose particularly when staffing levels were low. One school nurse also felt that problems might arise from a lack of understanding of what different agencies could and could not do, although this had not yet been a problem as they had not been asked to undertake anything thus far that was beyond their existing remit.

Cost-effectiveness

The head of service felt that the amount of funding was adequate and that the challenge was to use the funding that was available wisely and '*in pursuit of strategic and operational targets*'. S/he felt that the funding for the schools programme in particular was well used since schools' understanding of the broad health agenda had improved and there was evidence of their greater involvement in health education and health improvement. A widening of the role of school nurses, as mentioned by one of the school nurses themselves, was also noted.

The PSHE coordinator found it difficult to comment on cost-effectiveness, but stated that the service was free to the school and that they had received a lot of training, which could only be beneficial. One school nurse felt that, by rolling the programme out in the way they were to school nurses, this was a very cost-effective way of operating, as more people would be able to provide input to schools, rather than just the schools team, who were limited in number.

Key points

- A Government initiative was instrumental in initiating multi-agency working in this particular field of health promotion.

- The head of health promotion, by being employed by Health but located within Education, was able to develop informal links and relationships so that there was greater trust between the professionals within the two agencies.

- Working across agencies at strategic level can be particularly challenging, especially where those involved are accountable to more than one agency and there are not the structures in place to facilitate this.

- The flexibility engendered by joint funding may free up agencies to work more effectively and innovatively in a multi-agency way.

- Mapping where the objectives and targets for different agencies overlap and link to overarching agency plans can lead to the effective development of joint service delivery.

- The case study highlighted the different priorities of agencies, in this case concerning a child-focused approach as compared to working with and alongside professionals to develop their skills to help them work more effectively.

- Opportunities for informal, as well as formal, contact between professionals from different agencies can be beneficial and an effective use of time.

- Practicalities, such as the difficulties involved in getting all the relevant professionals together in the same place at the same time, can inhibit multi-agency working.

- Pressures of time and differing priorities mean that agencies sometimes return to their core business at the expense of multi-agency work.

CASE STUDY 4

A multi-agency strategic decision-making group focused on looked-after children, with a multi-agency operational team established to address their educational needs

Description

A strategic multi-agency planning group for looked-after children (LAC) and a LAC support team comprised of workers from Education and Social Services, which focused on addressing the educational needs of looked-after children. This initiative was originally classified as a multi-agency decision-making group since the strategic planning group was the main focus in Phase Two. However, in the case study, the work of the operational team was also examined in more depth.

Background

The LAC strategic planning group was originally set up in response to local concern about the educational performance of LAC and the need to take seriously the corporate parenting role of the local authority. However, as well as being developed in response to a recognised need, it was in part developed through individuals' personal interest: '*It was more grounded on people who were interested in getting together and doing something about it.*' According to the Education manager involved, for example, a move from Social Services into Education made him realise that '*you can't underestimate the value of education*'. Funding became available through a successful bid for Standards Fund money, although, even before this, a programme for LAC, run jointly between Education and Social Services, with two people involved, had been set up. When specific Standards Fund money became available for LAC, the allocation doubled. The initiative started with a multi-agency training course and, according to one interviewee, '*mushroomed from there*', but as this interviewee stated: '*It was the recognition of a need, money being made available and the right people in the right place at the right time to make it work.*'

Funding

Funding was provided by both Education and Social Services, although contributions were reported to vary with '*what people can afford*' and with '*what agency priorities are*'. Some Education money came from the base budget and some from the Standards Fund and, similarly, some of Social

Services' contribution came from the children's services budget and some from Quality Protects money. According to the Education manager, the funding differed from other multi-agency initiatives in that a large amount of money came from Social Services – they were '*falling over themselves to spend it*'. With this additional money, the funding for the team had increased to such an extent that it was now '*beyond the capacity of the team to manage the budget*'. As well as fiscal resources, incidences were also cited of professionals who had devoted time to the team. For example, an SRB-funded project worker had devoted some time to the initiative because his/her objectives tied in with the LAC team's objectives and, in return for the purchase of books, another service had offered reading mentor time for the young people.

Despite more than adequate funding, however, a number of issues arose. Although the manager felt that the team was quite innovative, s/he also felt that '*the budget is always lagging behind what they are trying to do, and it should be the other way round*'. S/he stated that '*you should be setting the budgets to meet the needs of the customers and the team rather than ... the team having budgetary demands put on them*'. According to the manager, the two separate budgets ran side by side with him/her responsible for one of them and someone in Social Services responsible for the other and there was therefore no one person responsible for making sure that the budgets were meeting the needs of the team. Funding structures were felt by the manager to restrict what could be achieved and to '*limit creativity*'. Such issues were therefore felt to be '*holding* [the team] *back*'.

Aims

The manager reported that, at least in the first instance, formal aims and objectives were not written in concrete. The overarching aim, however, was felt to be very clear – improving the educational attainment of LAC. One interviewee, when asked about aims, referred to equality of opportunity and LAC's entitlement to education. In the beginning, one of the main aims was to identify the children, where they were and which schools they attended. Since then, the team had focused on promoting their educational needs and encouraging professionals working directly with LAC to support them through advice and training, but at the same time they also provided support for individual children.

Agency involvement

The structure of the initiative is shown in the diagram in Figure 8.4, which shows strategic and operational level involvement of the different agencies. Whilst all three of the main agencies, i.e. including Health, and the voluntary sector were involved at strategic level, only Education and Social Services were involved at operational level.

Figure 8.4 Strategic and operational agency involvement in the looked-after children initiative

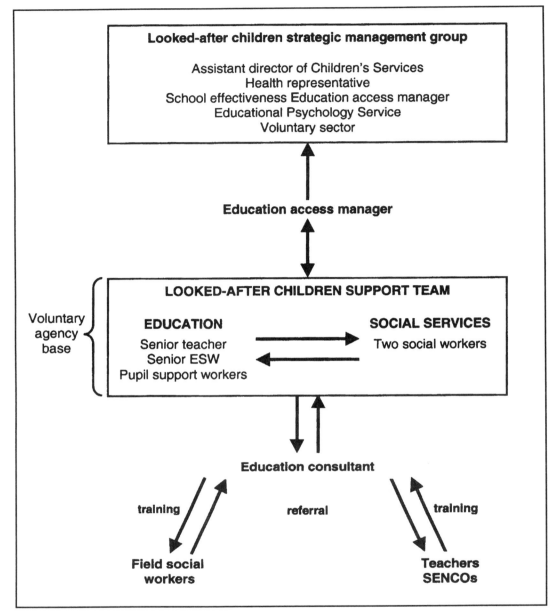

Strategic level

A multi-agency strategic management group involving Education, Social Services, Health and voluntary agencies had been established at strategic level. No specific comments were made about the relationships at this level. The Education access manager and the Children's Services manager from Social Services '*are basically in charge of this and decide where it should be going*' and therefore had overall responsibility for the team.

Operational level

The LAC support team consisted of a senior education social worker, two teachers, two social workers and two pupil support workers. Importantly, all team members had a background in residential care. A local voluntary organisation provided a location for the team.

Lack of Health involvement at operational level was felt to be '*a huge gap*' because '*nobody had made the connections between health and educational outcomes*', but this was felt to be only a matter of time. The manager felt that this would soon be an important political agenda and that it was vital for them to engage a health worker in the team as soon as possible in order to address the health needs of LAC. Whilst it was acknowledged that the team had not pushed enough for Health involvement at operational level, budgetary restrictions also made this difficult and they were trying to '*free the budget up*' so that they could '*involve more people*'. Potential partnerships with national, rather than just local, voluntary agencies and with other areas, such as Connexions and the Careers Service, were also reported to be an area for future development. In contrast, good links with other agencies were reported and close relationships with Social Services, in particular, were evident.

OBSERVATION

Context

The team concerned with the educational needs of children in public care met on a fortnightly basis. The meetings provided an opportunity to review children's progress on a case-by-case basis, to discuss any operational issues that affected the group (and its activities) so that these could be raised at strategic level and to inform and develop future strategy for the initiative overall. One of these meetings, which lasted approximately two hours, was observed as part of the case study. The meeting that was observed was the first of a new school term and not all of the staff who could have been present were there. This meant that only three staff were present, including the project manager for school improvement, the teacher and the senior education social worker attached to the LAC support team

Format of the planning meeting

Three members of the team were present, two of whom were based at the venue where the meeting took place, albeit in separate office space. The actual venue for the meeting was some way from the main centre of population within the authority and therefore away from any strategic agency base. It was held in a house formally used as a refuge from domestic violence and this venue added to the relaxed, although purposeful atmosphere. The overall format of the meeting was businesslike but informal. However, it did follow a very clear agenda that was informed by time constraints (two hours) and decisions were recorded as the members of the team took notes. The project manager for school improvement chaired the meeting and the other members of the team provided information, clarified points that were raised, raised related points for discussion and offered their professional assessment of any proposed resolutions to 'problems' or of proposed future strategy.

The first 60 minutes of the meeting were used to address the agenda items provided by the chair. The second 60 minutes concerned progress reports for individual children. Within this two-hour period, there was a short 'working break', where team members made tea or coffee and could go into the garden to smoke or stretch their legs. Throughout the 120 minutes of the meeting, the agenda was pursued by the chair and where items overran the time s/he had allocated to them (albeit not explicitly), s/he would ask members to defer resolution to another meeting. In this way the pace was balanced, but none the less quite firmly followed. The input of the members appeared to be equally valued, that is, each team member was given equal status within the discussions and the agenda served to facilitate debate, rather than to limit it or override it.

The individual members of the team on occasion disagreed and there was evidence of some tensions or conflicts, particularly concerning team members' responsibilities and issues around work space. Overall, the meeting was based on a democratic or consensual model, where the task in hand was to achieve progression towards goals that were not always articulated, but none the less appeared to be shared.

The time spent on different activities

Table 8.4 shows the rough approximations of the time spent on different activities within the session observed.

Table 8.4   Time spent on different activities

Activity	Time (mins)	Time as a percentage of the whole session
Informalities	10	8
Chairing	15	13
Presentation of information	35	29
Discussions/suggestions	40	33
Decision making	20	17

Percentages have been rounded to the nearest whole number, and therefore may not sum to 100
Source: *Observation in Phase Three of the NFER study, 2001*

By assessing the distribution of time across different activities, it was evident that the primary purpose of the group was discursive, with evidence presentation and resolution preceding and following discussion. Greater emphasis was placed on discussing the information than presenting it, but when this case is compared to others within the research, the presentation of evidence was clearly an important dimension of the meeting.

Evidence relating to the progress of individual children was **presented** on a case-by-case basis by the different team members; a substantial amount of time was spent in verifying this data, or validating it with information or evidence from other sources. In one example this concerned ascertaining the whereabouts of an individual pupil who had not been to school, or been seen in the area for some time. Both the senior ESW and the teacher exchanged the most up-to-date information within the context of the meeting, information sourced differently, but with the aim of ensuring the continuity of educational provision. Sources were cross-referenced in an attempt to close any gaps that the individual may slip through. The school improvement manager relied on their outreach role for information, whereas s/he sought to identify corporate responsibility for the child by checking the fiscal routes, pursuing any funding provided for that particular child at the strategic level. Therefore, where a child may have 'disappeared' within the system, the team shared information from a range of sources – agency-level data through to street sightings. The acceptance of various information sources recognised fallibility within current procedures, where children remain on school roll, but do not attend school, or where a child may leave care or foster provision, but remain in the area, living on the streets. Information was therefore the basis of discussion, but did not take precedence over discussion and any further decision making or resolution.

Discussion within the meeting was directed by the chair, but in a democratic manner that offered opportunities for all members to take part. A source of conflict within the team emerged when discussing a case where emergency foster care was to be withdrawn. The foster carers had stabilised a child who was attending school regularly and making progress after a difficult period, but Social Services were not willing to extend the placement and were seeking to place the child outside the area, in a residential school. The school improvement manager drew attention to the finite resources within Social Services and to the implications of blocking an emergency foster care option for other children. The senior ESW was critical of the impact of resources on needs. Within the team, there was some degree of frustration expressed concerning the use of placements outside the area, from which children may abscond, but not be able to return to a stable local environment. The teacher raised the issue of Social Services' commitment to education, arguing that their placement policies were based on 'where the beds were' rather than on an assessment of educational need. The school improvement manager was supportive of the concerns of other team members, and expressed a degree of empathy concerning their professional frustrations, but sought to mediate the negative impact of strategic decisions on operational teams by drawing attention to the necessity to move beyond individual cases.

Decisions were taken in tandem with discussion: where they were case specific, concerning future provision, they were recorded by all the team members; where they concerned issues to be raised at strategic level, they were primarily recorded by the school improvement manager. In one case, a decision could not be reached and was deferred to the next meeting. The brevity of the decision-making process was assisted by the presentation of information and discussions about it that preceded resolution. The ultimate arbiter in the decision-making process was the school improvement manager, albeit in a democratic context. Other team members sought his/her support for decisions they would like the team to take, whereas s/he expressed the will of the team, often by reaching or recording a decision on its behalf. In this respect, s/he was in authority, rather than an authority; the other team members were fully engaged in the decision-making process.

Chairing the meeting took up very little time (13 per cent), reflecting perhaps the emphasis on purpose. Informalities were restricted to the beginning and end of the meeting and the break period. These were largely based on humour and were evidence of familiarity within the team. For example, the chair drew the senior ESW's attention to some pictures in a box that she had 'rescued', thinking they would brighten walls of the office and meeting room. The senior ESW had to inform him/her that these were the ones that were up when they moved in; s/he had taken them down because they were so awful.

Key points

- ◆ The extent to which professionals may share evidence from a range of sources and use evidence as a basis for their decision making.

- ◆ The role of those staff located at the strategic/operational interface in mediating the tensions that arise between agencies within multi-agency initiatives.

- ◆ The use of case-level data in operational decision-making.

Evaluation and outcomes

The long-term absence of key personnel had meant that no formal evaluation, which had been planned, had yet been undertaken. According to the manager, however, the team was '*self-evaluating*', produced regular progress reports, but these had yet to be translated into evidence. A range of data was considered of interest, ranging from Government and service targets to young people's views of the service. The manager felt that s/he had to be open to criticism and that achieving a balance between offering support and not '*breathing down people's necks*' was sometimes difficult, involving a significant amount of trust at all levels. S/he felt that it was important for their own job satisfaction that the team was not always '*target driven*' and that targets were not '*the be all and end all*', although s/he acknowledged that they did focus people's attention and '*make people think again about why we are doing this job*'. GCSE results were acknowledged as an important indicator, as well as being easy to measure, but other things, such as lifelong learning, were just as significant but less easy to monitor:

> *We want the GCSE results, but the GCSE results are only an indicator of young people's ability to learn, and the ability to become lifelong learners and to be able to take advantage of the opportunities that the world had to offer. So that's only an indicator. You can't make the indicator the be all and end all. If you have to sacrifice the indicator for five years so that you work with the young person so in five years time they are able to take advantage of learning opportunities, then that's fine. But we don't have any easy way of measuring that. That's the difficulty; you can't measure that* (team manager).

As part of the case study, in addition to where interviewees were asked about the impact in Phase Two of the study, a SENCO in a local secondary school and a residential care manager for children with learning disabilities were interviewed about the support and training they had received from the LAC support team. With regard to the SENCO's role, whilst there was a designated teacher for LAC within the school with whom the team also had close contact, LAC were all considered to be on at least stage one of the Code of Practice and therefore part of the SENCO's remit as well. The remit of the residential care manager included children with learning disabilities or physical/sensory impairment. Some, however, were reported to have minor learning difficulties, but to be 'tagged' as children with emotional and behavioural problems. They included children who required mainstream and special school provision. Residential social workers contacted the team as and when they required advice and support. In addition, the manager was able to feed general issues through the planning group.

The benefits for children and families

The benefits to the children reported by interviewees in Phase One of the study included:

♦   improved educational attainment

♦   improved access to education

♦ maintainance within education

♦ individual attention for children

♦ the development of social skills

♦ improved liaison between school and home.

From an education perspective, the SENCO indicated that the team had provided one-to-one support for pupils with deep-seated problems who were having difficulties in school and had been effective in helping them access education. This was reported to be individual support that they might otherwise not have had, and the development of a close relationship with an adult in this way was considered key to their progress. The multi-agency approach adopted meant that children were aware that all the professionals involved were working in their best interests.

The residential care manager reported that the team's involvement enabled residential social workers to take a more proactive stance about children's education, to help them fulfil their role as corporate parents and, in this way, to improve children's access. Children were reported to receive appropriate educational provision more quickly since social workers no longer spent days on the telephone trying to identify the right contacts within the Education Department. Where children were excluded, for example, they were able to find out what to do quickly. A multi-agency approach meant that a holistic approach to children's needs was adopted and all those concerned with LAC were brought together to give a coordinated response.

Benefits for professional clients

The benefits reported by interviewees in Phase One of the study included:

♦ the raised profile of LAC

♦ raised awareness of responsibilities to LAC

♦ changed perceptions of LAC

♦ improved attitudes to children's education.

The team member with whom the SENCO had most contact was seen as part of the school team and someone with whom the school had developed an ongoing relationship. As well as offering staff training and advice, s/he was reportedly available for informal dialogue, attending individual reviews and helping to maintain home–school links for LAC. According to the SENCO, this service was better than before since the team worked more closely with the school rather than being a '*nebulous*' service and staff had no hesitation in contacting them for support. The multi-agency approach resulted in all those involved 'pulling together' so that there was a holistic and coherent approach, with open dialogue between them, rather than individual professionals working in isolation. This was considered important since there was now more pressure on schools to examine holistic needs and '*not just exclude*' children.

From the perspective of Social Services, the team provided residential homes with support for the educational needs of children and, as the manager interviewed stated, 'acts like a bridge between Social Services and Education' in an advisory role, as well as providing training. Advice and support from the team, reportedly, gave residential social workers the confidence to work within the school culture and to support the children with their education. It was felt that otherwise the school culture might be 'threatening' for some and this would prevent them representing children adequately and from tackling educational problems on their behalf. The team was felt to provide access to expertise from Education and to give them greater understanding of the processes and procedures involved so that they could approach schools 'in the right way'. The manager reported that residential social workers 'sometimes get bogged down in residential issues' and input from the team was felt to provide them with 'the bigger picture' and to widen their view so that it became 'more corporate rather than stuck in Social Services mould'. It was felt to extract them from a 'Social Services mindset', in which, for example, a child refusing to go to school might be left in bed. Previously, it was felt that social workers had been expected to fulfil this role without having the necessary links to Education, and there was felt to be lack of understanding between the two cultures. Social workers, for example, found it difficult to understand why they did not get an immediate response from teachers when they tried to contact them, and having the team reportedly 'gives them this angle'. The multi-agency aspect of the team enabled them to draw together an action plan for children and to make requests of senior managers in both agencies and therefore to be creative in their planning, e.g. the use of joint funding for out-of-borough placements, particularly where children had behavioural and social needs.

Cost-effectiveness

Generally, the Education manager felt that the team constituted a good use of resources. However, when asked about cost-effectiveness, this was reportedly difficult to gauge since there were several different 'customers' and a formal evaluation had yet to be undertaken. The SENCO interviewed was unaware of any cost implications for the school and felt unable to comment on cost-effectiveness as s/he had no idea overall of the numbers of children dealt with or their outcomes. However, s/he commented that the team had developed a good support network. From a Social Services perspective, the residential manager felt that the team was a good use of resources, since, without it, social workers would have no one to turn to in order to address educational issues and the support provided was 'massive'. However, the manager felt that cost-effectiveness might be improved by having a link worker attached to each children's home or to several.

Key points

- This case study illustrates that inflexible funding structures can inhibit creativity and innovation, as well as multi-agency working generally.

- The initiation of this multi-agency project was dependent, not only on identifying a need and having the funding available, but also on the personal motivation and commitment of individuals.

- Cross-agency collaboration entailed making the connections between the educational, health and social needs of children and establishing areas of overlap and joint priorities, i.e. there has to be seen to be something in it for individual agencies.

- Networking and collaboration with other agencies and having an understanding of the ways in which they work can be cost-effective in terms of the time saved for professionals.

- Those working in the multi-agency operational team had all previously been residential social workers, so they had some common ground, as well as bringing with them an understanding of the target group.

CASE STUDY 5

Coordinator-led service delivery involving an Early Years and Childcare Development Team, with a decision-making and an operational team element to it

Description

A multi-agency Early Years and Childcare Development Team with responsibility for implementing and monitoring the Early Years and Childcare Development Plan. A number of different initiatives fall within the remit of the team including: Sure Start; a parenting skills programme; the creation of new childcare places; support for new and existing childcare providers; training and recruitment strategies; early years education; a toy and resource library; and a Childcare Information Service. The team operates borough wide with a multi-agency brief developing strong links with the statutory, private and voluntary sectors. A partnership with representatives from all sectors then acts as a Steering Group for the team. Although the team manager felt that the initiative had both a strategic, decision-making element and an operational element to it, s/he affirmed that coordinated delivery was the most appropriate classification: '*I would say we coordinate an approach ... I would think very much the individual people around the table would coordinate a range of things on their own*' (team manager).

Background

On reorganisation to a unitary authority in 1996, Social Services and Education began as new departments. Although multi-agency activity had been taking place, the council set out to have '*a corporate approach to its business*', rather than having rigidly separate departments. Thus Social Services and Education worked closely with each other from the outset, with other partnerships developing over time. An Early Years and Childcare Partnership was set up between the two agencies in recognition that the work they were doing needed to be brought together in a coordinated and an integrated way '*because our interests coincided*'. They also began to work closely with Health. At that point, an Early Years team was only a vision: '*We knew what we wanted to do and we actually lobbied the various agencies because we knew that they were going to have to put people in, in kind or cash, to actually generate the Early Years Team*' (team manager).

The Government's agenda for the Childcare Strategy was then introduced which meant producing the Early Years and Childcare Development Plan. At that point, it was felt that everything needed to be pulled together, and an Early Years and Childcare Team which drew from all the different aspects of the council departments and Health seemed '*a natural progression*'. The team came into being in August 1999.

Funding and resources

The team was made up of core staff from the three agencies, Education, Social Services and Health. Initially, the team was jointly funded by Education and Social Services, both making in-kind contributions of personnel, office space, telephones and stationery. The DfES made an initial allocation, which had grown steadily, and other avenues of funding became available at regular times throughout the year. Specific projects, such as Sure Start and Parenting Plus, then had their own funding. Although welcome, the additional pots of money that became available created difficulties in terms of having to review existing plans:

> *You've actually written an implementation plan for the year based on the resources that you know are available. And then they give you some more money and they tell you to do something additional* ...[you] *have to review the plan* (team manager).

In addition, this money was criteria specific, coming in for a particular purpose and only to be used for that purpose, something that had been '*a learning curve*' for some involved in the initiative.

Aims

The overarching aim of the Early Years and Childcare Development Team was to ensure the provision of high-quality early years provision and childcare within the borough and thus meet the targets set in the Early Years and Childcare Development Plan. Within that, the team's objectives, as stated in this plan, were to:

♦ provide multi-disciplinary advice to single agency provision, particularly the involvement of a qualified teacher in settings where this was currently absent

♦ promote the sharing and dissemination of good practice

♦ stimulate multi-agency professional debate about the best way to provide high-quality education and care

♦ promote and coordinate the further development of integrated education and care provision in the authority and other initiatives such as the parenting skills programme and books for babies

♦ manage and support the development workers and any additional staff

♦ administer the partnership including progress reports and yearly reviews of the plan

♦ identify and monitor funding opportunities.

Agency involvement

A diagram portraying the strategic- and operational-level involvement of different agencies is presented overleaf in Figure 8.5.

Strategic level

The team was managed by the Early Years and Childcare Service team manager, who was previously a team manager within Social Services but had been seconded to the Education Department, and paid a 'top-up' salary between the substantive post and the team manager role and responsibility. Line management was through the senior assistant director for Education but the team manager was also responsible to the assistant director for operations in Social Services. The team operated at a more strategic level with, as Figure 8.5 shows, a very flat structure. Team members were responsible for coordinating a range of activity within their particular remit.

Operational level

Operational-level staff were then involved in delivering a range of services within the wider partnership, for example Sure Start, the Childcare Centre, the toy and resource library, information services, etc. Other agencies would be pulled in depending on the particular theme or activity: '*There's a good network in* [the authority] *for working on the ground together.*'

Figure 8.5   Strategic and operational agency involvement in the Early Years and Childcare Team

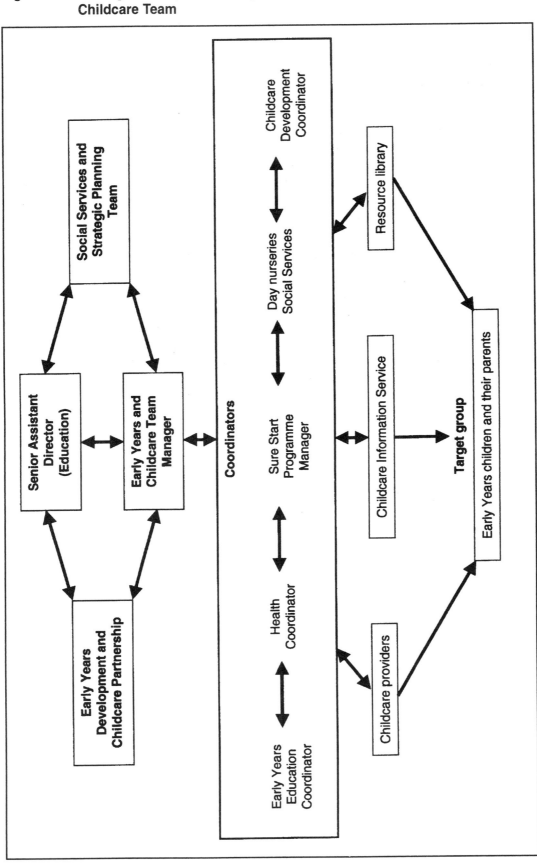

OBSERVATION

Context

The team met monthly to exchange information and focus on any issues that needed to be addressed as a whole team. Additional meetings included the senior assistant director of Education. One of the monthly team meetings was observed, which took place in one morning typically over a two-and-three-quarter-hour period. Present at the meeting were the team manager, the childcare development coordinator, the Parenting Plus coordinator, an information officer from the Childcare Information Service, the Education coordinator, two development officers and the senior Sure Start manager.

Format of the meeting

The team manager started off the meeting by welcoming everyone and introducing the NFER researcher, who explained his/her purpose for attending the meeting. Each member of the team was then asked to give a short presentation on their work, thus providing an update since the last team meeting. This information giving formed the focus of the majority of the meeting, with some time at the end, approximately 20 minutes, to discuss other issues such as quarterly action planning and the development of Neighbourhood Nurseries.

The time spent on different activities

Table 8.5 shows the approximate amount of time spent on the different activities that took place within the observed session.

Table 8.5   Time spent on different activities

Activity	Time (mins)	Time as a percentage of the whole session
Informalities (offering support/ affirmation)	3	2
Chairing	5	3
Presentation of information	157	95
Suggestions/problem solving	0	0
Decision making	0	0

Percentages have been rounded to the nearest whole number, and therefore may not sum to 100
Source: *Observation in Phase Three of the NFER study, 2001*

As evidenced in the post-observation interview, the purpose of the meeting was primarily to facilitate the sharing of information; therefore it was perhaps not surprising that almost the whole meeting (95 per cent) was devoted to the **presentation of information**. Members of the team took it in turns to update the rest of the team on their work in the intervening period since the last meeting. This was also seen to assist colleagues in making links with their own work:

> Although you meet each other every day, sometimes you miss bits, so when you sit round a table like this, you can actually start seeing what everyone's doing and what links there are. We get quite a lot out of these meetings (childcare development coordinator).

During each presentation, other participants asked questions or made comments, which sometimes evolved into a conversation between a few members of the team. Despite the indication in the agenda for the meeting that each presentation would last for five minutes, in total, the presentations by team members and associated discussion took all but 20 minutes of the meeting. The lack of strict timekeeping was commented on positively in the post-observation interview, as it was seen to be part of the relaxed, informal atmosphere. The remaining 20 minutes of the meeting also involved the presentation of information on specific issues.

Chairing the meeting was the responsibility of the team manager. Examples of 'chairing' were interspersed throughout the meeting, but took up only a small proportion of time (approximately three per cent). Chairing behaviours included:

- outlining the format of the meeting
- asking for volunteers to start off the proceedings and then inviting particular people to give their presentation
- thanking individuals for their input
- prompting a speaker, e.g. 'Maybe just touch on ...'
- negotiating the overall structure and timings, by suggesting a refreshment break in the middle and being aware of the time constraints at the end of the meeting.

As already mentioned, the supportive atmosphere of the meeting was commented on in the post-observation interview. **Informalities** such as the offering of support and affirmative comments were evident throughout the meeting, often from the team manager, e.g. 'Very good'; 'an exciting development'. At the end of the meeting, the team manager affirmed the work of all team members: 'You're all working incredibly hard'. Although difficult to calculate a percentage, approximately two per cent of the meeting could be attributed to this activity.

Although team members entered into discussions regarding the issues presented and some comments may have been seen as suggestions, there were no specific examples noted of practical suggestions, problem solving or offering expertise. Equally, the focus of the meeting was not on decision making as this occurred in other forums, for example in 'topic-specific' meetings. This view was confirmed in the post-observation interview when the team manager described how team members tried to keep focused in the team meetings, rather than being drawn into talking about planning.

It's very difficult not to launch into something like planning and to really focus on some of the issues that need to be addressed in team meetings, whereas it would be easy to start forging and creating in that environment. I think we do some of that, but I think we then have to say we'll stop, we'll have an actual topic-specific meeting on particular ideas, because there's a lot of detailed planning that needs to take place which shouldn't take place in a team meeting.

Other participants also noted that the team meeting often led to other meetings, as these could actually be arranged then: *'it might be the only time that you're together with your diaries'* (Parenting Plus coordinator).

Key points

♦ The flat structure of the team was evident in the fact that everyone was given the opportunity to contribute to the meeting.

♦ Coordinator-led multi-agency working often involved a large number of people and different projects and for this reason it is important that meetings address specific issues.

♦ There was a recognition that all involved had skills, knowledge and experience from their own agencies to offer; thus there was a lack of 'preciousness', a breaking down of hierarchical barriers.

Evaluation and outcomes

The initiative was due to be part of a 'Best Value' review, which would be completed within the next 15 months. This would measure processes and outcomes, and whether the services offered in-house were competitive to the outside market. The LEA's Early Years Development and Childcare Plan (1999–2002) set out the arrangements for maintaining quality assurance within early years education, namely through OFSTED inspections of all settings; the inspection of all nursery settings within schools by the attached school adviser and/or Early Years adviser; and the inspection of all settings within the private/voluntary sector by the Social Services Registration and Inspection Unit. The plan goes on to note that these settings are also given support through the Early Years Education coordinator together with the Early Years Development and Childcare Team. Playgroups are reported as being also supported by the Playgroup Network.

During its inspections, the Registration and Inspection Unit conducts a review of any training undertaken by childcare workers. At the same time, a similar review within the childcare sector had been conducted by development workers working as part of the team, which had resulted in the introduction of a training programme for childminders together with a range of topic-specific workshops.

As part of this study, in addition to Phase Two interviews, professionals from each of the referring agencies were interviewed and asked what they thought of the service.

Benefits for children and their families

In Phase Two of the study, team and partnership members commented that the work of the team had improved and increased services for children and families. Several initiatives had '*blossomed*' as a result of the focus on early years provision, which in turn was leading to '*far-reaching effects on the readiness of young children to learn when they go into school*' (senior assistant director, Education).

Interviewees from referring agencies were unanimous that the main benefit to children and their families was the fact that the team provided one point of information. Therefore, when there was a problem, the relevant support could be accessed much more quickly and effectively.

Benefits for the referring agencies

In Phase Two, team members commented on the benefits to other agencies in terms of the advice and training that was available to them. One member commented that, although fairly well established, it was still early days as far as agency awareness of what the team could offer was concerned: '*it's amazing how slow it is to percolate through*' (team member, Health). A benefit to the voluntary sector was identified as the fostering of a sense of inclusion, an awareness that the team was there to support, rather than being seen as a source of competition.

Interviewees from the agencies involved reiterated this benefit to the voluntary sector, affirming that it had raised the credibility of this sector, thus allowing it to develop and have '*a stronger voice*'. Of great benefit to referring agencies was the fact that they could just pick up the telephone and access a whole range of contacts, advice and information – this was believed to be '*invaluable*'. At the same time, the efficient transfer of information limited the duplication of services. Another benefit was perceived to be the raised profile of early years and childcare within the authority. This had led to a real understanding of what was going on across the authority in this area – it was much clearer, whereas before it had been segmented. Finally, other agencies remarked on an improved understanding of what different agencies did, which in turn had developed into an awareness that, although different agencies had different strengths and different problems, it was possible to work together to achieve the same aims.

Cost-effectiveness

The team manager considered that the initiative was well resourced although s/he pointed out that they were very aware that this may well not be the case long-term, so the emphasis was on building up a structure to enable it to continue should the funding stream dry up. The team was believed to offer good value for money in terms of the amount of work it completed and the other initiatives that it generated. At the same time, by supporting and empowering parents, it could remove the need for intervention by agencies such as Social Services at a later date.

> *So those parents who would hit Social Services at a low level because of neglect, not coping with their children, will actually go to Sure Start or Parenting Plus or be picked up in that team in another way, perhaps a playgroup. If we can help on the periphery, then we save the agencies money in the longer term* (team leader).

Interviewees from referring agencies also believed that the initiative was cost-effective, because it avoided duplication of services. One interviewee commented that the team provided a resource that could be tapped into when necessary, rather than individual agencies having to provide the expertise themselves, which would thus greatly increase their overheads.

Key points

♦ This case study illustrates that local reorganisation can be instrumental in bringing agencies together to work in more creative ways and to look at relationships afresh.

♦ Multi-agency working, in this case, was also influenced by Government agendas that encouraged the agencies involved to focus together on specific issues.

♦ This type of coordinator-led multi-agency working involved a large number of people and projects and, for this reason, it was seen to be important that meetings addressed specific issues that were relevant to all those involved.

♦ The linking of funding to the development of constantly changing plans was reported to be challenging, requiring continual readjustment to ensure multi-agency working.

CASE STUDY 6

A mental health decision-making strategy group with a number of operational teams and consultation and training at other levels

Description

This case study focuses on a mental health strategy group primarily comprising three local authorities and the coterminous Health Authority. The result of this strategy group was an operational team in each area, one of which, a project to address young people's behavioural problems, was a specific focus for this study and which was observed. Originally the initiative was classified as a strategic group – the original focus being on the multi-agency strategy meetings between the three local authorities and the coterminous Health Authority. However, there were several different layers of decision-making groups – at both county-wide, and individual local authority level – and each local authority also had an operational team as a result of their implementation of the strategy. The chair of the strategy group explained how the model of delivery adopted by one of the authorities fell into the operational team category when s/he said: '*they're a bunch of staff ... they're not based together, but they coordinate their delivery together ... operationally they work directly together*'. Consultation and training also resulted from the implementation of the mental health strategy. However, there was no evidence of centre-based delivery, or a central coordinator role in the implementation of the strategy in any of the three local authorities.

Background

The strategy group, consisting of senior-level strategic personnel (assistant director level) from each of the partner agencies, in each of the local authorities, met together to develop the mental health strategy. Within this group, there were also subgroups and working parties who met to address more specific aspects of the strategy. Decisions were made within these groups which were then presented for approval at the full steering group.

The strategy group was formed initially in 1992, before local government reorganisation created the three separate local authorities involved. A written strategy document was formally produced in 1997, and this strategy had just been through its three-yearly revision. The aim of the strategy, in general terms, was to provide a more coordinated approach to addressing the mental health or mental wellbeing of children across all three local authorities.

This involved all areas of work; however, the operational team which is the focus of this case study was created to address a recognised gap in service for families with children under the age of 12 who were not currently receiving adequate provision through the Social Services Access Team. One member of the team explained that they were able to provide a preventative, early-intervention service. As a leaflet produced by the team states:

> *Health, Social Services and Education have formed a new multi-disciplinary service to help families. This is funded by national and local government and involves teachers, educational psychologists, family workers and primary health workers working in collaboration. The aim of* [the initiative] *is to get involved at an early stage to prevent difficulties becoming worse, helping parents and staff who work with children become more effective in managing behaviour.*

Funding and resources

The chair of the steering group described the financial extent of this multi-agency project by saying: '*I am not aware of a bigger multi-agency initiative than this in this particular arena. In CAMHS I'm not aware of any other group, any other type of project or service that is spending £800,000 on multi-agency funding.*'

The funding came from a wide variety of different sources across the three local authorities and the Health Authority. The largest percentage of the funding for the project came directly from the CAMHS Innovation Mental Health grant, which was conditional on the local authorities providing an additional 30 per cent. The Health Authority contributed a large amount from their mainstream funds, with additional Joint Finance money being used to support the local authorities in providing their 30 per cent funding required for the Innovation grant. Some of the money from Health and the Innovation fund was specifically earmarked to pay for a detailed independent evaluation of the operational projects set up in each area.

The chair of the steering group explained that there were some difficulties around funding because Health were able to contribute relatively easily from their mainstream funding, whilst Education and Social Services relied much more heavily on targeted project funding which was often time limited. This sometimes caused problems of long-term planning, and placed additional pressure on these agencies to maintain their input to the project. S/he said that '*their anxieties and the need to worry about managing the replacement of a specific piece of funding can take up unnecessary amounts of time that you really want to focus on keeping the projects on track and continuing to develop*'. This was something that the steering group wanted to address during the process of moving the operational projects forward from being a geographically limited initiative to a mainstream service.

Aims

The aims of the project were formally summarised in the original bid for money from the CAMHS Innovation Mental Health grant, and quoted in a progress report of the independent evaluation:

> *To provide a team of family aides to offer early intervention to support families whose children are presenting behavioural difficulties or experiencing problems linked to neglect or poor emotional care. The emphasis will be on offering practical and emotional support and direct work to improve the parenting skills through advice and guidance and role modelling. This will form part of a multi-agency behaviour intervention initiative targeted at Tier 2 of the HAS model working in collaboration with Primary Mental Health workers.*

When asked about aims in Phase Two of the study, the following were identified:

♦ to improve coordination of services so that any gaps in provision are addressed

♦ to identify children's mental health problems at an earlier stage

♦ to provide a range of services to meet a range of mental health needs

♦ to address children's mental health needs in a more integrated way

♦ to enhance professionals' ability to deal with mental health issues

♦ to make mental health issues the responsibility of all agencies

♦ to develop multi-agency practice and improve lines of communication.

Agency involvement

Figure 8.6 shows the involvement of the different agencies with both the strategy group and the operational team in one authority shown. However, it must be recognised that this diagram does not show the consultation and training elements, nor does it show the implementation of the strategy in the remaining two local authorities in any detail.

Strategic level

The initial strategy group was set up prior to local government reorganisation in 1997, which had the result of dividing one local authority into the three that are now involved. Good relationships were retained between the authorities, and there were also apparently good links with the Health Authority (which was originally coterminous with the single authority, and now covers the three separate authorities).

The chair of the steering group, the children's strategy manager for the local Health Authority, explained that relationships were good between the individuals on the steering group – particularly as many had been involved for a long time. However, s/he also said that it wasn't *'a place for the faint-hearted ... there are an unusual number of highly opinionated people with lots of experience ... a group of very strong-willed representatives ...'*. He explained that between the agencies, the Health Authority often provided an independent arbitration role – because it was seen as removed from the three local authorities. Sometimes there were tensions between the different authorities, or the different agencies within those authorities, and the Health Authority were often able to find solutions appropriate to all partners.

Operational level

At operational level, each local authority was responsible for implementing the mental health strategy in their area. In practice, this had allowed each area to tailor the implementation to their particular needs and fit in with local structures. The chair of the steering group felt that this flexibility was beneficial in allowing each authority to respond within their own context.

In the local authority that forms the focus for this case study, Social Services had already begun to consider the mental health problems of young people, particularly with regard to management of their behaviour within both school and family settings. It was decided to implement the joint mental health strategy by forming a new team which included primary mental health workers, teachers and educational psychologists working alongside members of the Social Services team. However, it was agreed that team members would also continue to function within their own agency, as well as acting on behalf of the team, and that team members would not be based together in any physical sense. The objective of the new team would be to address cases where multi-agency working would be beneficial. As the lead case manager said: '*... the objective is that at the end of that there is then some shared responsibility for meeting the needs of that child, so typically it would be a case which is slightly more complicated ...*'.

The chair of the steering group described his/her concern that this arrangement allowed Social Services to dominate the team, which could have created problems of access for families who did not wish to be assessed through the Social Services access team route. However, this problem has, to a certain extent, been addressed as children and families can be referred through any of the team members, or other strategy group partners (including school nurses, health visitors and voluntary organisations).

Figure 8.6 Strategic- and operational-level involvement in the mental health initiative

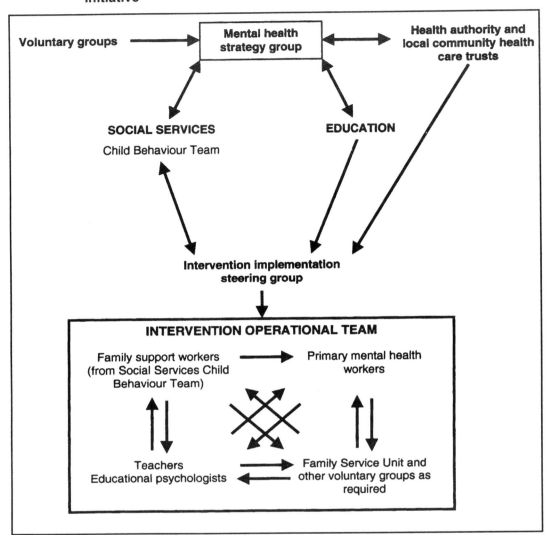

Note: there is a similar structure with operational teams in the two other local authorities as discussed in the text but these have not been included for ease of presentation.

OBSERVATION

Context

The observation centred on a case conference meeting of the operational team in one of the three local authority areas. The meeting that was observed was a regular case conference meeting of the operational team held once every two weeks, over lunchtime. Those who attended were the senior case manager for the team (chair of the meeting), a senior primary mental health worker, two primary mental health workers, a Social Services family support worker, and an educational psychologist. Prior to the meeting, a list of specific cases for consideration had been circulated to allow participants to prepare information about their own agency's involvement with the case in advance. This allowed them to check whether anyone from their own agency had had contact with the child or family in the past.

Format of the meeting

The meeting was held in a small room with comfortable chairs in a circle surrounding a low coffee table. Members of the group arrived and chatted informally amongst themselves until the senior case manager started the meeting. The situation was clearly informal, with several people eating packed lunches. This informal stance was maintained throughout the meeting, although informalities were not allowed to detract from the cases to be considered.

Six cases of individual young people, from the agenda, were addressed during the meeting, accounting for between four and 23 minutes each. A further case, not on the agenda list, was introduced at the end of the meeting. At the start of each case, the lead case worker was invited (by the senior case manager) to present an update of the case (each member of the team was allocated individual cases to manage). Sometimes the senior case manager would also add an update from the perspective of the rest of the team.

During the presentation of information, and immediately following, discussion of the case would ensue. This often included the rest of the team asking questions of the lead officer or the senior case manager in order to elicit further information or clarify particular points. Individuals from other agencies would also contribute their own updates of the case, explaining their own agency's previous involvement with the child or family. The discussion then moved to consider practical solutions to the problems, with team members brainstorming possible ways of proceeding with the case. This discussion progressed seamlessly into the group making decisions and developing action points.

Each case followed a very similar pattern, although the amounts of time spent on each phase – presenting updates, discussion of issues, brainstorming solutions, and decision making – depended on the nature of each case, and the complexity of the problems to be solved.

The meeting was closed after an hour and 25 minutes, after seven cases had been considered and the senior case manager had told the group about other meetings and events that were happening over the next couple of weeks. Some members of the group left immediately in order to go to other meetings, whilst some members of the team made arrangements for joint visits, or attending other meetings together.

The time spent on different activities

Table 8.6 shows the approximate length of time spent on different types of activities within the meeting observed.

Table 8.6   Time spent on different activities

Activity	Time (mins)	Time as a percentage of the whole session
Informalities	2	2
Chairing	4	5
Presentation of information	18	21
Discussion/suggestions	56	66
Decision making	5	6

Percentages have been rounded to the nearest whole number, and therefore may not sum to 100
Source: *Observation in Phase Three of the NFER study, 2001*

From the table it can be seen that **discussion and suggestions** formed the main component of the meeting, accounting for two-thirds of the total time. However, it was often difficult to distinguish where this began and ended – each case progressed from individuals presenting information about a case, through discussion and problem-solving activities, to decision making. However, the greater part of the meeting involved all members of the team discussing each case and providing alternative ideas for progression. The amount of time taken up by **decision making** belies its importance – there were regular instances of decision making throughout the meeting, although these were usually short and very focused.

Presentation of information also accounted for a relatively high proportion of the time. Each case had a lead officer who presented the background history and what had been done to date. Following this, other members of the group were able to give updates from the perspective of their own agency. For example, a child or family may be working with a primary mental health worker as their lead officer within the team, but the family may also be known to Social Services, or the child may have had input from educational psychology in the past.

Chairing the meeting was an activity which accounted for very little of the meeting time. The lead case manager did occasionally encourage the group to move on from one case to the next, but generally the meeting progressed with very little intervention. There was a clear agenda based on the list of cases to be discussed, and there appeared to be sufficient time to discuss each case in detail. It was also clear that the meeting always followed the same format, and that the team had operated in this way long enough to establish how long each case warranted, and thus move on naturally from case to case.

Informalities accounted for very little in the way of formal time during the meeting – only occurring before the meeting had really started, while people were still arriving. However, the members of the group clearly knew each other well and addressed each other on a very informal basis. Following the meeting, one of the participants explained that they had gone beyond the difficulties that resulted '*because we didn't know each other, or each other's agencies, and we didn't know how to make this thing work ...*'. However, now that the group had been meeting for a while, they had started to work better together, and the meeting was very informal and chatty throughout. The informality was demonstrated particularly by the way in which members of the group ate packed lunches during the meeting, and at one point the lead case officer sat on the floor and spread his papers out around him.

Key points

♦ Having adequate time to discuss each case in detail minimised the need for a lead chairing role.

♦ The need for firm chairing was also minimised because the team had worked together for some time, and understood the purpose of the meeting, and the amount of time warranted by each case.

♦ Multi-agency working allowed the team to look holistically at individual cases and decide on the best course of action from the perspective of a range of different professionals.

♦ Providing an agenda of cases for consideration in advance allowed all participants to contribute information about a case from the perspective of their whole agency.

Evaluation and outcomes

A local university had been contracted to conduct a formal evaluation of the impact of the implementation of the mental health strategy through the operational teams that had been established. This was not yet completed, but two progress reports were available. The chair of the steering group, members of the operational team, and several of those who referred clients to the team (including a member of the Social Services access team, a headteacher and a health visitor) also made statements expressing their perceptions of the benefits and cost-effectiveness of the initiative.

Benefits for children and families

Members of the team, referrers and the independent evaluation cited benefits of the service for the children and families who are able to access it. The fundamental improvement appeared to be that families who were previously unable to access services, for a variety of reasons, were now able to obtain support in dealing with their children's behavioural problems within the home.

A member of the Social Services access team described the benefit of providing a service which was not branded directly as Social Services when s/he said: '*people are much more willing to accept a service that doesn't involve a social worker ... they* [the operational team] *are perceived very differently*'. Interestingly, the social worker in this instance didn't see an access issue arising because the initial assessment was conducted by a Social Services access team worker – primarily because they describe themselves as members of the operational team when they are conducting this work.

The benefit of the team conducting most of their work within the family home was also identified, again removing the stigma of seeking support, but also allowing the operational team to make changes to the home situation in ways not open to other agencies. A headteacher explained: '*We have all sorts of strategies, in our school, because of the sort of catchment that we've got, for working with children with challenging behaviour, but we cannot change what goes on in the home.*' Prior to this team being formed, other agencies would work individually with the families, but would only make initial visits to the home, rather than working entirely within the home situation.

Other benefits included the impact of early intervention with families and children who would not currently meet the severity criteria for support from the mainstream services. The manager of the team explained that early intervention can often prevent the need for further mainstream support, but also removed pupils from waiting lists for more dedicated services who could be helped by this team. The operational team were able to act quickly to 'nip problems in the bud', rather than having to wait a long time on a mainstream service waiting list (if they met the criteria), during which time the problem could become severely exacerbated.

Benefits for referring agencies

The referrers who were interviewed described a number of benefits for the children and families that are discussed in the previous section, although these benefits clearly had knock-on effects for the agencies themselves. A health visitor described how the team provided an alternative avenue for them to refer to if their own work with a family was not having a positive impact. Before the team were formed, s/he explained that health visitors would have to continue to support a family even where they felt their support was not having a positive impact.

There was a sense, from all the referrers interviewed, and the team themselves, that communication between agencies had been improved as a result of the initiative. The manager of the team identified an improvement in agency communication and cooperation as a result of working together, and this was supported by the educational psychologist on the team, who explained that: *'the same few people keep meeting and talking about issues, so even if it's not directly to do with a case ... people from other agencies might learn about the way Education go about things, which is not the same as Social Services or Health'*.

The referrers also explained that the team were better at communicating with them and providing feedback on cases that had been referred. The social worker interviewed also cited instances where she had spoken to the team about an individual case and received their advice in an informal consultation-type way, which she felt had been beneficial to her own work.

Cost-effectiveness

The chair of the steering group described the substantial extent of resources that had been committed to this initiative, and this is discussed earlier in this chapter. However, in terms of cost-effectiveness and value for money, s/he said: *'it's not as effective as we would like, but it is still very effective'*. This was the most tentative view received. His/her concerns lay mainly in the way funds were managed and allocated, and s/he explained that this was something for future review. S/he said:

> *At least five agencies are directly accountable for different parts of the funds to different bodies, and some are responsible to more than one body for different aspects of different sums as well ... this means it is very hard to stay focused on what we really are spending, and turning that into a clear link between that spend and outcomes, and effective or efficient use of that money is hampered a bit if no one has a true picture of the resource levels at any one time.*

Despite these reservations, s/he also said:

> *It is providing a good level of service for the money that is being invested. Each of the key agencies involved is reporting, at this stage, good feedback about hitting targets. So, if you are the mental health service, every area that has got* [an operational team from this initiative] *does not have a waiting list for the specialised services ...*

The manager of the operational team explained that the independent evaluation progress reports had provided them with statistical evidence of *'parents feeling a lot more comfortable about the way they are managing individual problem behaviour that they had identified at the beginning of our involvement'*, leading him/her to have *'no doubt in my mind that they are benefiting'*. S/he also referred to other cost-saving benefits for the agencies involved:

*It potentially saves us time ... you get information, or you get a
route forward where you have to spend time banging your head
against a wall otherwise ... it's only an hour a fortnight ... it's not
an expensive way of doing things, you know. We're meeting with
a very clear idea about what we want to talk about, what our
objectives are ... it works, and it works very speedily; that's what
I like about it.*

When referrers were asked whether the service was cost-effective many,
were uneasy about responding, on the basis that they were not aware of
how much the service was costing, or where the funding was coming from.
However, their comments clearly suggested that they found the service
'*invaluable*', and that they felt it was a definite improvement on the previous
ways in which young people's challenging behaviour had been addressed.

Key points

♦ Providing consultation and informal advice from one agency to
another may be a useful way of widening the skill base of an agency,
as an alternative to direct work with children, where perhaps this
may not be relevant or may not be an option.

♦ Multi-agency working, in this case, was instigated in response to
an identified gap in service provision, so was very much needs led.

♦ Interagency working was felt to be an effective way of providing
services, particularly for children who had complex needs that were
unlikely to be addressed by a single-agency approach, and was
particularly helpful where cases were entrenched or 'stuck'.

♦ Agencies, particularly Social Services and Education, were
sometimes limited in the resources they were able to provide for
multi-agency working since funding was so target led.

♦ Where working alongside Health, coterminous boundaries were
considered an influential factor in facilitating multi-agency working.

♦ The more professionals worked together, the greater their
understanding of other agencies and the more informal their contact
became.

♦ It was felt that funding could become complicated to track and the
project difficult to monitor and evaluate since a range of different
agencies were accountable for different funds. However, the
advantages of generous funding for multi-agency work was clear.

♦ Multi-agency working was facilitated where consideration was
given to addressing single agency targets as an integral part of the
overall plan.

CONCLUDING COMMENTS

This study of multi-agency activity has highlighted once again the complexity and also potential of 'joining up' services. It has revealed the investment needed, in terms of finance, time and staff resources to develop new ways of working and interagency collaboration. Indeed, the attitudinal shift required in successful initiatives is an important finding. The kinds of challenges inherent in all joint service activity have been clearly laid out and, along with key factors in effective practice, should provide a useful checklist to reassure professionals (at both policy and practitioner level) that multi-agency working is not easy or easily achieved.

Equally, the study has revealed a new and 'hybrid' professional type who has personal experience and knowledge of other agencies, including, importantly, these services' cultures, structures, discourse and priorities. This understanding would seem to be a vital *sine qua non* for successful interagency collaboration. It may be that such familiarity needs to be offered to many others during initial training and in continuing professional development.

Finally, the models of multi-agency working offered in this report intimate the enormous variation in initiatives and practice that are operating under the nomenclature of 'multi-agency'. This suggests there might be value in refining descriptors and vocabulary associated with interagency activity to advance general awareness and understanding of its processes and outcomes.

REFERENCES

ANGELE, M., HEARD, R. and KENNEDY, I. (1997). 'Inter-agency co-operation – virtual reality?' *Education Journal*, **17**, 13.

AUDIT COMMISSION (1998). *A Fruitful Partnership: Effective Partnership Working* (Management Paper). London: Audit Commission.

BLOXHAM, S. (1996). 'A case study of inter-agency collaboration in the education and promotion of young people's sexual health', *Health Education Journal*, **55**, 4, 389–403.

BUTTERFOSS, F.D., GOODMAN, R.M. and WANDERSMAN, A. (1992). 'Community coalitions for prevention and health promotion', *Health Education Research*, **8**, 315–30. Cited in: BLOXHAM, S. (1996). 'A case study of inter-agency collaboration in the education and promotion of young people's sexual health', *Health Education Journal*, **55**, 4, 389–403.

CABLE, C. (1997). 'Supporting refugee children – working across departments', *Multicultural Teaching*, **16**, 1, 31–2, 34.

CAPEY, M. (1997). *'Pupils with Emotional and Behavioural Difficulties: Multi-Agency Working*. Slough: NFER, EMIE.

CLINE, R. (1989). 'Making case conferences more effective: a checklist for monitoring and training', *Children and Society*, **3**, 2, 99–106. Cited in: NORMINGTON, J. and KYRIACOU, C. (1994). 'Exclusion from high schools and the work of the outside agencies involved', *Pastoral Care in Education*, **12**, 4, 12–15.

COLE, R. (1995). 'Managing values and organisation climate in a multiprofessional setting.' In: SOOTHILL, K., MACKAY, L. and WEBB, C. *Interprofessional Relations in Health Care*. London: Edward Arnold. Cited in: BLOXHAM, S. (1996). 'A case study of inter-agency collaboration in the education and promotion of young people's sexual health', *Health Education Journal*, **55**, 4, 389–403.

DELANEY, F.G. (1994). 'Muddling through the middle ground: theoretical concerns in intersectoral collaboration and health promotion', *Health Promotion International*, **9**, 3, 217–25.

DEPARTMENT OF HEALTH, HOME OFFICE and DEPARTMENT FOR EDUCATION AND EMPLOYMENT (1999). *Working Together to Safeguard Children: a Guide to Inter-Agency Working to Safeguard and Promote the Welfare of Children*. London: The Stationery Office.

EASEN, P. (1998). 'Partnership approaches to deep rooted problems in local communities.' Paper presented at the British Educational Research Association Annual Conference, University of Belfast, Belfast, 27–30 August.

FULLAN, M. (1999). *Change Forces: the Sequel* (Educational Change and Development Series). London: Falmer Press.

GREAT BRITAIN. PARLIAMENT. HOUSE OF COMMONS (1989). *Children Act 1989. Chapter 41.* London: HMSO.

HALLETT, C. and STEVENSON, O. (1980). *Child Abuse: Aspects of Interprofessional Cooperation.* London: George Allen and Unwin. Cited in: SCRINE, J. (1989). 'Multi-professional education and the experience of social work students', *Maladjustment and Therapeutic Education*, **7**, 3, 158–62.

HARRIS, J. (1999). 'Multi-professional decision making: the myth of the rational', *Educational Psychology in Practice*, **14**, 4, 246–52.

HORNBY, S. (1993). *Collaborative Care: Interprofessional, Interagency and Interpersonal.* London: Blackwell. Cited in: BLOXHAM, S. (1996). 'A case study of inter-agency collaboration in the education and promotion of young people's sexual health', *Health Education Journal*, **55**, 4, 389–403.

MACHELL, J. (1999). 'The lost boys or the great unwashed? Collaborative strategies to address disaffection.' Paper presented at the British Educational Research Association Annual Conference, University of Sussex, Brighton, 2-5 September.

MAYCHELL, K. and BRADLEY, J. (1991). *Preparing for Partnership: Multi-agency Support for Special Needs.* Slough: NFER.

NORMINGTON, J. and KYRIACOU, C. (1994). 'Exclusion from high schools and the work of the outside agencies involved', *Pastoral Care in Education*, **12**, 4, 12–15.

PAYNE, J. (1998). 'The attractions of joined up thinking', *Adults Learning*, **10**, 4, 12–14.

ROGERS, D.S. and WHETTEN, D.A. (Eds) (1982). *Interorgansiational Coordination: Theory Research and Implementation.* First edn. Ames, IA: Iowa State University. Cited in: DELANEY, F.G. (1994). 'Muddling through the middle ground: theoretical concerns in intersectoral collaboration and health promotion', *Health Promotion International*, **9**, 3, 217–25.

SCRINE, J. (1989). 'Multi-professional education and the experience of social work students', *Maladjustment and Therapeutic Education*, **7**, 3, 158–62.

SCRIVEN, A. (1995). 'Healthy alliances between health promotion and education: the results of a national audit', *Health Education Journal*, **54**, 2, 176–85.

WHETTEN, D.A. (1982). 'Objectives and issues: setting the stage.' In: ROGERS, D.S. and WHETTEN, D.A. (Eds) *Interorganisational Coordination: Theory Research and Implementation*. First edn. Ames, IA: Iowa State University. Cited in: DELANEY, F.G. (1994). 'Muddling through the middle ground: theoretical concerns in intersectoral collaboration and health promotion', *Health Promotion International*, **9**, 3, 217–25.

ZAPKA, J.G., MARROCCO, G.R., LWEIS, B., McCUSKER, J., SULLIVAN, J., McCARTHY, J. and BIRCH, F.X. (1992). 'Interorganisational responses to AIDS: a case study of the Worcester AIDS consortium', *Health Education Research: Theory and Practice*, **7**, 31–46. Cited in: DELANEY, F.G. (1994). 'Muddling through the middle ground: theoretical concerns in intersectoral collaboration and health promotion', *Health Promotion International*, **9**, 3, 217–25.